1978

TELEVISION

TECHNIQUES

TELEVISION TECHNIQUES

By HOYLAND BETTINGER

Revised by SOL CORNBERG

WITH DRAWINGS BY BOTH AUTHORS

HARPER & BROTHERS *Publishers*

NEW YORK

Library of Congress Catalog Card Number: 55-6964

CONTENTS

~~~~~~~~~~

PREFACE

~~~~~~~~

There are many ways of building a house. Variations in the use of materials, in the treatment of mass and proportion, and in the application of design are infinite. But unless the house is built on a solid foundation, it will not long endure. Unless the workmen know how to use their tools, it will be a crude affair. Unless the design is conceived with due consideration for the combining of materials, for the requirements of locale and setting, and for the functional demands of the tenants, it will not be much of a house—either to look at or live in.

The same things apply in building a television program. It must be built on a solid foundation or it will fall apart. The workers must know how to use their tools. The materials of which it is constructed must be chosen with feeling and understanding. It must be suitable to the time and place, and to the audience it is intended to reach.

The purpose of this book is to provide a foundation on which to build. First, I have tried to orient the reader to television—to its limitations as well as its great potentialities, in order that he may make the most effective use of the medium. In describing television techniques, I have endeavored to make their psychological and aesthetic significance clear and understandable; to show when and how certain techniques may or should be employed, and the effect on the audience produced thereby. But above all, I have attempted to set forth in usable form the underlying principles which govern this complicated art; principles which have stood the test of time and will remain in force long after the dust of battle over color versus black-and-white has settled, and friend again shakes the hand of friend.

Purposely avoiding the how-to-do-it approach, I have chosen the much more difficult task of dealing with fundamentals, hoping thereby to provide a solid foundation on which the worker in television may build his own house. I have endeavored to analyze the factors entering into virtually all types of program production and to bring out the basic principles involved. I have tried to clarify the application of these principles and to set them up in such a way that the reader may apply them according to his own tastes and in his own way.

Though it is trite to say that there is nothing new under the sun, it seems apropos in the case of television. And, if one may take the typical, present-day program as the criterion, it becomes clear that a crying need exists for a realization that the basic factors of television showmanship are not new, but are as old as the arts from which they are derived. Furthermore, that a thorough schooling in these derivative forms is as essential to good program production as the electrons themselves. It is toward this end that my efforts have been directed, for it seems to me that, in order to do good work in any medium, one must be familiar with the basic principles that govern it and with the methods and techniques employed by masters and expert craftsmen, past and present, in achieving noteworthy results. There exists a vast fund of experience in television's derivative arts. We have only to study the growth of these forms and profit by the experiences of the past to avoid making the same blunders all over again.

In the treatment of this most complex and fascinating subject, in which almost every art and technique imaginable is used in one way or another, I have endeavored to simplify each situation and boil it down to basic terms. I am aware that it may seem almost frightening to the reader to realize how many things must be taken into account in producing a high-rating television program. Also, that the rapid pace at which these situations transpire—without let-up, would seemingly make it impossible ever to stop and think of basic principles and reason out the best solutions.

Well, the situations and problems are there, and they can't be "faded out" by sticking one's head in the sand. They must be handled for better or worse. Certainly, if the individuals dealing with them have had a thorough groundwork of study and experience, they will come up with better solutions than those who attempt to meet them on a catch-as-catch-can basis. Hence I have taken the position that the only effective answer is adequate preparation. Preparation on the part of the individual for his job. Careful and intelligent preparation of the program in all its phases. Planning and more planning—not only for the planned effect but for the unexpected that usually happens.

If this book is helpful in any small way to the many who, in the next few years, will cast their lot with television, I shall feel well repaid for the effort it has taken. And this, gentle reader, as authors say in prefaces, has been considerable—either through my own awkward groping for truth or the complexity of the subject.

The book is directed to all who make use of the medium: the sponsor and his representatives; script and continuity writers; studio and control room production crews; remote pick-up and motion picture field units; actors and performers, for they should be on speaking terms with all aspects of the medium; and, finally, the producer, on whose shoulders all of the problems are heaped. There is something, I hope, of value for all of them.

For the uninitiated and novices in the use of the medium, it will have to be read and re-read in order to be absorbed. Even then, the principles and techniques enumerated will amount to little more than an enumeration unless they are brought to life by actual use, so that they become a part of one's working equipment. For the classroom, perhaps the most beneficial use of the book will be to assign script writing and program production problems employing the techniques and embodying the principles described, actually demonstrating the application whenever possible, and opening the problem up for general discussion. No book can take the place of a capable teacher, of dynamic classroom discussion, or of actual experience. It is but a jumping-off point for a thrilling expedition on one's own, and a Baedeker for occasional reference along the way.

To the many friends who have been patiently helpful in the preparation and collection of the material, I am deeply indebted. I am grateful for the courteous permission to use quoted passages from published works, and for the kindness and cooperation of all who furnished photographs.

HOYLAND BETTINGER

New York City
January 15, 1947

PREFACE TO THE REVISED EDITION

~~~~~~

Television is all that Mr. Bettinger had hoped for when he wrote this book in 1947—and more. It has entered into the daily lives of peoples in this country and abroad wherever they have been privileged to come in contact with it. The miracle of television, the ability to project a picture—in motion, talking, and now in color—from a point of origin into the homes of millions many miles away, is now taken for granted by the public.

The uses to which the miracle is being put will continue to be questioned; and that is good. Television as a tool, a force, in the art of communications—information, education and entertainment—has never been equaled in history. It is incumbent on intelligent people to become a party to television lest it fall into the hands of the selfish and short-sighted. When television deals in mediocrities, of which no art form is free, it may be in contact with perhaps four million people; but a program of substance may have an audience as large as seventy million. No other art form is so rewarding in terms of audience numbers.

It is with this belief that I have assumed the responsibility, left by the untimely passing of Hoyland Bettinger in 1950, of updating this book, that it may continue to serve the growth of television into a distinctive art form, dedicated to service.

SOL CORNBERG

New York City, May 4, 1954

TELEVISION

TECHNIQUES

Chapter I

TOOLS OF THE TRADE

ALTHOUGH a technical understanding of television is not necessary in writing or producing a program, an insight into its workings is a definite aid. Certainly a working knowledge of the equipment used is essential. The sponsor, agency man, writer, actor, director, and others concerned with the program's preparation or production should know how the equipment is used, what it will do, and what it will not do well, if they are to make the best use of the medium. It is only through such knowledge—coupled with a keen awareness of the "personality" of television—that good programs can be conceived and produced. And so, before delving into the details of program production, let us become familiar with the tools of the trade.

Many of the tools of the television trade—perhaps the most important ones—are intangible. They are the aptitudes, talents, and special abilities requisite to good work in a creative field. A few richly endowed mortals seem to do superb work instinctively—though it usually will be found that they acquired much of the "know how" through painstaking effort and study. The purpose of this book is to outline the guiding principles and basic factors on which good television programming depends, and to give the practitioner a solid foundation on which to build his own individual accomplishments.

We are dealing with factors as old as the arts from which television stems—fundamentals gleaned throughout the centuries from a rich harvest of picture-making arts and the drama, from fifty years of motion picture experience, and from twenty-five years of radio. Television, to be sure, added a new dimension—immediacy. This was true for too little time until television, technically, became aware of the fact that it could reproduce old and new recorded programs, specifically those on film.

I

The public was then subjected to a barrage of out-dated and purposeless programming, only because it was available on film. The miracle was working. Pictures were reaching the far corners of the community, but the very essence of television—immediacy—was being bypassed. It is with pleasure that we note the return to programming which has as its basis immediacy, specifically The National Broadcasting Company's shows *Today, Home,* and *Tonight:* and the Columbia Broadcasting System's programs *Person to Person,* and *See It Now:* as well as the enlightening revelations of Government functions. But the factors which govern its use as an art of communication are as old as human nature, and they are subject to revision only to the extent that we from time to time alter our desires, tastes, and habits. Television simply gives us a new emotional outlet and some new electronic tricks. Our reactions to visual and aural stimuli are as ancient as man.

What Is Meant by Electronics?

Radio is an *electronic* device. So is the X-ray machine and the electric eye that opens doors. The term is applied to a long list of devices in which *electrons* are put to work. Television is but one of the products resulting from years of electronic research.

Many years ago scientists discovered that all matter is made up of atoms. They thought then that an atom was the smallest possible division of matter. But later it was found that the atom is, in effect, a tiny universe like our solar system, with a central nucleus around which still smaller particles move. These particles were named *electrons* because they were found to be negative charges of electricity.

We do not know what an atom really looks like, for the scientists thus far have been able only to study its behavior, but it is usually expressed symbolically as in Figure 1.

Every substance in nature has a definite number of electrons in its

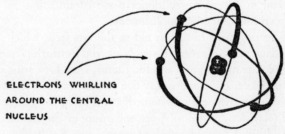

ELECTRONS WHIRLING
AROUND THE CENTRAL
NUCLEUS

FIG. 1. An Imaginary Close-up of the Atom.

atom. Uranium, for instance, has ninety-two. Hydrogen has only one. It so happens that, in certain substances, the electrons are not firmly held by the attraction power of the nucleus. The electrons can actually be driven out of those substances by heat or light. It is on these phenomena that television depends.

In the vacuum of an ordinary electric lamp, electrons are continually boiling out of the tungsten filament, because of the heat produced by the electricity. Thomas Edison discovered this effect many years ago. Fleming and De Forest came along and put these electrons to work, thus giving us radio. Other scientists perfected ways of controlling the action of electrons in vacuum tubes, and they found so many useful applications for this "magic in bottles" that we now live in an electronic age.

How Does Television Work?

Although television is a complex process and beyond the full comprehension of the layman, it is both possible and useful to form a mental picture of its workings.

The first thing to bear in mind here is that the picture and the sound are transmitted separately. In a television set there is the same sort of apparatus that is found in an FM (frequency modulation) radio for

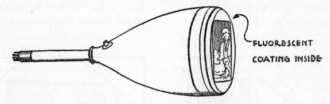

FLUORESCENT
COATING INSIDE

FIG. 2. A PICTURE TUBE.

receiving, amplifying, and controlling the sound. In addition to this, there is apparatus for receiving the electrical pictures that come over the air and converting them into visual pictures. How these pictures are formed in the receiving set may be simply described as follows:

Certain substances, called *fluorescent* materials, become luminous and glow with light when placed in the path of electrons. In a television set, regardless of whether it is of the direct view or the projection type, there is a vacuum tube, coated on the inside at the picture end with some form of fluorescent material. (See Figure 2.)

The picture is produced by electrons, falling on the fluorescent material and causing a glow of light. The amount of light at each minute point of the picture area depends on the number of electrons which impinge upon it. The whole trick of television lies in controlling the number of electrons which bombard each point of the picture. Bombard is an apt word because the electrons are literally fired out of a "gun" at the other end of the tube. As to how this is done the layman needs to know little more than can be visualized in the sketches in Figure 3.

This action takes place at lightning speed. Even then, an objectionable

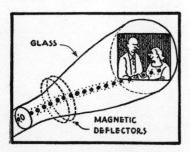

1. In an electric lamp the electrons boil out of the filament, in all directions, and return to it again. In a television tube they are boiled out of a cathode. . . .

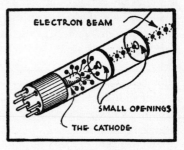

2. . . . located in the gun end. From here the electrons are drawn through small openings, until they form a tiny stream or beam, directed toward the picture area.

3. By a magnetic method of control, this beam is caused to move in straight lines, from left to right, as the eye does in reading.

4. Thus the beam scans the whole picture, point by point, thirty times each second, making the fluorescent material glow with patterns of light, exactly as in the original scene.

FIG. 3. HOW THE PICTURE TUBE WORKS.

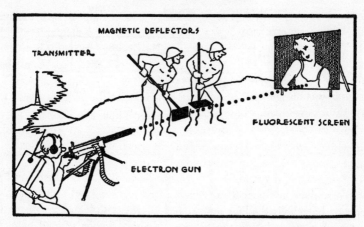

Visualize a machine gunner, on orders from some distant point, firing
electron bullets which are being deflected in precise, military regu-
larity across the surface of a picture target. At points where the picture
is black, no electrons are fired. The spots where the brightest lights
are get a terrific burst. All the shades of gray in between these ex-
tremes are bombarded with electrons in proportion to the amount of
light.

FIG. 4. A PICTURE TUBE—WITH GESTURES.

flicker would be observed were it not for the fact that the human eye for
a fraction of a second retains an image of what it sees. This is known as
persistence of vision, and it is this which makes us unconscious of the
flickering of both motion pictures and television.

The lay person is likely to flounder hopelessly in any technical explanation of such a complex subject as television. Usually it is helpful to
resort to some simple analogy, even though it may verge on the absurd.
We therefore present another sketch (Figure 4) to explain further what
goes on in a picture tube, believing the analogy not too far-fetched.

We may visualize a similar sequence of events in the tube of the
television camera, but with this striking difference: In the camera tube,
although there may be an electron gun and a beam of electrons similar to
those in the picture tube, a different function is performed. Here, instead
of patterns of electrical impulses being converted into visual pictures,
the opposite occurs. The patterns of light and dark in the scene being
televised are converted by the electron beam into *electrical patterns*.

There are a number of types of television camera tubes. For the sake
of simplicity and clarity of understanding in bridging between black

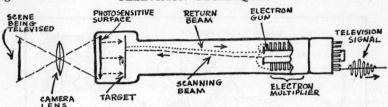

FIG. 5. IMAGE ORTHICON TUBE.

and white (monochrome) and color television, we shall describe only one of them, the image orthicon tube (Figure 5).

In appearance, it resembles a large size flashlight. At one end is a flat photo sensitive glass surface on which a lens focuses a light image of the scene to be televised. The appearance of the visible image instantly creates on a target inside the tube an identical image formed of electrons. The number of electrons at each point of this invisible image correspond to the intensity of the light at that point in the original scene.

Next, this electronic pattern is to be "read" so that each unit area in its composition can be evaluated and then transmitted to receivers. This is done by scanning this charged image by a beam of electrons shot from a "gun" at the opposite end of the image orthicon. This beam, pinpoint small, scans the electron image from side to side and top to bottom just as the human eye scans a printed page, but a thousand times faster. When this beam reaches the image it loses different amounts of electrons depending on the charges it meets, and then returns to a spot near the "gun," where the electrons are amplified millions of times and let off to the transmitter in the form of an electric current. This alternating current forms the heart of the television signal, which is radiated into space by the transmitting antenna, and may be pictured as in Figure 6.

Thus we see that the television picture is sent out on the air, bit by bit in single file, and reassembled in the home receiver. The patterns of light and dark in the televised scene produce identical electrical patterns in the signal that is broadcast to the antenna of the receiving set. Here these modulated electrical impulses are converted back into the original patterns of light and dark.

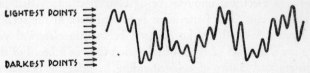

FIG. 6. AN ELECTRICAL PICTURE.

In today's black and white television, the image of the scene is, in effect, divided into 525 horizontal strips, each a small fraction of an inch in width. The scanning rates and other operating specifications of black and white television have been standardized by the Federal Communications Commission, hence the signal from any television station can be received by any television receiver within range.

When color is added to the black and white images, more information must be carried by the television signal without exceeding the operating specifications as laid down. A brief description of color and its relation to vision may impart an inkling of how this is accomplished.

Hue, saturation, and brightness are the three terms that define any color scientifically and indicate a color's probable effect on the human eye and brain. Brightness is the basic information of the monochrome signal. To this must be added hue and saturation and these must be added in such a way as to be compatible to black and white receivers.

To assemble a complete color signal, a color television camera breaks up the image into three primary colors—red, green, and blue. With these primaries any color in the visible spectrum can be described electronically by selecting the proper values of hue, saturation, and brightness. The sensitivity of selection is at such a point even now in the infancy of color television that a wider range of colors is available to the creator in color than is available in any other known palette.

By adding a certain amount of each of the three primary colors, the impression of white can be produced in the eye. Green and red together give an impression of yellow; red and blue result in purple. An absence of all three primaries produces an impression of black.

Color picture tubes of various technical arrangement have been developed. One version (Fig. 7), the tri-color picture tube, has three electron guns—one for each primary color—which scan and stimulate color phosphers on the viewing screen. The tiny phosphor dots—there

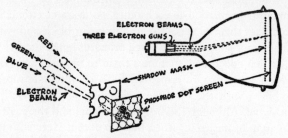

FIG. 7. TRI-COLOR PICTURE TUBE.

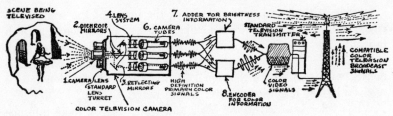

FIG. 8. PICKUP AND TRANSMISSION.

may be 600,000 of them or more—are arranged in clusters of three, a red-glowing, green-glowing, and blue-glowing phospher in each group. A shadow-mask between the guns and the viewing screen has tiny perforations in it so positioned that the stream of electrons from each gun can fall only on its appropriate color phosphor. The beam that "part paints" red information will only strike the red phosphers, etc.

The lens (1) of the television camera collects light rays in full color from the scene being televised. The full-color image is focused into a series of mirrors. In the center are two dichroic mirrors (2) made of specially treated optical glass which has the property of reflecting one color while passing all other colors. The first of these mirrors reflects the red light, while the blue and green light pass straight through. The second dichroic mirror reflects the blue but passes the green. Thus three images, one in each primary color, are created. With the aid of regular reflecting mirrors (3) and the lens system (4), the three primary images are focused on the faces of three television camera tubes (image orthicons). In front of the camera tubes are color filters (5) which assure that the color quality of each primary has the precise value for the system. The electronic beam in each camera tube (6) scans the image pattern which has been formed on the tube screen, thereby producing a primary color signal. The three primary color signals from the three tubes are now processed for transmission. Samples of these signals, in proper amounts in relation to each other, go to an electronic adder (7) which combines them to make the brightness or black and white signal. At the same time, samples of the three primary signals are fed to another unit (8) which encodes or combines them to produce a signal carrying the hue and saturation information. This color-representing signal is then combined with the brightness signal to form the complete color television signal. Although the brightness signal and the color-representing signal are transmitted together, they do not interfere with each other.

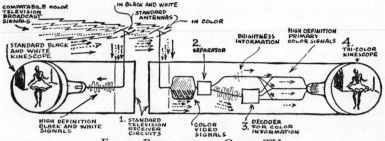

FIG. 9. RECEPTION OF COLOR TV.

When the color television broadcast signals reach a black and white receiver, the electronic data pertaining to hue and saturation are ignored by the receiver's circuits and only the brightness signal remains effective. Unless the viewer were informed in advance, he would not realize that the scene on his receiver started out from the studio as a signal in full color. When the color television broadcast signals flow down a standard antenna lead-in and through standard television amplifying circuits (1), the receiver separates (2) the color-representing signal from the brightness signal. Next, the color information is decoded (3) so that when recombined with the brightness information, a series of high primary color signals are produced, ready to be applied to the color tube (4).

ABOUT TELEVISION EQUIPMENT

The equipment with which we as program people are concerned consists of (a) television cameras, (b) motion picture and slide projectors, (c) lights, (d) microphones and sound pickup, and (e) that portion of the control room equipment which is utilized by the director or producer. In addition to this there is a considerable amount of special equipment used for producing "effects."

In subsequent chapters we shall deal specifically with most of this equipment, but for the benefit of those who may never have been inside a television studio a brief résumé will be given.

The Television Camera

In the work it will do, the television studio camera differs little from an ordinary professional movie camera. Like its counterpart, it is heavy and, to make it readily mobile, it is mounted on a rolling platform or base—usually referred to as a dolly. The dolly is so constructed that the camera can be quickly and smoothly raised or lowered, tilted up or down, or swung in an arc.

Some cameras mounted on pedestals are pushed around by the cameraman himself, the camera head being raised or lowered by counterweights or hydraulically. In others the cameraman rides the dolly, which is moved around by an assistant, called the dollyman. Motor driven dollies which carry the cameraman, the dolly operator, and a monitor to see what the camera is picking up are in use but take an extraordinarily large amount of studio floor space for their operation. The cameraman wears headphones through which he receives instructions from the director in the control room as to the camera position desired.

The lens system is not at all unusual. There is a means of focusing the picture on the mosaic. The diaphragm can be opened or closed for different intensities of light. There are lenses of varying focal length.

In remote pick-up cameras, such as are used for sporting events, lenses up to 40-inch focal length are used, just as in the newsreel camera. The remote or field camera is lighter than the studio camera and is used on a standard newsreel camera tripod. Two to four cameras constitute the usual field unit.

In shooting a scene in the studio, as many as three or even more cameras may be focusing on it at the same time. Any one of them may be put on the air. In the control room the technical director, as he is called, switches from camera to camera in accordance with instructions in the script. What is more, he can intercut shots from motion picture or slide projectors located in the projection room.

Motion Picture and Slide Projectors

Every complete television studio has a projection room where motion picture and slide projectors are mounted so as to focus the projected picture directly on the mosiac of a television camera. In the case of motion pictures, which may be either 16mm or 35mm, the difference in the projection speed of 16 or 24 movie frames per second and 30 television pictures per second is compensated for in the design of the projector.

Motion pictures or slides are used to embellish a live-action show in many ways—for instance, in introducing variety of locale, creating time transitions, moods, and so on. A common technique employed in title sequences is to use movies or stills, sometimes superimposed on a shot from one of the studio cameras.

Control-Room Equipment

The control room is where the program is "edited" and put in the form it takes on the air. It corresponds to the cutting room of the motion picture studio. In a movie cutting room, camera shots and sound track can be juggled around at will and retaken at leisure, if necessary. But in television there are no retakes. Though the director can cut from one camera to another, he is forced to take what the cameras are seeing and the microphones are hearing *at the moment*—for better or worse.

As in radio, the early control rooms in television were designed to allow the director and engineers to look down into the studios to see the action. However, operating practice shows that the volume of scenery used more often than not blinds the control room to the action on the studio floor, and therefore the control room operating personnel must resort to the medium in which they work—television—for the view of action. The control room has the usual radio control and mixing console, where the audio engineer sits and manipulates the sound. In addition to this, there is the video engineer who controls the picture quality, and also produces such visual effects as fades, dissolves, and superimposures. In monochrome televising one video engineer can handle three or four camera outputs efficiently. However, in color televising, where each camera, at this time, is three image orths, one video engineer is required for each camera.

From here the director or producer of the show guides its destiny. He, together with the video and audio engineers, are in constant contact, by means of headphones, with the cameramen, the stage manager, and others on the studio floor. Furthermore, they can see at all times what each camera is taking, and what is being sent out on the air. This is accomplished by what amounts to a receiving set for each camera and one for the picture being sent to the transmitter. These are called monitors. Any one of the cameras can be put on the air; in fact, the pictures from two or more of them can be superimposed one upon the other.

Since the director's instructions to the cameramen and stage manager are brought to them over their headphones, they are not heard by the home audience. Nor are his side remarks to the control-room personnel.

Microphones and Sound Pick-up

Television sound, although it is broadcast in the same way as radio, presents pick-up problems more closely related to those of motion picture production. Whereas the radio player stands more or less in a fixed spot, close to the microphone, the television player is usually wandering all over the place. Hence in the television studio the microphone must follow the player. This is achieved by hanging the mike on the end of a long boom that can be readily and noiselessly maneuvered by an operator.

The operator stands on a movable boom pedestal which can be shifted from scene to scene. By means of ingenious cranks and levers, he orients the microphone in such a way as to pick up the desired voice or sound. The sound or *audio* engineer in the control room lets him know, through his headphones, how he is doing.

In addition to the boom mike, (wireless included) other microphones are placed at advantageous points, to be used for announcing, narrating, or introducing sound effects. In the control room, music and sound effects can be picked up from records. Such sound may be either mixed in the control room or played back into the studio through speakers when it is desirable for the players to hear the sound.

Lights

Television originates and terminates in light. It is no wonder, then, that the lighting equipment used in a television studio is extensive and that it must be skillfully used. The kind and amount of light depends on the sensitivity of the camera tube and on whether the broadcast is in black and white or in color. We shall take up these matters in detail in the chapter on lighting. For the time being it need only be established that the lighting equipment, in general, is like that found in a motion picture or photographic studio.

These are the tools of the television trade. They are good tools and in the hands of good craftsmen will turn out a good product. The television camera will tell the audience what it sees; the microphone will tell what it hears. But the equipment, no matter how wonderful it is, possesses no creative or selective ability. That is the function of the program department.

A television program involves three steps—three distinct and equally important processes: first, *selecting the material;* second, *organizing and arranging* this material so that it has continuity and meaning; third, *producing the program within the limits of the medium.* It is to the solution of these three problems that this book is devoted.

Chapter II

~~~~~~

THE MEDIUM

THE prime requisite for success in television program production is an awareness of the medium's inherent "personality." To make the most effective use of this medium one must know what it can do, what it does best, and wherein its weaknesses lie. Its limitations as well as its great potentialities must be taken into full account.

Stemming as it does from the stage, the screen, and radio, television possesses many of the limitations and potentialities of all three. And yet it is greater than the sum of all of them, for in reality it is an extension of two of our senses—sight and hearing. Therein lies its greatest potential.

Television is a medium of communication which, like theater, motion picture, and radio, has the ability to provide education, information, and entertainment. It is in a real sense a powerful sociological force. Like radio, it reaches into the home and thus into the heart of the nation. It forms attitudes. It conditions thinking. It establishes and nurtures cultural standards.

To protect the best interests of the public in this field of influence against abuse, the Federal Communications Commission exercises rigid control over television broadcasting, as it does over radio.

Since television is such a potent factor in home life, in the formation of attitudes, in setting standards of taste and judgment, and in molding public opinion, it is imperative that all who work in it are cognizant of the power they hold in their hands. To use it wisely, then, will in the long run pay the highest return to the industry as a whole.

VIEWING HABITS

Before any constructive thought can be given to television program techniques, a comprehensive study of the preferences and habits of the audience must be made. We must know where the potential audience is during broadcast hours, what they are doing, and to what extent they will give (a) visual and (b) aural attention to the program. We must be familiar with their home routine and social habits. We must know how television is integrated into those habits.

Though it is not within the scope of this book to treat the whole subject, we shall discuss certain aspects of it which have a direct bearing on the techniques of program production.

Reaction to Visual and Aural Stimuli

Since television demands the simultaneous use of two of our senses—sight and hearing—it carries a double impact. This, of course, accounts for its double effectiveness as an entertainment and advertising medium. At the same time, its dualism of appeal can easily degenerate into a weakness, if control is not intelligently exercised over the *attention balance* between the visual and aural. This necessitates an understanding of our reactions to visual and aural stimuli.

The human mind can concentrate on only one thing at a time. It cannot concentrate with the eyes and the ears simultaneously. To be sure, we can look and listen at the same time, but that is not concentration. Consequently, if the attention of a television audience is to be held, the focus of attention must be shifted back and forth between picture and sound.

In a television play, for example, it is unwise to ask the audience to concentrate closely on either the picture or the sound exclusively for too long a period of time. Rest periods should be *planted*. The eye and the ear should be given alternate periods of relief. When the strongest impact is carried by movement, action, business, or any form of picturization, the dialogue should be restrained. Conversely, when the dialogue is more important than the action, the visual treatment should be passive. Through this device the audience is conditioned for high, climactic situations wherein both picture and sound, for brief moments, are played with all stops out.

We do not react the same ways to both picture and sound. In the matter of fatigue, the eye is the more susceptible of the two. It demands more frequent relief from concentration.

Any form of concentration causes fatigue. In life, we continually shift our eyes from point to point, thus lessening fatigue by a change of focus. This relief is not possible while the eye is focused on a television screen, though the condition can be ameliorated to a considerable extent by maintaining pictorial variety. In life, we shut out sounds by mental control, or we move away from them, if they are too tiring. It is important, therefore, that the fatigue factor be taken into account in building a television program.

In stimulating the imagination, the ear is more effective than the eye. The latter is apt to take what it sees literally. Sounds conjure up more associations than does the eye. We hear the sound of a distant train whistle and are reminded of some nostalgic childhood scene. We hear the scream of a siren and our mind's eye sees the police car in pursuit of the gangster. The use of sound, then, as a device in stimulating the imagination, in establishing moods, and in the association of ideas is of great psychological importance.

In the exchange of information or the transfer of knowledge, the eye is the more potent organ, for two reasons: first, because we are more picture- than ear-minded, since most of our knowledge has been gained visually; and, second, because visual memory is more lasting than aural.

In carrying conviction, the picture does the better job, for we are apparently guided by the old adage, "Believe nothing you hear, and only half of what you see."

It should be borne in mind that we can look without seeing and listen without hearing. In addition, scientific study focuses on the fact that there are those of us who partake of information orally, or visually, as well as kinesthetically. Various television techniques make it possible to take advantage of these facts and, by shifting the focus of attention to either picture or sound, to create powerful dramatic effects.

LIMITATIONS OF THE MEDIUM

Success in the use of any medium is dependent on recognition of its inherent limitations and on working within them. Television, like every other form of expression, possesses certain limitations and weaknesses. We are concerned here, not with the transitory limitations of a technical nature which are continually being weeded out by scientific and engineering progress, but with those inherent in the medium itself. The limitations we are about to discuss are not serious in themselves. They become so only when they are not recognized and when intelligent steps are not taken to circumvent them.

1. *Time.*

First of all, there is the limitation of time. This is encountered in a number of forms. There are limitations imposed by the length of time that can be allotted to a given program segment; by the disparity between the time when an event takes place and the time when the audience is available to see it; by the time zones into which the country is divided; and by the insufficient time which is ordinarily available for adequate program preparation.

We go to the theater prepared to devote a considerable period of undivided attention to the presentation. In the home, on the other hand, we may or may not be willing or able to devote a like amount of complete attention. Also, in the home we can, in effect, jump from theater to theater by the mere turn of a dial. The television producer must capture the attention of the audience instantly—during the first few critical moments—and hold it in the face of all the distractions that prevail in the home, without knowing whether the audience was there for the unfolding of the plot or whether they were diverted during its development. This means that in television the pace must be faster than in the theater, even to the point of imposing limitations in plot development, exposition, characterization, and picturization.

The sponsor pays for a specific block of time, and the fact that the program must fit this block, and hit it to the second, constitutes a very definite limitation as anyone who has worked with the medium knows. Often the time allowance actually does not fit the material to be broadcast, and to be successful in this case the producer must have learned the trick of sacrificing material without weakening the over-all effect and of padding without diluting.

The foregoing time limitations result in what amounts to some of the most troublesome features of television program construction. The visual aspect of television makes it dependent on action. Picturized action consumes an amount of time that is not always in proportion to the contribution which the action makes to the total effect. A bit of stage business is frequently time-consuming but difficult to eliminate. Often there is not as much time for story development as the writer or producer would like or as the story demands. As a result, ingenuity of the highest order is demanded of the producer.

In radio, where the action is not seen, it can be moved along as rapidly as the ear can keep up with it, merely by the use of words or sound effects. But in television it takes just so many valuable seconds for the villain to drag the body across the stage, remove the preshus jools, and make an upstage exit. If he is not allowed time to perform visually at least some of the things that a dastardly villain is supposed to do, he cannot be a very good villain.

Yes, time is the villain of the television program, and his depredations can only be foiled by heroic planning. It's 29:40 or bust.

2. Space

There are space limitations, too, which must be circumvented by clever handling. The television camera is limited to *monocular* vision—seeing with only *one* eye. This throws linear perspective out of balance and makes it difficult, at times, to show objects as they appear to the human eye. Since we normally have *binocular* vision—seeing with *two* eyes—we see things in a different perspective than the one-eyed camera sees them. Perhaps you have taken a photograph of someone stretched out on the beach; the feet—by accident or intent—were toward the camera and near to it. The feet, you will recall, came out size twenty-six and the head the size of a peanut.

In motion pictures, where only one scene is shot at a time, the camera can be set up at the most advantageous angle. In live television this is not always possible—even with the use of a number of close-up cameras. Certain shots—sometimes shots that are badly needed—have to be eliminated.

Space limitations are encountered in other ways: In studio live production there are limitations of space imposed by the size of the studio and the number of sets required; there are restrictions placed on the movements of talent in the direction toward and away from the camera, because of the focal depth of the camera lens; there are also cross-stage limits of movement, both as to distance and speed, brought about by the necessity of shooting in continuity and by the lack of time and space to get the best camera set-up.

3. Light

The most serious limitation is experienced in lighting effectively for television because of the element of sustained production. Yet it is light that makes television. Light causes the modulation in the picture signal that is transmitted to the receiver; light causes the screen to glow with a visible image; and it is by painting with patterns of light that the lighting director gives the screen image meaning—both intellectual and emotional. Through the manipulation of light and shadow, pictorial composition is achieved; detail is accentuated or repressed; moods are established. The picture can be made good or bad by its lighting alone.

Screen technique calls for the display of *surface* emotions—the flicker of feeling that plays across a face. For such a subtle visual effect to be felt by the audience it is necessary to light the face with subtle modeling. Usually only one position of the head—one angle of tilt—in relation to the lights will give this. With the limited number of camera angles that are possible in the continuity shooting of television it is often difficult, if not impossible, for the producer to get the shot he wants. He may rehearse and re-rehearse the action, but it may not be possible for the lightmen to get the light where the cameramen can catch it. Consequently the producer must create his effect in some other way.

Whereas in motion pictures there is almost no limit to the lighting effects that can be created, because the lighting can be carefully set up for each scene, the effects possible in television are much more limited; therefore it calls for clever direction by the producer, willing co-operation from the talent, and adroit handling of camera and lights in order to circumvent the limitations thus imposed.

4. Sound

Another set of obstacles inherent in sustained production is encountered in live sound pick-up. In a dramatic program, for example, the actors are moving about the playing area, throwing cues in all directions; dialogue and sounds are coming from here and there. This presents pick-up difficulties in that the microphone, whether used singly or in multiple, sometimes cannot be at the right place at the proper time. As a result there are undesirable changes in sound level. Furthermore, it is often difficult to maneuver the boom mike into the proper position for good pick-up without its casting a shadow on a player's face.

In motion picture production these difficulties are avoided by breaking the action up into short takes, by re-recording the sound, and by prescoring—either making the sound track first and then playing it back while the picture is being made, or "dubbing" the track in afterwards.

In television the only solution is to be found in skillful direction, the co-operativeness of the players, and alertness on the part of the technical staff. Careful rehearsal directed specifically toward this end is essential.

SHOWMANSHIP OR ELSE

The very nature of television calls for showmanship of the first order. The television program director must be a showman. What is more, this quality must permeate the entire production staff—technical and program alike.

To be a showman the producer must understand the twists and turns of human nature. He must know people and how to make them laugh and cry, think and reflect, relax and enjoy themselves. The good showman has (a) sense of *structure and form*, (b) a keen sense of *continuity*, and (c) a highly developed sense of *timing*. He is endowed with originality and the ability to devise new ways of presenting "the tried and true"—of giving old ideas new twists. He knows how long it is safe to sustain a mood, when to change the pace; how often to repeat the familiar, and when to introduce the novel. He knows what people want and like, and how to give it to them.

The good showman also knows his medium—its potentialities and its limitations. Is he born or made? Who can say? This much is certain, the most important item of his stock in trade is experience. The fundamentals with which we are dealing are the foundation stones of showmanship.

Chapter III

~~~~~~

PICTORIAL COMPOSITION AND CONTINUITY

SINCE we are dealing with a subject that is essentially visual, it is logical that we begin with a detailed study of the fundamentals that govern visual continuity and pictorial composition.

Visual continuity is television's "reason for being." Its very existence depends on the production of good pictures selectively chosen and woven together into smooth continuity. Considering the hundreds of pictorial arrangements that flash on the screen during a television show, it might seem that carefully worked out compositions would be humanly impossible. This is not the case, provided the producer is equipped with two essentials: first, a working knowledge of pictorial composition; second, a carefully thought out plan for building the continuity.

Every television production can—and should—be built around the *key picture situations* which constitute the essence or high points of the program. These key pictures are the ones that will have the strongest appeal for the audience, and they are probably the only ones it will remember. They can make or mar the show. Therefore these are the pictures on which the producer should concentrate. His very first step should be to analyze the production and determine the key picture situations around which it revolves. This will provide a safe structure on which to build the intervening continuity. Knowing the pictorial arrangement and how the players are to be placed in the key situations, the producer has only to plan the action and stage movement which leads up to them.

It is with the composition of these key pictures and the planning of continuity around them that this chapter is concerned. The principles with which we shall deal will be recognized by many as being the basic principles underlying all the picture-making arts. The gifted producer uses them perhaps instinctively. The same is true of the photographer, the cameraman, and the artist who has been specially endowed. But the average person engaged in television production must needs prepare himself through study for the art of picture making.

Good pictures are compounded out of time-tested principles of art and the laws of what we call composition. Pictorial items thrown together without the application of these principles may have statistical value, but they certainly have no pictorial significance. The piano keyboard is able to produce many different musical notes. If struck at random, there is no music; but, if it is played by someone who knows how to put the notes together, people stand in line at the box office.

Unfortunately there are practically no rules for composing pictures. The few that can be laid down "hard and fast" are negative rather than positive. They are "don'ts." There are, however, guiding principles which may be learned and used as working tools.

PSYCHOLOGICAL FACTORS

A picture is an arrangement of shapes. Shapes are made up of line, mass, and form. Our emotional reaction to shapes is very pronounced. We react differently to the huge, bulky shape than we do, let us say, to the petite blonde. It is on the *known reaction to shapes,* coupled with other psychological factors, that we compose pictures to produce definite —and predictable—responses on the part of the audience.

If, then, a picture is something more than an arrangement of objects to entertain the eye, if it is a device for reaching the emotions, is it not vitally important that television pictures be well composed?

The arranging of shapes into pictures that will convey a story or mood requires an understanding of the psychological factors which control our response to pictorial effects. These factors can be traced directly to our reactions to things commonly experienced in life. To make this clear: when in a prone, relaxed position—more or less horizontal—we rest or go to sleep; hence, the picture in which horizontal, quiet lines predominate gives us a feeling of restfulness and repose, whereas the picture built on strong diagonals gives us something of the same reaction we get from watching violent action.

From this it will be clear that the *basic structure* of the picture—the abstract form around which it is built—*governs our emotional response to* it. Such basic forms or structures can be listed, described, and memorized. Before considering them in detail, however, we should become familiar with the significance of line, mass, and form.

SIGNIFICANCE OF LINE, MASS, AND FORM

1. *Line*

Line, as it is thought of in a picture, is formed by the edge of a mass or an area. It may be a line that is actually seen or a line that is suggested by a repetition of spots. Such lines are called transitional lines—a means of getting from one place to another. Our mental reactions establish lines where none actually exist. We "feel" a line running from head to head in a scene involving a number of people, provided they are arranged in some geometrical pattern, such as a triangle. Line may also be felt by direction of movement.

We think of lines as being straight or curved or broken, and as being horizontal, vertical, or diagonal. Each has its psychological meaning.

The scenic artist uses the psychology of line in set design. He must fit the linear design to the mood. If the content of the scene is light and informal, he will use broken horizontals—perhaps in combination with curved lines. If the feeling is formal and dignified, the linear structure

(a) *Straight lines* give a feeling of directness, rigidity, masculinity, and the like. They should be used where those feelings dominate a scene.

(b) *Curved lines* express charm, grace, movement, and femininity. The curved line is the line of beauty and graceful movement.

FIG. 10. THE PSYCHOLOGY OF LINE.

(c) *Broken lines* express informality, indecision, disorder, and similar states. Broken lines may be used to give a feeling of informal casualness.

(d) *Horizontal lines* express repose, tranquillity, and stability. They are monotonous if used to excess.

(e) *Vertical lines* are expressive of importance, uplift, aspiration, and spirituality. They possess more attraction power than do horizontals.

(f) *Diagonal lines* are the lines of force, action, aggressiveness, and change of movement. They are the most dramatically exciting lines, because of their power to attract and hold attention.

FIG. 10. (*cont'd*) THE PSYCHOLOGY OF LINE.

of the setting must be formal. He will not design his sets merely to look well as sets, but to contribute to the effect which the producer wishes to achieve.

The cameraman uses line as the structure of his shots. If a feeling of stability is desired, he grabs on to a near horizontal for the lower part of the composition. He watches out for the distracting vertical that divides his composition centrally into two pictures. He looks for transitional lines that will hold the picture together.

The producer uses line psychology in the placement and movement of his characters, in the disposition of properties, and in the lighting effects.

Since line is produced on the television screen by contrasts of light and dark along the edge of masses, it will be seen that linear structure can be regulated in two ways: (1) by utilizing the degree of contrast in the objects themselves, that is to say, by putting a light object against a darker one, or vice versa; and (2) by lighting the edges of objects so that they separate from what is behind them.

We must also think continually of the *intensity* of the line, because the same linear structure can produce two different psychological effects. Brightness, gayety, and excitement are expressed if the shapes are "edgy" and the lines strongly felt; calmness, solemnity, and peace if the lines are soft and diffused.

2. *Mass or Psychological Weight*

Mass in the dictionary sense is a quantity of matter. Pictorially, mass is used to denote the *psychological weight* of an area, an object or a group of objects. We intentionally or instinctively group individual shapes into masses, because the arrangement produces an emotional

Fig. 11. Mass.

response. We are moved by the wide expanse of the sea, by the precipitous drop of the cliff, by the majesty of the mountain. We speak of cathedral pines, for we associate the regular massing of tall verticals with things spiritual.

Our emotional response to mass is definite, as a few examples will prove. The virile, dominating husband playing against the weakly submissive, frightened wife could not seriously be cast with a puny, dried-up specimen of a man against a big, raw-boned, Gashouse Gertie hunk of a woman. It would not feel right. Conversely, its absurdity could be turned to advantage in a comedy.

Fig. 12. Contrast in Mass.

A graceful, informal massing of living-room properties induces nostalgic feelings of ordered domesticity, but bring a jumbled group of characters into the room and disorder prevails.

The character of masses, their relationship one to the other, and their distribution, together with the linear structure of the television picture, play a vital part in establishing the mood. These factors are present in every picture; they should therefore be carefully analyzed and used in a way that will create harmony between content and treatment. If not, they may induce contradictory emotions.

3. Form or Aesthetic Shape

Form, in the sense we are using it here, is the *aesthetic shape* of the areas and masses which make up the picture. Whereas we think of mass as being light or heavy, slight or bulky, we think of form in a more specific way, for we instinctively associate form either with our knowledge of things or our emotional response to them. For instance, we speak of Venus as "the form divine," of the "tubby" man, of the "tow-

1. The Square expresses equality of interest or formality.

2. The Right Angle expresses opposition of interest or informality.

3. The Triangle expresses unity of interest, stability, or climax.

4. The Circle expresses continuity of interest or continuous movement.

FIG. 13. BASIC FORMS OF COMPOSITION.

5. The S Curve expresses variety of
   interest, grace, or beauty of movement.

6. The Z Shape expresses excitement
   of interest or extreme change.

7. The Cross expresses merging of interest or cohesion.

8. The Radii express concentration of
   interest or intensity of focus.

FIG. 13. (*cont'd*) BASIC FORMS OF COMPOSITION.

ering" giant; we associate the square with honesty, the circle with continuity, the scales with justice. Form calls to mind *conscious* associations and *subconscious* reactions. For this reason it is imperative that the pictorial forms used be compatible with the intent of the scene.

We use form in two ways: first, in the individual picture units; second, in the *structure or basic* form of the picture as a whole. A picture affects us in two ways: our minds take in its content; our emotions respond to its mood. The one is concrete and obvious; the other is abstract and not apparent to the uninitiated. But the *abstract form of the picture is what makes it what it is,* and the selection of the right basic form is the first step in composition. It is the abstract structure—the framework —on which the picture elements can be arranged.

It will help in grasping the significance of these basic forms if the mind is kept closed to recognizable shapes and if they are looked at in the abstract, as line, mass, and form.

All the foregoing forms may be used in perspective as well as in the two-dimensional vertical plane. In other words, the picture may (and should) be composed *in depth* by applying the same principles. Too often the *spatial* composition is completely disregarded.

1. *How to Use the Basic Forms*

One of the first considerations in planning a television program is how to present it visually. The solution of this problem will be found in the answer to the following questions: (1) What is the basic character of the program as a whole—formal or informal, light or serious, factual or imaginative, charming, bizarre, gay, or macabre? This will determine the over-all feeling which the pictorial continuity should have. (2) What is the mood pattern of each scene, and what specific effects are desired? (3) What basic forms of composition will produce those specific moods and effects? (4) In each situation, throughout the program, what treatment of line, mass, and form will be best suited to the content?

Just as the actor must think of the appropriate gesture, so must the writer, producer, set designer, cameraman, and lighting and technical director think of the appropriate picture. This means thinking of the picture in its *abstract* form.

The procedure should be to *start with the abstract and work through to the concrete.* It will be somewhat difficult for the novice to think in abstract terms at first, but once he has caught on and acquired that habit it will become almost instinctive. Then he will be prepared for catching good visuals "on the fly" in the heat of production, where there are no retakes and excuses do not count. That is what television demands.

How may these eight basic forms of composition be applied to a television program? Let us take a specific case—a dramatic situation in which contrasting moods and emotional conflicts exist.

2. Example of Application

Our problem is a scene of domestic, middle-class family life. As the scene opens, a mother and three children are engaged in quiet conversation. An air of peace reigns. Suddenly the drunken father enters and a conflict ensues between him and an older son, as the father threatens the youngest child. She, a little girl, runs out of the room in fright. Soon, offstage, the screech of brakes is heard. We cut to the scene of the accident; the injured child is lying in the street. One of her brothers picks her up. Then, back to the room as the child is brought in and laid on the sofa.

As a first step, suppose we figure out as literally as possible how we may apply the basic forms described on pages 24 and 25 to the *key situations* in the foregoing dramatic episode. Later we shall put our reasoning down on paper in *visual* form.

As the action begins we wish to convey an atmosphere of pleasant domesticity; consequently, in the disposition of the characters, we may use the triangle (3) for its stability and *unity of interest*. By opening with a series of triangular structures, we shall establish the close friendship and unity of the mother and her three children. If they are then brought into a *circular* arrangement (4) seen as a tight four-shot, and if we follow this with a long shot in which the characters are still in a closely knit family circle as the drunken father enters, we shall have built a strong situation. The breaking up of the family circle will make an effective dramatic contrast.

If the father is directed now to assume an isolated position facing the other four characters, who have moved into a triangular group with the older son forming the apex, we heighten the feeling of opposition by the use of the *right angle* (2).

The sequence of medium and close-up shots which next ensues for the conflict and turmoil will be built on strong *diagonal* lines and a rapidly changing focus of attention from one character to another. For the child's frightened exit, a long line of movement cutting across a medium long-shot will shift the interest to her emotional reaction. Following her exit there should be a brief period at a lower level of pace and pitch. To achieve this, we can make use of the stability and *rigidity* of the square (1). The characters are held momentarily in rigid posi-tions as the screech of brakes is heard offstage.

The action shifts to the scene of the accident. Here we make use of Z forms and the opposition of the right angle, thus employing *intensity of line* and *dramatic contrasts of mass,* for we wish to point up the help-lessness of the small child against brutal forces.

Back in the living room we compose on *horizontal* lines with the focus on the child lying prone on the sofa. We wish to bring out the solemnity of the occasion, and the horizontals will accomplish that. Through a shift to the *cross* form (7) the interest can be made to merge in the possibility that the child's injuries may perhaps be fatal. By a transition to the *radial* structure (8), the interest is still further con-centrated on the child, and we have built to our climax, which, if it runs true to form, will consist of the ghost of a smile flitting across the face of the child as she dies.

This is the skeleton of our picture plot. It is not complete, of course, because we shall take care of small details in rehearsal, but we have gained a big advantage over the un-thought-out method of program construction; we have laid a sound foundation and built a good frame-work. The attention can now be focused on finish and finesse.

But we should carry our planning a bit further and get it down on paper. This requires the making of simple sketches showing how char-acters and properties can be arranged in the key scenes, in accordance with the basic composition forms which we have found the story de-mands. It is to be expected that at this point many will come forward with the argument that they "can't even draw a straight line." It will be found, however, that if one can *think straight* he will be able to draw "straight" enough for the purpose. Furthermore, we are suggesting not the making of finished drawings but merely rough outlines to crys-tallize one's thinking.

Nor is it to be implied that it is necessary to make a drawing for each camera shot, or even many of them, but there is no contradicting the fact that a few simple line sketches (no matter how crude) of the *key scenes* is of inestimable value in planning visual continuity. Often it will save time in the end as well as make for better productions. The skilled producer may be able to do all or much of this planning mentally. But the student and the novice will find it helpful to adopt a visual method along the following lines.

a. A Method of Visual Planning

Think, first, of the emotional content of the scene—the feeling that is to be conveyed. Then, select the basic form or combination of forms (Pages 26 and 27) that will express that feeling. Finally, think in concrete terms of properties, characters, and acting, and fit them into the abstract structures, applying the psychology of line, mass, and form.

A situation from the opening of the play just analyzed may be used as an example. It occurs prior to the father's entrance and after a feeling of pleasant domesticity has been established. We wish to sustain that mood and develop the feeling of unity and closeness that exists. We are going to build a sequence of three-shots and four-shots in order to create that effect, for by such a device the interest can be passed from one character to another, with the resultant feeling of family unity.

Starting with a triangular structure that will include the four characters, proceed as shown in the illustrations of Figure 14.

Anyone who can write his own name can acquire the manual dexterity to make adequate sketches. Anyone who is visually minded can use this method of planning, and unless one is visually minded he has no place in television program planning. There is this to be said, however: many have more of a talent for visualizing than they realize, and this faculty, like other skills, can be developed by practice. Through continued application of the method suggested, the student will acquire the ability to analyze a situation and give it visual significance. As he gains experience he will be able to do more and more of this planning mentally. Let us apply the method to the key situations in our dramatic problem.

b. Demonstration of the Visual Method of Planning

If you refer to page 29 you will find the plot outline and the analysis of the basic forms of composition indicated by the dramatic content. The treatment could be worked out in other ways, but we shall take the following as an example. As to the design of the set, we shall assume that the producer has talked it over with the scenic artist and outlined the moods and effects he desires. The floor plan of the set will have evolved from the requirements of the action and the number of characters. Only one important downstage playing area is needed—a sofa

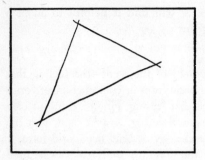

Draw a rectangle in the proportions of 3x4. With light lines, place in it a triangle of a shape and size that will allow an informal, pleasing arrangement of the four characters.

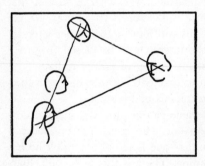

Now decide on the distribution of the characters. Since the mother has the lines and is the principal character, she might be placed with her head at the point of the triangle on the right of the picture. The other three may be placed with the older son at the upper point, the little girl at the bottom, and the other son just above, all looking at the mother. Draw ovals for the heads, adding features only if you feel able.

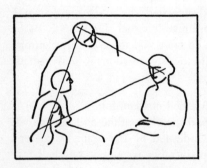

It is not necessary to carry the sketch further, because the general plan of the scene is by now fixed in mind, but the addition of a few lines will make the possibilities of the scene more clear. With this as a key shot, the whole sequence revolving around the dialogue between the mother and children can be planned—how the focus may be shifted from one to the other, and how this establishing shot may be followed by others, ending in the circle form as mentioned.

FIG. 14. A METHOD OF PLANNING A KEY SCENE.

with space around it for movement. An upstage door is required at which a number of strong situations are played; consequently its placement is important. The set might be arranged as shown in the first illustration of Figure 15.

Informal balance is used, with broken horizontals, quiet verticals, and pleasing curves to give a feeling of coziness and friendly informality. The basic form is the right angle in combination with curved shapes.

Any one of a number of opening shots may be thought of, but, since the climax is to be the death of the little girl, suppose we open with a close-up of her, stretched out on the floor, reading aloud from a story book. We then dolly back to reveal the first key picture—the establishing shot of the mother and children. We shall scatter the characters and maintain diffused focus of attention,

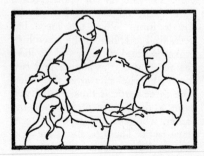

until a line from the mother motivates movement toward her ending in this triangular arrangement, which is used for its stability and unity of interest. This is followed by a sequence of three-shots and one close-up of the mother, all in triangular form, the focus being handed from one to another at a leisurely pace.

FIG. 15. A STORY-BOARD TREATMENT.

We pull them more compactly to-gether in a circular composition to heighten the feeling of close relation-ship between them, and to set the stage for the contrasting mood of the drunken father's entrance.

On his entrance, the circle breaks dramatically to this right-angle form of opposition. Note that the mother and children are grouped in a mass that counts as a vertical. The direc-tion of their attention forms a line of opposition to that vertical as it leads directly to the father at the door. The action resulting from his entrance will be built on Z construction terminating in . . .

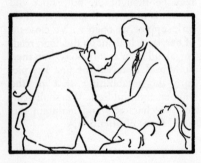

. . . the conflict between father and son, which is a brief, rapid sequence built on sharp dynamic diagonal lines leading up to the terrified exit of the little girl. This is relieved by . . .

. . . an interval of slowed-down pace, built on the rigidity of the square form. When this mood has been well established, the screech of brakes is heard offstage, and we have the reaction of the mother and two sons, who rise—one after the other. The three verticals thus created will form a dramatic contrast with the father, who is still slumped down at stage right. These positions are held momentarily, then the older son exits.

FIG. 15. (cont'd) A STORY-BOARD TREATMENT.

At the scene of the accident, we must use strong lines and dramatic contrasts of mass to point up the helplessness of the fragile child against strong forces.

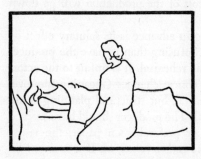

Back in the living room, after the child has been brought in and laid on the sofa, we compose on horizontal lines. A shift to the cross form stresses the solemnity of the situation and merges the interest in the possibility that the injuries may prove fatal. After this thought has been planted . . .

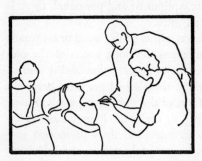

. . . we shift the characters to a radial structure, to concentrate the interest on the dying child. We have now built to a climax and doubtless will not be able to resist dollying in for a close-up to catch that faint, tear-impelling smile as the eyelids close.

A concluding shot suggests itself: a close-up of the little girl's open story book, with her doll near it, on the floor, just as she left it in the opening scene.

FIG. 15 (*cont'd*) A STORY-BOARD TREATMENT.

c. Why Is Visual Planning Necessary?

Television program production is a complex and expensive process. In camera rehearsal a lot of equipment and many pay-roll members as well as high-priced talent are tied up. Minutes count, and yet enough time must be spent on rehearsal to insure good production. There are only two answers: (1) *preplanning;* (2) *more preplanning.*

If sufficient time has been devoted to planning prior to rehearsals, and furthermore if this planning has anticipated and resolved the visual as well as the aural problems, the cost of the production will go down and the quality will go up.

Another valid reason for planning in advance is its salutary effect on actors and talent. Nothing is more confusing than to have the producer continually changing his mind during rehearsal. It is unfair to the actors and detrimental to production. Of course changes (meaning improvements) are definitely a part of rehearsal, but structural planning is not —this should be done before rehearsal. The producer should have worked out definitely, either in his mind or preferably on paper, the visual structure of the production *before he calls a rehearsal.* If it is an *ad lib* show and he is going to tie up studio equipment and personnel, there is all the more reason for planning in advance.

Visual planning involves picturization, either in the mind or on paper. As time goes on and as visual mindedness develops, much of the picturization can be planned mentally. But to develop that ability and to insure top ratings even with the ability, the method proposed here will be found helpful. It is a simplified form of the story-board method used extensively in Hollywood, particularly in the Walt Disney studios. Its application is even more necessary in television than in motion pictures, for the reason that there can be no retakes when the television show goes on the air; it is good or bad in direct proportion to the way it has been *planned.*

In some television station set-ups it is not inconceivable that the management will find that it pays to employ one or more artists whose main function is to prepare these skeleton story-board treatments, for in this way the program manager can see and evaluate how the production will look—even before it has been started.

But we have not finished yet with the problems of pictorial composition, and, although the subject cannot be encompassed in less than a book or two, we can at least outline the most important considerations.

We have learned something of the significance of line, mass, and form and how to apply them to the basic forms of composition. We have learned how to adapt these basic forms to story content and how to use them in production planning. Now let us consider the fundamental principles which underlie all the arts and are particularly applicable to picture making—principles that should be part of the working equipment of all who are engaged in television program production.

PRINCIPLES OF PICTORIAL COMPOSITION

The ten basic principles of pictorial composition are: unity, variety, harmony, balance, rhythm, pace, proportion, emphasis, dominance, and continuity. These principles apply not only to the individual camera shots but to the flow of pictures in continuity. At first glance their relevance to television may not be apparent. They are, in fact, seldom used with conscious thought. Nevertheless they are the cornerstones of all the creative arts, whether used instinctively (as some gifted people are able to do) or as the result of study and training.

Pictures may be classified as to the various purposes they serve: (a) the *story-telling* picture, in which the shapes are recognizable and put together in such a way that they bear a relationship to some realistic experience in life; (b) the *imaginative* picture built on fantasy, in which the shapes are realistic but put together out of sheer imagination; (c) the *mood* picture, which reaches out to the emotions more than to the intellect; (d) the *factual* picture, built to convey information and nothing more; (e) the *abstract* picture, in which the shapes may or may not be recognizable, designed to convey some abstract idea and appeal to the subconscious.

Each of these pictures has a specific use:

a) The *realistic picture* is used where the content of the story does not go beyond the bounds of realism. Using this type will contribute to clarity of exposition and make it possible for the picture to carry much of the story. When this condition obtains, the attention of the audience is of necessity held to the screen.

b) The *imaginative picture* has tremendous interest value because it provides an escape from realism and stimulates the imagination of the viewer. It can add variety and relief to the broadcast day.

c) The *mood picture,* since it asks little or nothing of the mind but instead reaches out to the emotions, can be used either to hold the attention of the audience or to give visual relief. Exciting, dramatic, or farcical moods tend to hold the attention at high pitch, if they are not sustained too long. On the other hand, calm, tranquil, restful pictures, if cleverly interspersed among the others will give the audience an opportunity to relax and even to look away from the scene while merely listening. This device of planting rest periods for the eye while sustaining aural interest, and then calling the eye back to the screen for the important visual sequence, is an excellent means of making sure, of capturing complete attention when it is wanted by the producer.

d) The *factual picture* seeks only to inform. To be successful it must be clear and concise and have the focus of attention led *directly* to its important elements. There must be no confusion, and the picture should not attempt to tell too much. Variety should be found in continuity.

e) The *abstract picture,* through its appeal to the subconscious, has a variety of applications in television. It can serve as the visual treatment for music spots, which are in themselves abstract. When it is used creatively, with taste and finesse, fascinating effects can be produced. The color organ is an excellent example. The kaleidoscope is another.

The choice of picture type is, as we have said, the first step in pictorial composition. Then follows the application of the ten fundamental principles. We shall take them up separately.

1. Unity

A picture, like a sentence, must have unity. It should tell only *one* story. There should be nothing in it that is not needed or does not add to the over-all effect, either in thought content or in line, mass, or form. Any irrelevant elements will raise doubts in the mind of the viewer as to what the picture is supposed to say.

2. Variety

More than anything else it is variety that holds the attention of the audience. It must be kept under control, however, or the state of unity may be disrupted. Not only is this quality essential in individual shots, but variety of type, mood, pace, and proportion are essential in building continuity. In the linear structure of the picture there should be variety in the kind of line, the direction, the spacing, and the accent.

Variety, however, is not employed for its own sake; it is used for aesthetic reasons dictated by our subconscious reaction to rhythm and to space and measure. The proportions of the television screen—3 by 4—in themselves have variety. In putting a picture on this rectangle, what we do essentially is to cut up the enclosed surface into areas—into *spaces and measures.* The process is called space-cutting. Whenever two lines cut through and join, a picture or design has been started, and every other line that is added must bear a relationship to this. If the first two lines break the rectangle up into equal divisions, as shown below on the left, we cannot proceed in developing variety. The same lines, however, placed as they are in the righthand sketch, introduce space-cutting variety.

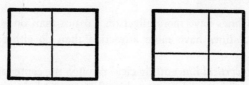

FIG. 16. VARIETY IN SPACES AND MEASURES.

In composing a picture the beginner will tend to look at the objects of which it consists, whereas it is the *spaces between them* and/or the *shapes of those areas* which make the picture what it is. This is particularly true in television, because most of the pictures consist of medium close-ups of people. Over and over again the same shapes are used. Only by constantly varying the spaces and measures can this amount of repetition be tolerated.

3. *Harmony*
Harmony involves both unity and variety, for it implies the *putting together of related things.* This is the element that holds the picture together psychologically.

4. *Balance*
Balance is so intimately tied into our physical state that we are subconsciously aware of any condition of unbalance. Through the functioning of the internal ear, a state of balance is maintained that enables us to stand or move about without toppling over. Hence subconsciously we demand a state of balance in pictures.

To understand how this may be achieved, it must be realized that a picture is made up of separate units each of which has *weight,* in the sense of pulling power or attraction to the eye. These units consist of line, mass, color, and direction or speed of movement. All these elements must be kept not necessarily in complete balance but close to it, except in those instances where, by departing from balance intentionally, a specific effect is achieved. By keeping in mind that each unit of a picture has weight due to its attraction, one can see that balance is achieved through the control of the *relative attraction power* of lines, masses, colors, or movement. Attraction may be controlled by placement, contrast, emphasis, or repetition and, in the case of movement, by direction and speed. By way of further amplification the following statements can be made:

a) *Vertical* lines have more effect on balance than do horizontals.

b) *Diagonal* lines have more attraction than do either verticals or horizontals.

c) *A strong vertical line* cutting clear through the *center* of the picture makes it impossible to achieve anything but formal balance, and this is bad, because it cuts the picture in two. A horizontal cutting of the picture into equal parts is not quite so objectionable but should be avoided.

d) *A large mass* may be balanced by a *small* one by placing the latter in an *empty area*. This is the principle of the lever or the seesaw.

e) A unit in an empty area *near the edge* has more attraction than one in the center.

f) *A unit in the foreground* has less attraction than one in the middle distance, provided the contrasts are the same.

g) An area surrounded by a *hard edge* has more attraction than one of which the edge is soft.

h) *Repetition* of a unit *weakens* its power of attraction. The exception to this is seen when a principal character in the foreground is supported by others directly in back of it. Then the attraction is strengthened by repetition.

i) *Black against white* or *white against black* has more attraction than if the contrast color is gray.

j) *A small white unit in a large black area* will have more attraction power than the reverse, for the reason that the eye instinctively seeks light.

k) The eye goes first to the *point of strongest contrast* in value or color or to the strongest line; in the case of movement it is attracted by a *change in direction*.

l) The eye is attracted to *geometric or symbolic shapes*, particularly if they seem to be formed by accident.

m) Emphasis may be achieved by a *gradation in tone*. The eye will follow this gradation in a direction *toward the light*.

Importance of Horizontal Balance

Since the television screen forms a horizontal picture, horizontal balance is more important than vertical, though the latter should not be entirely neglected. The placing of the dominating vertical line or mass is extremely important. If it is dead in the center it is either bad or monotonous. If it is too far to the right or left it makes the picture too heavy on that side. A picture should be so balanced that it will "hang" *from its center.* But balance may be obtained in ways that are not obvious. Take the case of the single head and shoulder composition. If the person is looking straight ahead, with the head *placed off center* in a vertical position, it will not look well (provided the background contributes no balance). But, if the head is turned, or even if the eyes only are turned so that the person is looking *across* the center line of the picture, a feeling of balance is established.

Acceptable   Bad   Good

FIG. 17. THE PLACEMENT OF A SINGLE FIGURE.

Balance, then, can be gained or lost through suggestion and association, for, as in the instance cited, the suggested line formed by the direction in which the person in the picture is looking has enough weight to balance the off-center position of the head.

Since we are dealing with a visual subject, it will be found helpful, wherever possible, to *visualize the principles* involved. For instance, a mental picture of balance itself as applied to pictures will be of assistance, especially in times of stress when it is necessary to compose on the fly. The analogy of the scales as illustrated on the following page is apt, because balance is the relationship of weights. We should therefore carry in our minds symbolic images representing formal and informal balance as it is used in both the vertical and the horizontal (perspective) plane.

5. *Rhythm*

The word rhythm suggests music or the dance. Though its application to pictorial composition is not obvious, it is actually of vital importance,

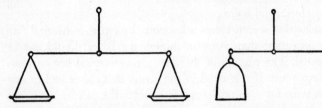

Formal balance. Equal weights at equal distances from the center or fulcrum. This conveys a static feeling and hence is more often applied to decorative design.

Informal balance. Unequal weights at unequal distances from the fulcrum. This is the form most commonly used in television because it gives a feeling of variety.

Informal balance in the vertical plane.

Informal balance in the perspective plane.

FIG. 18. PICTORIAL BALANCE.

and the analogy of the dance is apt. Take the rhythm of the waltz: one-two-three-one-two-three, or more particularly the accented rhythm—*one*-two-three-*one*-two-three. Think of this in terms of movement rather than cadence of sound—in terms of eye movement as it goes from one line or shape to another in looking at a picture. Now apply it to one of the commonest pictures in television—the three-shot. (See Figure 19.)

Note that by merely shifting the positions of the three characters and lowering the camera to get variety in height, we have made the arrangement interesting by adding rhythm. In fact, we have created three rhythms: By moving two of the heads closer together, the accented rhythm of the waltz—*one*-two-three—has been introduced in the spacing. By having one of the characters seen in profile and the other two in three-quarter view, we have produced rhythm of body position. And again, by the change in head level, still another rhythm has been added.

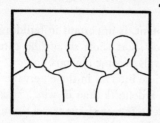 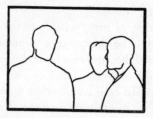

Uninteresting because there is no rhythm.

Interesting because of the accented rhythm.

FIG. 19. RHYTHM IN SPACING.

Frequently it is necessary to compose a scene involving a number of people. Let us say it is a cocktail party of seven. We wish to focus the interest lightly on one of the characters and have it rather equally diffused over the others. Surely if the heads are equally spaced the arrangement will be dull and the focus confused. Structure is needed. This can be obtained by rhythmic spacing.

Rhythm is particularly effective when applied to line pattern and to movement. A rhythmic pattern in the linear structure of the set, when it

FIG. 20. RHYTHMIC SPACING IN A GROUP SHOT.

echoes the rhythmic disposition and movement of the characters, produces the ultimate in effect.

In building continuity it is by means of rhythmic patterns that moods are controlled. The intervals used in cuts, fades, and dissolves and the cadence in the flow of picture continuity have a very definite effect on the emotions induced. For this reason it is important that the rhythmic pattern of the continuity be in harmony with the program content.

6. Pace

Variety of pace, suitable to the content, is important in building continuity. The pacing of a sequence of short shots should be carefully analyzed, because otherwise the intervals become obvious.

There is also the factor of pace or time interval in the observation of a picture. In each composition there is a definite time in which it can be taken in, and there is a more or less definite rate of eye travel through it. Hence for the picture that is to be held on the screen for only a short time the eye travel must be fast, whereas for one of long duration the pace of observation may be as leisurely as desired.

Pace of eye travel is subject to control. It may be made fast or slow depending on the number and placement of the shapes involved and the use of transitional lines that lead the eye from one place of interest to another.

7. Proportion

It is axiomatic that everything should be "in proportion"—in life and in pictorial composition. Subtle proportioning of shapes, lines, colors, and gradations of light gives a picture distinction and contributes to its effectiveness. It would be wonderful if a set of formulas could be written for making things with good proportions, but it cannot be done—such things must be felt instinctively. Some people have an innate feeling for proportion. If you have it, you are fortunate; if you do not, the only alternative is to be observing of things around you and to study the proportions in pictures that have stood the test of time.

8. Emphasis

The actor emphasizes important words and phrases in order that they will stand out from the rest. The same principle applies in picture construction. In order that the eye may be attracted to the important parts of the picture, it is necessary to give them emphasis. This can be accomplished by the use of line, by contrasts of light and dark or of color, by isolation, by repetition, by placement, and by movement.

By referring to the list of factors contributing to balance on page 40 you will find the most frequently used methods of obtaining emphasis, for balance and emphasis are closely related.

9. Dominance

To tell a story effectively, to create a mood, or to convey information, a picture must have a dominant theme and one spot or area of attraction to which the eye is irresistibly led. If the picture is to be held on the screen for only an instant, the eye must find this place instantly; there must be no doubt or wavering as to the intent, or the scene is lost. If, on the other hand, the scene is long, the eye must be given other areas of lesser attraction, so that it may be led from one to another, always coming back to the dominant area. This may be done through the use of repetition, similarity, or counterpoint in which some contrapuntal theme or pictorial form supports the main theme.

Dominance almost always involves the sacrificing of interest in certain areas, according to their relative importance. The greater the number of interesting shapes a picture contains, the more difficult the problem of control becomes. Therefore, except in skilled hands, the safest rule is to keep the picture simple.

10. *Continuity*

As pointed out at the beginning of this chapter, television involves not only the composition of separate camera shots but the putting of those shots together in continuity. No matter how good the shots are, they will fall apart in a badly constructed continuity.

In the section above we spoke of eye travel from one place of attraction to another. This is continuity within individual pictures. In television the flow is so continuous from scene to scene that the whole program is, in effect, one picture. This means that we must apply to our continuity the same principles on which the individual pictures are built.

These, then, are the ten mileposts to good composition. They mark out the route which must be traveled in arriving at pictorial effectiveness. They apply to every segment of the program day and to every picture in it. The telling may have made them seem complicated, but the same is true in learning to drive a car; through familiarity and practice the process will become second nature.

SPATIAL COMPOSITION

On the television screen, except for titles and special effects, we attempt to convey a three-dimensional feeling on a two-dimensional surface. The inherent limitation of the camera lens—its one-eyed vision—poses certain problems, but there are others which are a part of pictorial composition. At this time we shall concern ourselves only with the latter.

Depth in a picture is controlled by perspective and also by spatial balance, which we shall consider first. It must be understood that the principles of balance apply to the *spatial depth* of the picture as well as to its width and height. In any picture expressing depth, balance must be maintained between the foreground and the background. If the focus of interest is in the foreground, there should be no item of equal interest in the background, and vice versa. If a feeling of great depth is desired, there must be a foreground, a middle distance, and some device that will push the background into the far distance.

Distance or depth is gauged by the eye through perspective, of which there are two kinds—linear and aerial. *Linear perspective* is readily identified in the merging of the railroad tracks as they vanish in a point in the distance. Glance about and you will observe that all horizontal lines that are above the level of the eye appear to be sloping down, while the ones below eye level are sloping up. By noting the slant of these lines we judge distances, though we do it subconsciously. In set designing the *forced* (exaggerated) slanting of horizontal lines is one of the devices used to create depth and make a small set look large and spacious.

Aerial perspective is present in all views of the out-of-doors. It is indicated by the haziness that objects take on as they recede in the distance and by the softness of edge and the tendency toward blue and purple. We can control aerial perspective, therefore, by softening edges and by diminishing contrasts of light and dark and of color as we go toward the background.

COLOR

The ten principles of composition are all applicable in the use of color. In addition there are other considerations which should be evaluated here, particularly the psychology of color. We react emotionally in definite ways to different color harmonies. First there is a relation between our reactions to heat and cold and to the various colors. Since blues and purples are the predominant colors of the winter landscape, we associate these colors with conditions of coolness. On the other hand, we think of red and orange as the warm colors because they are found in the warmth of the fireside glow. Through other associations we think of reds as being exciting and of greens and blues as restful. White is linked with purity, and black with sadness and death. We are excited by strong contrasts of lively color, and we are quieted by the subtle harmonies of analogous color.

We must therefore, in using color, be sure that our color harmonies are in themselves harmonious with the content of the program. There are books devoted to color harmonies which will be found helpful, and the techniques used in the better colored films can be studied to good advantage. By and large, however, the handling of color should be left to those who know how to use it effectively.

A FEW DON'TS TO REMEMBER

As stated earlier, the few hard-and-fast rules that can be laid down are negative rather than positive; they are *don'ts*. He who can fly in the face of the *don'ts* and reverse them as a change of pace may also make a mark. Here are the more important ones to remember:

Don't tell more than one story at one time.

Don't tell too much at one time.

Don't use a picture type or basic composition form that conflicts with the purpose or feeling of the scene.

Avoid dividing the picture on a center line in either direction, thus making it into two pictures.

Avoid horizontal lines that run all the way across the picture without interruption and near the bottom edge. The effect is even worse if the line is almost but not quite parallel with the frame line.

Avoid compositions in which the weight is all on one side. A slight pan (described on page 63) to the left or right will usually correct this.

Avoid barriers in the immediate foreground that act as "do not enter" signs. Lead-in lines are desirable, as are foreground shapes which add to the composition, but not if they block the entrance.

Don't let a line or shape form an awkward attachment or extension, as in having a clock on a rear wall, a lamp shade, or a bowl of flowers directly over a player's head as if it were being worn.

Avoid having a prominent line in the background become tangent to the edge of an important foreground object—especially a person's head.

Don't let a long diagonal run out of the exact corner of a picture.

Don't frame figures with the feet resting on the bottom frame line or with the top of the head just touching the upper frame line.

Chapter IV

~~~~~~

VIDEO TECHNIQUES

I N DEVELOPING video techniques that will capture and hold the attention of the audience, imagination and creative expression should be leavened with logic and practicality, for it is well to keep in mind that the audience is not interested in technique for technique's sake. Furthermore, where technique becomes tricky and self-assertive, attention is directed toward the trick and away from the story or subject matter.

We may state as a premise then: that *video technique should be logical; that it should grow out of the story or theme;* and, that *it is not an end in itself.* This does not mean that the full bag of television tricks—of which there are many—cannot be used; rather that they be used in the right place, at the right time.

The opening of a program is the crucial period. It is then that the audience decides whether to stay with it or dial another station. Here the producer can go "all out" in the use of imaginative treatments; he may use trick effects, superimposures, montage, or any device that is fitting. Though for the most part he should be straightforward in the body of dramatic, factual, or sports programs, he is not limited in the use of imagination in the treatment of transitions. Musical and dance programs afford the greatest opportunity for the use of creative techniques. We shall have more to say about these special applications in a later chapter.

BASIC CONSIDERATIONS

1. *Eye Fatigue*

Eye fatigue is a factor worthy of careful consideration. If the flow of pictures is trying on the eyes, it will be difficult to hold the attention of the audience. The same thing will hold true if the visual focus is kept at too high a pitch or if no relief periods are planted throughout the performance.

Certainly the video techniques employed—that is to say, the types of camera shots, the pace at which they occur, and the manner of using cuts, fades, and dissolves—will very largely determine the fatigue factor. The eye of the viewer can be effectively relieved by planning the flow of the picture patterns so as to vary the scale and arrangement of shapes. An occasional sequence of short close-up shots, the intercutting of big close-ups and medium shots, and the planting of quiet, restful scenes following an exciting sequence are some of the methods that can be employed.

2. Audience Orientation

Some producers forget that the audience at home has not read the script, has not had the advantage of attending rehearsals, has not seen the sets, and may be totally unfamiliar with what is being presented—particularly if it is a play. Hence when camera shots, taken from all possible angles, flash in succession on the screen the audience finds itself wobbling in a daze of meaningless confusion.

With three or more cameras available there is a tendency for the untrained producer to shoot the scene from every possible angle and to use *too many cameras* and *too many cuts*. By so doing he feels that he is being cleverly original, whereas more often than not he is wearing the audience out; what is worse, he probably is confusing the story.

Change of camera angle has come to be an accepted device in motion pictures. But if the beginner will study the technique he will find that the camera angles are so planned that the audience is convincingly *oriented to the scene*. The basis of this technique is to be found in the dictum that *"the camera should be the eyes of the audience."* When the cameras are used in this way, the sequence of pictures will follow the visual habits which we exhibit in our daily life: We take in a scene in its entirety; we see something in it that interests us particularly; we move up to examine it; perhaps we move around to study it from all angles; we may even pick it up for closer examination; often we move back for another chance to see how it looks in relation to things around it; then we move on to the next item of interest.

In effect, the producer's function is to do all this for the audience without asking them to move out of their seats. But the whole point is that he should make the audience feel that they themselves are seeing it in their own way with their own eyes. As a matter of fact, one of the greatest potentials of television is its ability to get into the essence of a situation and, by camera selection, make it more vivid and more expressive than if the human eye with its wide-angle, all-inclusive vision were seeing it firsthand.

3. *The Essence of a Scene*

Practically any subject can be made into an interesting picture *if there is an opportunity to compose it and light it properly*. Even when this is not possible, there is usually some quality in the subject matter that can be brought out, either by the angle from which it is viewed or by its scale and positioning on the screen. The problem of the producer is to search out the essence of every scene and present it *with as little dilution as possible*.

The essence of a subject usually lies *beneath the surface;* often it manifests itself only vaguely on the exterior. Picturization at its best is concerned not so much with the exterior appearance as with the *interior essence*. Take portrait photography as an example: the usual results are superficial, but in the hands of a Steichen the camera reveals the character of the inner man. This is the *subjective* approach.

The very nature of television—its intimacy, its immediacy, its opera-glass technique—makes it an ideal medium for character analysis.

TELEVISION'S BAG OF TRICKS

Television technique falls into two main divisions: (1) *live origination,* from cameras either in the studio or with remote pick-up units; (2) *film or slide projection,* from cameras located in the projection room. In Chapter IX we shall discuss motion pictures and film integration in detail. At the moment we are concerned mainly with live production. Since control-room technique applies to both live and projected picture signals, it is logical that we begin there.

1. *Control-Room Video Technique*

From the program standpoint there are two principal control operations related to the picture: (1) *monitoring and shading* the picture being picked up by each camera; (2) *switching* these picture signals "onto the line." An engineer is assigned to each of these operations. The one who does the switching is usually referred to as the *technical di-*

rector, and he is actually responsible for all aspects of the technical end of the program. Since we are not concerned with engineering or technical matters, we shall consider these operations only in so far as they pertain to program production. It should be noted that if the camera tube is of the image orthicon type the shading operation is eliminated.

a. Monitoring and Shading

In most stations there is a picture tube—or *monitor*—for each camera channel. This enables the producer or director to see what each camera is getting and thus to direct the cameramen and studio personnel. These camera monitors are arranged side by side on the *shading desk* and so stituated that both the producer and technical director can see them readily, along with the *line monitor,* which shows what is being transmitted.

The shading or video engineer, by means of many dials, controls the quality of the picture electronically. He can make it light or dark, or sharp or soft, and can even vary its size and proportions. He can produce a number of effects useful in program production. The principal ones are as follows:

1) *Electronic lighting effects.* Suppose the script calls for a night effect or a dimly lighted room; this can be handled better by shading than by mood-lighting the set. A dark, low-lighted set will cause what is known as edge flare (light areas around the edge of the picture tube). Electronic shading does not have this defect. In a scene where low light is to be simulated, the lighting on the set should be at a high enough level to prevent edge flare, and the desired effect should be created on the shading desk.

2) *Reversing the picture.* It is possible for the engineer to change a "positive" picture to a "negative." In the case of motion picture projection, negative film may be used, and by electrical means the image can be reversed to form a positive picture. Certain interesting trick effects can be achieved by this means. For instance, a title card lettered black on white can be reversed so that the letters become white. This signal can then be lap-dissolved over another camera shot.

b. Switching

The technical director who sits at the control desk has an array of buttons and dials by means of which he is able to switch any camera or combination of cameras "on the line." He also introduces the optical effects—cuts, fades, and dissolves—which in the movies are produced by the "cutter" and the optical printer.

In remote pick-up of sporting and news events, since it is not possible for the producer to work from a tight script he must "call" his cuts. But, in all except the *ad lib* type of studio show, camera cuts and effects should be carefully worked out and thoroughly rehearsed. The script should be set up on the page so that everything is clear and distinct, for during the telecast nervous tension is high and all the editing operations must be executed with split-second timing.

Bad control-room work—sloppy cutting, bungled dissolves, and missed cues—can ruin a production. Good television depends on good editing, executed with rhythm and precision.

2. Editing the Picture

Operations vary in different stations, but the usual procedure is for the technical director to do the switching, working either from the script or on verbal cues from the producer or director. Let us analyze the aesthetic and psychological factors involved in these editing operations.

a. Fades

When the outgoing picture is reduced to black level by turning the video gain dial down, a fade-out is obtained. By reversing the operation the incoming picture is faded in. The *fade-in* is commonly used at the beginning of a sequence to indicate that something new is to follow. The *fade-out*, by the same reasoning, is used at the conclusion of a sequence or section of the program, in effect bringing that chapter to a close. The two are ordinarily used in combination and can be as long or as short as desired.

b. Cuts

The cut is the most frequently used (and misused) effect. It consists of nothing more than a direct switch from one camera to another. But the emotional reaction it is capable of inducing should not be underestimated; it can produce sudden shock if the change of visual image is extreme. For this reason it should be used intelligently and—as in the case of all optical effects—for a definite purpose. What are some of its purposes?

1) *Variety*. This is such an obvious use of the cut that it might be

dispensed with in a word or two were it not for the fact that it is so often misused. Visual variety is essential for audience interest, but it must have regard for audience orientation, smoothness of visual continuity, and fatigue. Cuts used merely for variety should be logical—not confusing. They should not be obtrusive.

2) *Pace and rhythm.* The time interval—the relative length of camera shots—has definite *emotional value.* By rapid cutting, the tempo of a scene can be speeded up. Short flashes occurring in rapid sequence are stimulating and exciting. Slow cutting lowers both tension and tempo. If cutting is executed in rhythm with the action portrayed and if the cuts add lucidity or production value to the continuity they are justified, otherwise they are not.

Every production has its own rhythm. Cutting has rhythm. The two rhythms should harmonize. The rhythm of both music and the dance is obvious—so obvious, in fact, that if the accompanying optical effects are out of rhythm the result is irritating. Though the rhythm of dialogue is less obvious, the sensitive director will feel it and time his cuts accordingly. Rhythmic cutting adds that much-desired touch of perfection.

3) *Comparison and contrast.* In plot exposition and in factual programs, the device of *intercutting* can often be used to advantage. Suppose someone is demonstrating the advantages of the all-electric kitchen. The joy of cooking in modern surroundings could be effectively pointed up by intercutting contrasting scenes from a cold-water, coal-fired kitchen of the old days. In plot exposition, a character is describing some antecedent action. As he talks we show what he is describing by a series of rapidly cut scenes.

4) *Psychological effect.* A cut can be used specifically for its powerful psychological effect. The sudden shock of a cut in a suspense scene following a period of low tension will inject a surprise element and lift the scene by its effect of sharp contrast. Or there may be a situation where, without resorting to dialogue, we wish to advance the story by visual means: Two people are in heated dialogue and one of them steals a glance in a fixed direction; we cut to the face of a clock and, through association of ideas, we know that the person is playing for time.

Intercutting for psychological effect has infinite possibilities. Its value lies not only in its emotional impact, but also in the fact that *it draws the audience into co-operative activity* (audience participation) with the situation. By being allowed to discover portions of the story for themselves, they get increased satisfaction and enjoyment. The ability of the audience at home to participate with and in what they see coming over the glass eye is the essence of successful television program making.

Here are a few suggestions regarding the use of cuts:

Have a reason for cutting.

Time each cut according to the picture content, action, or dialogue. If the picture needs time for recognition, or if it introduces new subject matter, it must be held longer on the screen. Close-ups can be cut more tightly than medium shots for this reason.

In cutting from widely different angles be sure the audience remains oriented to the scene.

Cuts on action or business should ordinarily be taken while the action is in progress, and it is usually better to have the cut come *just after* the action has been started, so that it may be sustained throughout or completed during the subsequent shot or shots. In other words, it is ordinarily not good practice to cut near the end of an action unless there is some reason for doing so. The important thing about action, of course, is its *result*. Cuts, therefore, should be made and timed for the purpose of showing *how* and *where* or *why* the action was started and *what the action resulted in*.

Cuts on dialogue must be timed to the situation and the dramatic content.

In cutting to a reaction shot, showing the listener rather than the speaker—one of the most important reasons for cutting, by the way—the cut should be made *a split second ahead of the reaction*. For instance, a smiling reaction or one of anger is much more effective if we see the face *change* from its normal expression than if the cut is taken to a face already smiling or mugging an angry scowl. In ordinary dialogue, if we are holding a medium two-shot and are to cut to a close-up of one of the characters, followed by a close-up of the other, we should cut to each close up *just before* the character speaks—not during his first word.

Cut to the tempo and rhythm of the sound. If it is music, cut to its rhythm. If it is dialogue, follow its cadence. Certain sound effects make ideal cutting points: A crash of falling dishes is heard; *simultaneously* we cut from the dinner guests to the door of the butler's pantry, which timidly opens to reveal the terrified cook. Cuts made on such sounds as the screech of brakes, a factory whistle, or a burglar alarm are all extremely effective.

c. Dissolves

The outstanding characteristic of the dissolve is its smoothness. For this reason it is used where that psychological effect is desired. It is accomplished by the manipulation of dials on the control desk. The video gain on the incoming picture is lowered to black level; then it is switched onto the line with the outgoing picture; by reducing the gain on the latter while at the same time increasing the strength of the incoming picture, the two are made to merge in a smooth transition. The length of the dissolve can be made as short or as long as desired. A normal dissolve is from two to three seconds.

A *fast dissolve* approaches the cut in psychological effect but is less abrupt. Its duration is ordinarily something less than a second. Its use is usually restricted to fast sequences—particularly a rapid montage.

A *slow dissolve* should not last over five seconds as a rule. Its length will of course be regulated by the tempo and mood of the scene.

The principal function of the dissolve is to maintain the flow of a scene. We may cite the dance as one example. Here fluidity of movement is often heightened by dissolves, whereas it is destroyed by the abrupt shock of cuts. Contrariwise, there are moments in a dance routine when cuts are indicated—for instance, at changes in tempo; during a repetitious passage; during a pause; or when it is desired to come in for a close-up.

Since the net effect of the dissolve is to cause one picture to appear to grow out of another, it can be effectively used to indicate transitions. A character is denying that he saw the murder weapon; suddenly his expression changes to fright; we dissolve to a shot showing him picking up the gun involved in the crime, and we know he is thinking of his fingerprints. The very fact that the shot appeared to "come through" him as he was speaking shows how logical a dissolve is in such cases. If, on the other hand, he were to say, "Wait. I picked up that gun myself . . ." a direct cut would be better.

In general, dissolves should be used where fluidity and smoothness are necessary to the continuity. They may be used to create time or mood transitions and to show paralleling action. They are trying and ineffective if used to excess.

d. Matched Dissolves

The matched dissolve is a useful and pleasing device. It consists of exactly matching the positioning of two similar or identical shapes, one on each camera, so that when the dissolve is made a metamorphosis appears to take place. For example, in the Dr. Jekyll-Mr. Hyde situation, the camera on Hyde is lined up with the one on Jekyll, so that when the dissolve is made, one head is exactly superimposed over the other.

The device has many applications. To mention only a few: In a dance routine, when going from a medium long shot to a medium close-up of a single dancer, it is effective to use a matched dissolve—in fact, it is disturbing if the incoming shot shows the dancer in some other part of the screen. The matched dissolve can be used in speeding up action when demonstrating how a thing is made or put together; also in showing a variety of treatments of the same thing, as in costume design or interior decoration.

e. Lap Dissolves

The lap dissolve consists of fading in one image over another, holding it for a period of time, and then fading it out. It is useful in *stream-of-consciousness* effects and in fantasy. A character under emotional strain is plagued by the spirit of an antagonist; his leering face fades in above the person's head. Or perhaps a ghost appears on the screen; the person may be relating some terrible experience, and a montage of what he is describing is lap-dissolved in by means of motion picture film.

From a production standpoint the lap dissolve is not always practical. There must be sufficient contrast range in the two pictures to make it effective. In the instance cited first above, the upper part of the picture showing the person speaking would have to be rather dark and the face to be lap-dissolved rather light (preferably against a black background) in order for it to work effectively.

f. Superimposures

The term superimposure is used for a technique midway between the lap dissolve, which fades in and out over another picture, and an effect that is switched onto the line as a fixed double exposure. It is frequently accomplished in title sequences by superimposing a title card over a live action shot or film loop. It has many applications in commercials, for instance in bringing the sponsor's name or trademark in over another camera shot or film sequence. It is a good device for time signals, weather reports, and the like.

Being a trick effect, the superimposure should be confined to uses that are legitimate and not plain silly. In addition to the things mentioned above, the abstract quality of double images opens up many ways of embellishing musical and dance programs; the much-used trick of using two cameras to show a piano keyboard superimposed on the screen in two diagonals is only one example.

We have thus far covered the optical effects produced in the control room. Now let us move to the studio and see what can be done there in the way of video effects other than straight camera work.

g. Electronic Effect Unit

Electronic effects units are available which enable the montaging of one camera's picture into the picture of a second camera through a number of different shapes, horizontal and/or vertical wipe, diagonal wipe, second picture blossoming out of center of first picture, second picture enveloping first picture from all edges, etc.

3. *Special Video Effects*

The special effects which can be produced on television are limited only by the necessities of sustained production. For this reason some effects must be either put on film or produced in combination with projected images. The more important special effects are as follows:

a) *Title effects* produced by various mechanical devices—pull-through, roll-up, drop-card, and revolving titles; the wipe and the dissolve.

b) *Smoke, flame, rain, snow,* and other similar phenomena.

c) *Miniatures* either treated realistically or designed for sheer fantasy.

d) *Process screen effects* produced, as in the movies, by rear projection on a translucent screen, in front of which the television cameras pick up the live action.

e) *Animation* approximating the results obtained in animated movies and produced by specially constructed mirror boxes.

f) *Puppets and marionettes.*

g) *Detail sets* used for picking up details on the full set which the cameras can not catch.

h) *Kaleidoscopes* and other mechanical devices for producing abstract, ever-changing design, including the *color organ.*

i) *Foreground projection,* specifically instrumentation known as Vistascope, which enables the montaging of photographs of any description of any scene as foreground to actors standing in an empty properly lighted studio.

a. Titles

The purpose of the title sequence is to supply information that is not contained in the program and/or to identify the sponsor or product. This information can sometimes be given by a spoken announcement. When it is made visual·by a title sequence it ordinarily consists of giving the title of the program, the names of the cast, credits, and the name of the sponsor. All of this may be given in the opening title, or part of it may appear in the end title. Some stations follow the radio custom of giving cast and sponsor plugs both fore and aft.

A few basic factors should be taken into account in the design and preparation of titles. In the first place, the size of the average television screen demands that the titles carry the barest minimum of lettering and that the letters be simple in construction, with few flourishes for artistic effect. Legibility is the most important consideration. Certain electronic vagaries of the iconoscope make it necessary to observe these rules:

1) Do not use a solid white or solid black card for the background of the title. White causes "blooming"—an effect that tends to obliterate the lettering. Black produces "edge flare." The latter condition can be overcome by airbrush toning around the edge of the title cards.

2) Avoid too great a contrast range between letters and background. White letters on black or black on white cause *streaking*—an electronic condition in which bands of light are carried across the picture by the scanning beam where extreme contrasts occur. For this reason off-white and gray values should be used.

3) Because of this streaking tendency, letters must be spaced a little farther apart than would ordinarily be done, and the letter should not be too thin.

4) Do not fill the picture field with the title layout. Leave ample margins to take care of faulty centering in the home receiver.

Title design is a subject in itself and not within the scope of this book. The same is true of the structural design and mechanics of the many devices that can be devised to produce an endless variety of title effects.

From the standpoint of concept and treatment, a title sequence should be in harmony with the feeling or content of the program. Aided by its accompanying music, it should establish the mood of what is to follow. It should be smooth and rehearsed to perfection. It is better to be simple and precise than to make a bungling attempt to be clever.

b. Smoke, Flame, Rain, and Snow

It is often desirable—and worth the effort—to create the illusion of some of nature's moods and manifestations. In certain plays and frequently on commercial spots these effects are essential. They are useful also in creating mood transitions or "bridges."

The many devices and the devious ways by which the special-effects man portrays these phenomena can be studied, by those who are interested, in various books and publications. The most complete treatise to date on the subject of special effects as applied to television is to be found in William C. Eddy's *Television, the Eyes of Tomorrow*.[1] In this book Captain Eddy also gives a fairly complete description of the special equipment used in title work and the construction of miniatures.

c. Miniatures

Since television is a "one shot" matter and program production is time-consuming, it is always a moot question whether the preparation of expensive miniatures can be justified. In some cases their cost is less than to send a motion picture crew out on location, and where the results achieved warrant the expense it can be justified. For the most part, however, miniatures must be kept simple.

If a miniature set is to be convincing it must be realistic. If it is to be realistic it must be prepared with attention to detail. More than likely it will be a set devoid of motion (which would add to the cost) and will consist of a long-shot picture—neither of which contributes much in television. A good piece of art work will often do just as well.

It is useful, however, for a studio to build up an array of stock items: scenery, doors, windows, and architectural detail; street scenes; trees, shrubs, and bits of nature. Such equipment is subject to infinite combinations and is valuable in effecting transitions and moods—for example, rain on a deserted street, a store front, or a nameplate on an entrance, to name only a few.

d. Process Screen

With a sensitive pick-up tube it is possible to make use of the motion picture technique known as the *process* shot. This consists of projecting motion pictures (or stills) onto the back of a translucent screen, in front of which the "live" scene is acted—and the television camera picks

[1] Prentice-Hall, Inc., New York, 1945.

up the combined picture. It is necessary, of course, to obtain high illumination on the screen, which means the use of a carbon arc projector, in order to offset the "spill" light from the set. The pictures must be projected at the rate of 30 frames per second. And the light on the set must be carefully controlled, with cross and rim lighting for the higher light levels. Furthermore, the depth of focus must be sufficient to hold both the screen and the set in sharp focus.

One example of adapting the process screen to television may be cited as follows: We have a scene in a fleeing car, and through the rear window we wish to show the pursuit. A skeleton set is constructed showing the interior of the rear portion of the car. It is placed just in front of the rear-projection screen, so that when a stock shot of weaving street traffic, with oncoming cars, is thrown on the screen a convincing illusion is produced on the television tube.

The possibilities of process screen work can be readily visualized if one thinks in terms of a screen large enough to back up an entire set. All sorts of action—dramatic episodes, dance and variety routines, music interpretation—could be shown against out-of-door settings, drifting clouds, babbling brooks, and what not. The cost of such equipment, however, is so high as to place it in the realm of dreams.

e. Animation

By means of a special studio device known as an animator it is possible to approximate, in a rather crude but acceptable way, the effect of animated motion pictures. This technique has been used with considerable success on news and science programs. In its simplest form, maps can be animated by moving arrows and other symbols. Of current interest, on the day following the first radar contact with the moon, excellent use was made of animation in explaining how the lunar contact was achieved. On an occasion coincident with a news report of an earthquake, an animated story on the cause of earthquakes and how they are located and measured by the seismograph was made extremely interesting and informative.

The device makes use of the dual ability of a half-silvered mirror both to reflect and to transmit images. By the manipulation of lights it can do the work of two cameras: a map or diagram can be shown, with other images (in lighter value only) superimposed upon it and made to move or come and go at will. The success of this technique depends on the proper values in the contrast range and on proper lighting.

f. Puppets and Marionettes

Though puppets and marionettes can furnish a complete program segment, they are also useful in creating special effects. They have been successfully worked into commercials and used as continuity devices in plays. A small set with a fixed camera is the usual arrangement.

g. Detail Sets

Frequently it is impossible to bring a camera in for a close-up of some small piece of business without interfering with shots on the other cameras. In such cases one solution is the *detail set*. Suppose it is desired to show a hand depositing various objects in a wall safe located in a library set, where the principal action takes place. Later the safe is opened by a thief, and it is important to show what is removed in a big close-up. A small, full-scale detail set (on another camera) may be used for this bit of business. The hands, of course, must resemble those of the actor. The application of this technique will often solve troublesome camera problems and add richness of detail to the production.

h. Kaleidoscopes

The kaleidoscope, color organ, and similar devices which give a continuous flow of ever changing abstract patterns or designs offer opportunities for embellishing certain types of programs—particularly music.

CAMERA TECHNIQUE

Although television camera technique may appear, at first glance, to parallel motion picture technique, it actually hinges more on what the cameras *cannot be made to do* than is the case where retakes are possible and where the cutting room and optical printer can come to the producer's aid. It is best to recognize this in the beginning and work within the limits of the medium, asking the television camera to do only that which it can do well and not debasing the art to the level of the movies of 1900.

The visualization of program material is a highly selective process which calls for showmanship and a nice sense of continuity. It would be a relatively easy matter, with three or more cameras and a control desk, to string together a succession of camera shots and call it television. But to achieve any degree of perfection one must understand screen technique and know how to use the tools of the television craft. Let us first become familiar with the manipulation of the television camera.

1. *The Camera and What It Will Do*

A characteristic of the television camera that should be understood by all who write or prepare program material is the nature and extent of its mobility. Many program ideas have been projected which proved to be impractical because the cameras just could not do the things called for in the script.

First, the camera is mounted on a base that is heavy and takes up a certain amount of floor space. Second, a sizable cable is attached to the base of each camera, connecting it with the control room. The production has to be planned so that these cables do not become hopelessly tangled. Sequences must be worked out with a view to camera maneuverability.

Camera mounting falls into three general types: (1) *the tripod,* used for remote pick-ups; (2) *the pedestal,* a mobile base which the cameraman can push around (some pedestals have a hydraulic lift for raising or lowering the camera); (3) the *boom dolly,* which makes it possible to raise the camera to any desired height, depending upon the length of the boom. If, as is usually the case, the boom is mounted on a turntable, the camera can be swung in a complete circle. The cameraman rides the dolly, which is pushed around by a dollyman.

Remotely controlled camera panning heads are available on the market and one installation at the *Home Show,* NBC, New York City, has in service a remotely controlled ceiling mounted hydraulic boom with remotely controlled camera attached. The basic requirements of quick flexibility, smooth, noiseless mobility, and reliability have been adherred to.

The flexibility and mobility of the camera determine the results that can be obtained in the way of what we call camera work. If we accept the premise that the principal function of television is to make the audience feel that they themselves are present at the scene, then it is a basic requirement in good camera work to use the cameras as the audience would use their own eyes. At various times, depending on the field of interest at the moment, the cameras must show:

a) The whole setting, so that the audience is oriented and generally informed about the place where the action occurs;

b) Selected parts of the setting at closer range;

c) Minute details in big close-ups of objects, for purposes of information, plot exposition, dramatic effect, or entertainment value; and

d) The characters, personalities, or moving objects around which the interest centers, as seen at long range and/or near at hand.

The television camera can do all these things within the limits imposed by physical bulk, floor space, speed of movement from place to place, and the cables. Experience is the only teacher from whom these restricting factors can be learned.

2. *Camera Movement*

To use the terminology by which the various movements are designated, the camera can: (a) *tilt* up or down, (b) *pan* left or right, (c) *boom up* or *boom down,* (d) *dolly in* or *dolly back,* and also (e) *travel past* or *follow* the scene. All these movements can be performed with a boom dolly equipped with a turntable.

Any camera movement made "on the air" should be executed so smoothly that the audience is not conscious of it. All such movements should be *eased into and tapered off;* they should not start or stop with a jerk. Furthermore, *they should be anticipated* by the cameraman so that they are nicely timed with the action. The rate of movement should be adjusted to the dictates of the scene.

Since the camera usually is operated with a "free head," that is to say, free to move in any direction, and since it is dependent for stability on the steadiness of the cameraman's arm muscles, one danger is always present. Unless the camera is skillfully handled and moved only for a legitimate purpose, the audience will be made to feel that they are riding in a small boat on a rough sea.

a. The Tilt Shot

As its name indicates, the tilt shot consists of tilting the camera up or down. It is a shot that must be used intelligently and executed smoothly for the reason that otherwise it is apt to seem unnatural or to have been made to correct faulty framing. That will be likely to happen unless the shot is motivated by some action. Unless so motivated, a tilt shot should be made so slowly as to be scarcely perceptible, especially if it follows a fixed camera shot.

b. The Pan Shot

The term "pan" is a contraction of the word panorama and implies the horizontal scanning of a scene. The pan shot is more often used, however, for the purpose of following action or of giving movement to a scene that otherwise would be static. When made rapidly it is called a *whip shot,* a maneuver that is better reserved for special occasions, such as a dramatic shifting of interest from one character or thing to another. The whip shot can also be used to denote a quick change of locale.

The pan has two main functions: first, to direct the attention from one place to another; second, to follow action or movement. It will readily be seen that in the first instance the sense of movement is supplied *by the camera;* in the second, where movement is dominant *in the scene,* the camera is merely reporting, hence the pan should be made in a way that does not detract from the action. These two functions are sometimes combined. But, as a guiding principle to good camera technique, it is well to keep them in mind as having *separate* values, and to use them accordingly—with a definite purpose in mind.

Another common use of the pan is to readjust the composition when it is thrown out of balance by movement on the set. If such adjustments are made smoothly—if they seem to tie in with the movement of the players—they will hardly be noticeable to the audience. But they can be objectionable if not skillfully timed and executed.

In panning with a moving figure, it is usually best to *"lead with the camera."* Except in situations of a special nature, the figure being followed should be held to the *same spot in the camera field throughout the pan.* One useful exception to this rule occurs in the case of a shift of interest between two widely spaced characters: The camera is focused on one of them, and he starts to move toward the other; the camera begins to pan with him, but speeds up to the other character; the first player is then seen walking into the picture. A direct cut to the second character could be used, but panning as described might lend stronger dramatic values.

As a general rule it is not considered good practice to pan away from and directly back to the same point. It should also be borne in mind that it is better to pan *from a weak to a stronger dramatic situation* than the reverse—in other words, to build toward strength.

Like the dissolve, the pan shot can be used as a dramatic implement. Here is a case in point: A woman sits in suspense down stage right; we are holding her in a medium shot (head to hands); we see her head turn as she hears an off-stage noise; a look of horror crosses her face; immediately, the camera executes a *slow* pan in the direction she is looking. As the camera moves slowly on, suspense is sustained, and the dramatic effect is heightened when the camera reaches the door up stage left, revealing the cause of her terror. Compare the effect of this long, slow pan with a cut from character to character. Each has its use. The point being stressed here is that the camera work should fit the demands of the scene.

c. The Boom Shot

Pictorial variety can be added by the use of the boom in combination with the tilt shot. For example, starting with a low close-up of a pianist's hands at the keyboard, the camera booms up slowly, tilting down as it does so to hold the keyboard in the same centering. A maneuver of this sort increases the camera field, thus adding another touch of variety. The shot may be tightened up again by dollying in.

d. The Dolly Shot

The dolly shot is most often used for the purpose of "coming in for a closer look." Employed in this way, it follows the logic of first taking in a situation in its entirety and then moving closer to examine in detail that which is interesting. Sometimes, for dramatic reasons or for variety's sake, the essence of a scene can be more effectively emphasized by starting with a close-up of some characteristic detail, followed by a *dolly back*. Each method has its own dramatic or psychological value. The *dolly in* should be used when orientation to the entire field of interest is the item of first importance. The *dolly back* is indicated when the field of interest broadens pictorially.

It is important, before starting a dolly shot, to have the dolly *lined up* so that there will be no weaving during the camera movement. If the line of travel is not properly chosen, the cameraman will have to correct the error by panning. Though there are times when this is legitimate, it is not good practice for the reason that the multiple movement resultant on the screen is very noticeable. When extreme precision is demanded, the line of the dolly should be marked with chalk on the floor (start and stop points included).

It is also important to end a dolly shot at the *exact point* desired. Nothing is more amateurish than to overshoot the dolly travel and have to back up a bit.

The proper execution of any type of dolly movement on the air requires adequate rehearsal, clear and well-timed instructions over the headphones by the producer, and a good system of signals between cameraman and dollyman.

e. The Travel and the Follow Shot

A good example of the application of the *travel shot* may be seen in the showing of a display of merchandise arranged on a long table or mounted on a background. The dolly boom is at right angles to the platform so that the cameraman can ride the dolly as it is pushed along the line of the display.

The *follow shot* would be applicable to a situation such as the following: A character must be shown going from one room to another; the two sets are side by side, with a connecting door; the camera moves along with the actor, thus catching any business or reactions en route.

From the foregoing résumé of camera movements the reader should have deduced two all-important precepts of camera technique: (1) that *each movement of the camera has a psychological effect on the audience; a specific dramatic value;* and (2) that *all camera movement should be based on a definite purpose* inherent in the continuity.

In the foregoing we have been speaking of camera movements made *on the air.* The producer should always have an understanding with the cameraman regarding movements about to be made on the air. Cameras are being moved so continually to set up shots that, if the cameraman is not warned in advance of a move to be made on the air, he is apt not to be properly set for it. If it is an *ad lib* show, and as a safeguard on re-hearsed camera work, the producer's instructions should be something like this: "Get set to dolly in on the air for a close-up of. . . ." This will give the cameraman an opportunity to line up the shot.

3. *Camera Orientation*

If the cameras are to be the eyes of the audience, they must be oriented to the subject at angles and distances that seem satisfactory to the audience. Though there are an infinite number of choices, every scene has its optimum viewing angle and field. The selection of the best angle, and the decision as to how much to take in will naturally be dictated by the content of the scene or its contribution to the continuity. Unless a camera shot is made strictly for effect, the camera should be angled in a normal, straightforward manner.

As a general rule, it is not good practice to cut back and forth between cameras of the same focal length viewing the scene from *widely different angles.* It will throw the audience out of orientation. This, of course, does not apply to close-up sequences where it is important to catch the reaction of two or more characters. Nor does it apply, for example, to the picturization of a pianist or a dancer; orientation is not a factor here. But, in all situations where the positioning of one character to another or to the setting is important, camera angles should be selected with only one thought in mind—the effect they will produce on the audience and how each shot will contribute to the story development.

The psychological significance of camera angles can be brought out in the following comparisons: A theater performance is not quite the same when viewed from the dizzy heights of the second balcony as from an eighth-row-center seat among the ermine. By the same token, a football game televised from the press coop atop the stadium can be more adequately pictured than with cameras on the ground.

The foregoing examples, however, take into account only the matter of the audience being able *to see* all the action to the best advantage. There are equally important *psychological* factors involved: First, we get a definite reaction when someone towers over us. The very fact that we have to look up to him conditions our attitude; it may be one of respect for his views or strength, or it may take the negative form of submission to (or fear of) his power. Hence it will be seen that merely by the choice of camera angles it is possible (a) to buld a subject up; (b) to present it in a normal "eye-to-eye" manner; or (c) to play it down.

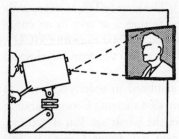 

FIG. 21. SHOOTING UP AT A SUBJECT MAKES IT DOMINANT; SHOOTING DOWN MAKES IT WEAK.

The second psychological factor has to do with *scale*—in other words, how large the subject will appear on the screen. Again we are speaking not of the presentation of the subject so that every detail may be clearly seen but of the psychological effect of scale or size. The selectivity of the camera lens, combined with the limited picture field, make it possible to build a subject up by filling the screen or, contrariwise, to render it weak by making it diminutive. If it is desired to stress the importance of a subject, to make it overpowering or just plain big, it should pretty well fill the screen.

FIG. 22. SHOWING THE EFFECT OF SCALE ON THE PSYCHOLOGICAL IMPORTANCE OF A SUBJECT.

There is more to the choice of the camera angle and the shooting distance than mere visual reporting. In the hands of a skilled craftsman the camera becomes a truly creative implement. Under the direction of a talented producer, camera work can be raised to a high art.

We shall now examine, in more detail, the factors involved in the choice of the shooting distance or, more accurately, of the picture field. In general, we break this down into the *long shot* (abbreviated as LS), *medium shot* (MS), and *close-up* (CU). The term *full shot* (not usually abbreviated) is used to indicate that the picture is to take in an entire set or a broad exterior view. There is also the *medium close-up* (MCU). And when, for instance, a face is to fill the screen the term big close-up (BCU) is used.

All these terms need to be further amplified in order accurately to describe a shot. To specify loosely a "long shot showing George standing by the table" might imply a long shot of the whole set. But if you say, "A long shot of George," the cameraman will frame George in full figure, regardless of whether he is standing or sitting. In standard practice a *medium shot* shows the figure from head to hips; a *medium close-up*, head and about half the torso; a *close-up*, head and shoulders; a *big close-up*, the face filling the screen.

4. *The Long Shot*

Where orientation of subject matter is desired, where the relationship between pictorial items must be simultaneously established, or when there is great breadth of movement, the long shot should be used. Accordingly it is commonly referred to as an establishing shot.

Because of the smallness of the television screen and the resulting loss of detail, the long shot should be used with discretion. Rather than show a full shot of the set, it is often possible to write a "stage cross" into the scene and use a *medium shot*, panning the entire set with the figure as it moves. This is a common device in the movies and valuable on two counts: first, because not too much detail is shown at any one time; and, second, because it creates anticipation. With this technique a large set may be used, thus providing a variety of playing areas.

5. The Medium Shot

The medium shot is the most frequently used shot in television continuity, for it is the basic shot around which close-ups are woven. When skillfully selected and intelligently interwoven it can carry the show. Since it is selective, it should include only such pictorial material as is pertinent to the action.

Admittedly it is not an easy matter to determine how much of the subject to include in a basic shot. It is difficult, in fact, without actually seeing a camera sequence to be more specific than in the general statement given above—include *only that which is pertinent to the action or mood*. Hence it is up to the producer or cameraman to analyze each scene, determine its contribution to the continuity, and compose it to the best of his ability.

6. The Close-up

The close-up, being still more selective, is more revealing in pictorial detail. Its function is to strengthen visual impact by focusing only on *relevant* detail. When watching a sporting event or a play, our wide-angle vision takes in the entire scene but our minds select the portion on which to focus. We tend to strain forward for a closer view. In television the camera lenses do that for us, and since the producer has a variety of focal lengths to choose from he can select as much or as little of a scene as is pertinent.

The close-up, therefore, is a means of *underscoring the essence* of a scene, of *stressing* some aspect, or *strengthening visual impact by eliminating unimportant detail*. When the producer exercises skill in this selective process the continuity is made strong and dramatically convincing. When the intermingling of medium shots and close-ups is smooth, logical, and so natural that it is completely satisfying and effort-less, the television medium is being properly used. Then the revealing intimacy of the close-up is performing its true function.

The camera close-up, however, accentuates detail—both the good *and the bad*—to such an extent that there are times when it is better to use a medium shot. In some situations detail is distracting. Sometimes a significant line is weakened by magnifying an irrelevant detail or a pointless bit of business. Because of its potency, the close-up should be carefully analyzed for its contributive value.

On account of the continuous production, it is not an easy matter to get consistently good close-up shots in television. It is not possible to interrupt the show and set up for proper lighting and picture composi-tion, which can be done in movie production. For this reason the close-up presents a greater problem here than the medium shot. Whenever possible the producer should carefully rehearse all intimate camera work and point out to the talent the necessity of maintaining camera orienta-tion and of duplicating on the air, as closely as is humanly possible, the shots *as they were rehearsed.* Even in an "off the cuff" show it is advisable (perhaps we should say *particularly* advisable) to work out close-up continuity *in advance,* using stand-ins.

One of the most troublesome problems in getting satisfactory close-ups results from the difficulty of catching them—on the fly—with proper lighting. Ordinarily, if a set is lighted so that the long shots look well, the close-ups will lack contrast and modeling. Therefore, if the program depends for effect on an appreciable number of important close-ups, it is best to light for the close-ups and sacrifice on the long shots. Further-more, under these conditions the talent *must play to the lights,* each person making sure that he does not cast unwanted shadows on other players and, when he is being taken in close-up, that he poses himself with regard for the lighting.

7. *A Few Suggestions Regarding Camera Technique*

Remember that each camera shot must be judged on two points: (1) its effectiveness as an individual picture; and (2) how it will tie into the continuity. Each shot in some way affects the one that precedes it and the one that follows.

Because of the foregoing, it is not good practice to cut from a long shot (say a full shot of a room) to a close-up (head and shoulders of one of the characters) unless there is some special reason for it. It is better television technique to introduce an intermediate shot or to dolly in.

Be sure that each shot maintains good continuity flow as regards scale of shapes, line structure, and tone quality. Sudden contrasts in any one or a combination of these three things are noticeable; sometimes this is desirable and at other times it is not.

Always maintain audience orientation. Particularly in close-ups, try to make the audience feel the presence of characters that are *out of the picture*. For instance, in cutting back and forth between "one-shots" of two or three characters engaged in dialogue, frame each shot so that the other characters are "felt" outside of the frame. This condition is defeated if each actor is seen in *full face*, apparently *addressing the camera* rather than the other actors. He should, of course, favor the camera (referred to as "cheating") but should *never break the contact* with the other characters.

In a series of shots built around one character (but involving others) avoid having the central character bob up *in different parts of the picture field*, with each succeeding cut, for no apparent reason.

Since television demands that players work in close proximity to each other, it is usually necessary to have them "give way" when taking a *one-shot* (close-up of one person) or a *two-shot* (two seen in a close-up), so that a portion of another figure will not "hang on the edge" of the picture—a very disturbing effect. This should be rehearsed until it is fixed in the actor's mind along with the accompanying lines.

Caution the talent against "weaving." There is not much the cameraman can do about it if a person is weaving back and forth on his feet—a habit many musicians have.

Since all but wide-angle lenses have a limited depth of focus, try to keep all figures within the field of focus. Naturally this cannot be done at all times, and the cameraman will have to exercise his best judgment in splitting the focus and favoring the important figure.

Move the camera only when camera movement is logical or contributive. Most of the movement should be supplied by the players.

ACTION AND REACTION

Action is enriched by reaction. The thing that makes action interesting is either what caused it or what it resulted in. The anticipation which precedes an act is as valuable dramatically as the act itself, and so is the reaction of one person to another's act. Often the *reaction* is the stronger dramatic element.

A remote pick-up of a horse race is greatly enriched if, between the parade to the post and the shout "they're off," we see a guy dashing up to a window to buy a ticket on a hot tip and forcing his way up to the fence as the race starts, and then, intercut with the race, shots of his face changing through hope in various stages to sheepish disillusionment as he tears up his ticket.

Although the reaction shot cannot carry the story, it will give it life and vitality. In dialogue it is often better to hold the camera not on the one who has the lines but on the character being emotionally moved by what is being said. This, of course, presupposes that the actor knows how to react *for the screen*. Doubtless much of the producer's time will have to be devoted to showing the actor who is inexperienced in television how and to what extent to act and react, for the reason that there is no way for the actor to see how he looks on the screen, except by film transcriptions.

The charm of television is its intimacy. In rehearsing talent, the producer should work for *naturalness*. In both action and reaction he should direct the players to *underplay*, as compared with their acting on the stage. The television actor must always be aware of the fact that he is playing not to thousands but to "two or three gathered together" by the fireside. Whereas on the stage the actor *projects* his characterization, on the television screen the condition should be reversed and the audience should be *drawn to the actor*—the viewer should project himself into the characterization.

Screen technique calls for *surface emotions that are recognizable symbols of emotional states*. Actually the number of these symbols used in facial expressions by the better Hollywood actors are surprisingly few, but they are subject to an infinite number of subtle variations because of the intimacy of the camera and its tendency to magnify little mannerisms.

THE CAMERAMAN

The ideal cameraman is a hybrid, resulting from the tripartite union of a picture-minded person, an elephant, and a mind reader. That he should be picture-minded is self-evident. That he should be an elephant stems from the fact that he is never supposed to forget any of the instructions the director gives him during rehearsals. His mind reading must tell him not only what the director is going to want but also what the talent is likely to do.

The cameraman and the director must work together as a team. The ideal condition is one of harmonious collaboration. They should both feel the production in the same way. Failing this, the director's way must dominate, for a good show can have only one head. At the same time, a good cameraman has a perfect right to ask why he is requested to get a shot that seems to him to be bad technique, though it is necessary for him to realize that he is seeing only the individual shots that appear on his view finder and not how they are woven into the continuity.

Good camera work is never obvious. It is so smooth and effortless that the audience is not conscious of it. To achieve this the cameraman must be picture-wise and in tune with the spirit of the production. He can improve and nurture his picture sense by making pictures mentally wherever he goes, by studying film transcriptions of his own work, and by critically analyzing other shows.

Since camera work provides the element which gives television its appeal, the cameraman is one of the most important people on the set. His work will either raise the production to high technical standards or pull it down to mediocrity. The good cameraman will always try to reach beyond the minimum requirements of merely *reporting* the scenes at which his camera is pointed. He will use his camera selectively, artistically, dramatically. He will approach each subject creatively.

Chapter V

~~~~~~

AUDIO TECHNIQUES

SOUND, whether in the form of music or sound effects, is one of television's strong points as an entertainment medium. But unless it is used with taste and finesse it can be glaringly absurd, amateurish, or just "corny." If it is appropriate to the intent and content of the program and is executed with artistry and skill, the double impact of picture and sound is raised to its highest point, for the power of suggestion which sound possesses is strong and emotional responses are readily aroused through the association of ideas. Ear fatigue is no less worthy of careful consideration than is eye fatigue in the case of those who partake visually.

Television sound is picked up in essentially the same manner as and with equipment similar to that which is used in motion picture production and in radio. Since the manipulation of sound is largely a matter of engineering, to which the motion picture and radio industries have devoted many years of intensive research and development, we shall touch only upon the non-technical aspects of sound as it applies to program building.

Following the procedure used in the foregoing chapter on video techniques, we shall begin our study of audio in the control room. Here we find an *audio engineer* seated at a control console, "riding the gain" (regulating the volume of the sound being broadcast), mixing and blending sounds picked up from various sources, switching from one source of origination to another, and performing the functions of final "fixer-upper" of the sound before it goes out on the air.

Close at hand are turntables for phonograph recordings or transcriptions, so placed that the audio engineer can operate them with or without the aid of an assistant. The audio engineer can communicate with the studio and projection room by means of telephones or speakers, and with the microphone boom operator through headphones. The boom man, by the way, hears the sound he is picking up, through his "high fidelity" headphones, and is thus able to judge the quality of the pick-up. The audio engineer, however, has a more accurate check on the sound quality, and from time to time he may have to suggest changes in the handling of the mike.

The audio engineer works from a script identical with that of the others but marked up especially for sound cues and timing. The information contained in it must be complete in every respect. It should give the entire sound plot—the cues for all music; the titles and sections or portions of all recordings, the cut number of all transcriptions; the nature and source of all sound effects; the order of mike switching; and any special notations as to particular effects requested by the producer. In addition to this standard production information, the audio engineer will add his own notations made during rehearsal.

The producer should confer with the audio engineer during the early stages of planning a program, in order that the latter may contribute his ideas and point out any insurmountable technical difficulties. The audio engineer should be present at the *technical rehearsal* so that he may analyze the sound problems and find out if any special microphone set-ups are necessary. Since the responsibility for the audio portion of the broadcast rests on his shoulders and his contribution to the success of the program is by no means small, co-operation between him and the producer is essential.

RELATIONSHIP OF SOUND AND PICTURE

We can form some idea of the relationship of sound and picture and of the wide variations that exist in the use of sound if we examine only a few types of programs.

a) The *news program,* in which a commentator is seated at a desk, presents a situation almost identical to those encountered in radio. The speaker is in fixed orientation to a microphone which can be advantageously placed for ideal pick-up.

b) The *remote pick-up* introduces another element—*extraneous* sound. We are no longer in a sound-proofed studio but out in the open, where all sorts of sounds—those we wish to broadcast as well as unwanted sounds—are sneaking into the microphone, (even though the announcer is using a "unidirectional" hand mike, which does a fairly good job of keeping out all sounds except his voice). In order to select only the sounds which are wanted, the engineers may employ a number of microphones placed as advantageously as possible. Balance between the various microphones is maintained by the engineer at the mixer.

c) The *audience participation* show, assuming it to be of more or less standard radio format, differs from that used in radio in that the emcee (master of ceremonies) and the participants here cannot work at floor mikes in fixed positions. Since microphones should not ordinarily be shown in the television picture, it is necessary to pick up the voices of the emcee and the participants with a boom mike, which follows them wherever they may wander. The emcee, of course, can be fairly well relied upon to maintain proper voicing and mike orientation, but the unschooled participants usually present a difficult and sometimes impossible pick-up problem. Yet the problem, like the two preceding ones, is only a matter of sound *reporting*, and in none of these cases will the home audience be too critical of the finer points.

d) The *television play* introduces some entirely new and complex elements. Here, in addition to the faithful transmission of sound, we are concerned with *emotional* factors, since the effect on the audience will depend largely on the *quality* of the sound. For one thing, in the voice of a character shown in close-up on the screen we wish to establish a feeling of closeness; a "faraway" quality would destroy the effect. Then, too, there are times when to achieve a feeling of realism we must have *perspective* in the sound—a sense of depth. Natural sounds are sometimes difficult to control; hence to make them "sound natural" we often must create artificial sound effects. Throughout the play we are concerned with the dramatic quality of the sound and its emotional impact. To this end, therefore, we must devote much attention to the voicing of the actors and, here and there, to heightening the effect with mood music and sound effects.

Whereas the radio depends entirely for its effect on voicing and the painting of word pictures, *in television the screen should carry the burden of the story, and the sound or dialogue should be reduced to the minimum needed for plot exposition, characterization, and total effect.* Actually the production problems are in few ways similar in the two media and *are entirely different as regards the purpose of the sound.* In radio the sound is the whole show. The tendency to produce a wordy, radio-with-pictures hodgepodge is regrettable, for it completely disregards the essence of television—its ability to tell a picture story.

SOUND AND SOUND PICK-UP

In the previous chapter it was stated that the function of the television cameras is to serve as the eyes of the audience. It should follow, then, that the microphones should play a parallel auditory role. At first glance this might seem to be a simple function to perform, for it is common knowledge that the microphone is capable of transmitting, with commendable fidelity, all the sounds which it "hears."

But therein lies the difficulty—the microphone picks up *all the sounds within its field of sensitivity*. It is not selective. The human ear, on the other hand, is highly selective; the mind blocks out unwanted sound and makes it possible for us to focus aural attention on the sounds we wish to hear.

In addition to this, our hearing is *binaural*—that is, we hear with two separate mechanisms. If a sound is registered more strongly by one ear, we instinctively turn the head until both ears pick up the sound with equal strength. In this way we determine the direction from which the sound is coming. Having oriented the sound, we judge the distance of its origination through our *experience* with sounds. We know the normal volume of a woman's scream when close at hand. If we hear it only faintly, we know it came from a distance; what is more, we are able to judge the distance with reasonably accuracy. The microphone, however, is *monaural*. It hears with only one ear and lacks a sense of perspective.

These two differences in the functioning of human hearing and microphone pick-up should be clearly recognized in handling television sound. In order to achieve a feeling of reality it is necessary to perform for the microphone the functions which the brain performs for the human ear. Since the microphone is not capable of blocking out unwanted sounds and focusing only on the sound to be transmitted, it is necessary to adopt the practices of acoustical engineering. And, since the microphone cannot indicate the direction of the sound, we must resort to visual means. As an example of the latter: Two people are conversing on a living-room set; a voice or sound is heard offstage; there are two upstage entrances and it is important to the plot to know from which the sound came. Since the microphone cannot supply this clue to the home audience, we should have one or both of the characters look in the direction of the sound. This is only one instance of how sound orientation can be achieved. The producer and audio engineer should be constantly alert to the ever present problems of point of sound origin and perspective.

1. Sound Perspective

The illusion of sound perspective is essential if a feeling of realism is to be gained. If a character is shown in a close-up, the viewing audience should feel the "nearness" of the voice. In a medium shot in which a number of characters speak, the illusion should be created that each voice comes from the proper speaker. In a long shot, the voices should seem farther away. To maintain realism: (1) the audience must be able to feel *space* and *spatial depth*; (2) there must be a sense of the *relative distance between* sounds; (3) the *distance into the picture* from the surface of the screen to the point of sound origin should seem logical.

Motion picture sound engineers, after years of experimentation, have pretty well solved this problem as it applies to that art. Unfortunately a comparable amount of engineering development has not been undertaken in television up to the present time. For this reason it is often impossible today to maintain good sound perspective throughout a production. This is caused principally by the necessity for continuous production, which makes it impossible, with present equipment and methods, to cut from a long shot to a close-up with *both picture and sound*. The boom microphone can in time be brought into the right position, but it is humanly impossible, when cutting rapidly from long shots to close-ups to medium shots, to shift the position of the microphone and orient it properly at that speed.

Therefore, until this engineering problem is solved, the producer must do the best he can in creating the illusion of sound perspective. The situation can be ameliorated somewhat through careful direction of the players as to voicing and microphone orientation and by co-operative effort on the part of the producer and the audio engineer. Incidentally, the cause of sound realism would be greatly advanced if a television receiver could be designed in which the sound actually came (or appeared to come) from the picture screen.

2. The Nature of Sound

Going back to the matter of selectivity, it will be useful to have some understanding of the nature of sound as applied to the microphone. Sound travels in waves. It can be transmitted by solids, fluids, and gases. In television sound pick-up we are concerned principally with the last form of transmission—through air.

Sound waves traveling through air fan out in all directions. Some of them travel directly from the point of origin to the microphone. These are heard most distinctly because they have traveled the shortest distance. But, since sound waves are reflected by hard surfaces, the microphone picks up not only the *direct sound* but all the reflected sounds which reach it. These are called *reverberant* sounds. Furthermore, since the microphone, unlike the ear, cannot focus on the desired sounds, it picks up all sounds reaching it—all the *extraneous* sounds (unwanted noises) and all the *reverberations* caused by reflection.

3. *The Control of Sound.*

Extraneous sound can be fairly well controlled in the studio by the use of noiseless equipment, by care in moving scenery, and so on, and by the usual precautionary measures, plus the use of directional microphones. In remote pick-ups, however, even though unidirectional and parabolic microphones are used, many extraneous sounds will be picked up and there will be much more reverbation than in the studio, where the walls are covered with sound-absorbing material.

Reverberant sound presents many bothersome problems of control, and here is where a knowledge of acoustics is of use. Although these are matters for the audio engineers to handle, we as program people cannot blithely pass the buck or we shall be asking them to perform the impossible. The engineers can give us directional microphones and can perform marvelous tricks of acoustical engineering, but they can go only so far in delivering the quality of sound which we want the audience to hear; we must exercise control over the way the sounds are produced (voicing, direction, point of origin, and so forth) and the settings in which they occur.

A certain amount of reverberation is desirable, otherwise the sound is "dead" and unreal. This, however, is seldom a television problem; there is usually more sound reflection than is desired. In radio, where the microphones can be placed in close proximity to the source of the sound and where the talent "hugs" the mike, the problem of unwanted reverberant sound is not acute. But in television it is a troublesome factor; so much so, in fact, that at the present time television sound leaves much to be desired and presents problems as yet unsolved.

The television studio walls and ceiling are treated acoustically to make them as nearly sound-absorptive as possible. But there are many other hard surfaces which are highly reflective—the floor, scenery, properties, lights, and cameras. In motion picture production there are many ways of overcoming sound pick-up difficulties. The continuity can be broken up into short takes to enable the sound men to make proper microphone set-ups. The sound and the picture can be taken separately, and adjustments can be made when the sound is re-recorded. In television, however, because of the need for continuous production and transmission of the sound just as it occurs, it is necessary for the producer to accept many compromises and to direct the production of voice sound, music, and sound effects so that the desired results are obtained within the limits of the medium. We shall consider a few of the controls which the producer has at his command, in the hope that it will lead him to the solution of other sound problems. They are as follows:

a) Have the microphone as close to the source of the sound as possible. The ratio of reverberant sound increases with the distance between the microphone and the sound source. In close-ups, where intimacy is desired, see that the boom mike is brought in as close as possible without getting into the picture. School the talent to speak with less volume during such scenes. This means that the talent will have to play to the microphone as well as to the camera; it is essential in television. To be successful in television, actors and performers must continually be aware of pick-up problems and must adjust their voices to changing conditions.

b) If the boom microphone cannot be brought close enough to an important bit of dialogue or business, plant a concealed mike. For example, in a courtroom scene the judge seated at the bench can be given a concealed microphone, and the boom mike can be used to pick up the scattered dialogue.

c) Avoid as much as possible having sound originate close to a hard, reflecting surface. If a speaker is seated at a desk or table, cover the table with cloth or some other sound-absorptive material if it is possible to do so. Keep actors or musicians as far away as possible from the hard walls of the set. If a considerable amount of important dialogue must take place close to the scenery, use draperies or a hanging on the near wall. Carpet the floor of any set where there is seated dialogue or where the set is large. Use carpeting for seated musicians, except in large groups where their clothing usually forms sufficient cushioning.

d) Avoid deep, three-sided, small sets having hard, reflecting walls. They are certain to give a barrel-like quality to the sound. The ideal set is one in which the walls are treated acoustically.

e) Be especially careful with the sounds made by properties. If a package is to be unwrapped, have the paper slightly dampened to avoid the disturbing rattle which dry paper makes. The same holds true of paper props such as newspapers. If a cartoonist is working on a large block of paper and is to turn the sheets over as he works, dampen the upper part where it folds over. A prop telephone should have black friction tape wrapped around the cradle so that a loud crash will not result from replacing the instrument. Hand tools, dishes, and parts being demonstrated should be handled quietly and cushioned whenever possible. Prop dishes can be provided with felt or cloth cushions where they come in contact with the furniture.

f) Sound effects and off-stage noises should be carefully produced and thoroughly rehearsed. They should be handled by someone trained to such work and should originate from sound effects equipment which is capable of giving the desired effect. More often than not the most realistic effects are produced by unrealistic means. The ideal condition is to have a separate sound-effects studio, where it is easier to control reverberations and where the proper preparations (often noisy in themselves) can be made without interference with the program. In such a room, equipped with a viewing monitor, talk-back, and headphones for the sound-effects man, showmanlike results can be achieved. The sound-effects operator can see the action on his monitor and cue in his sound effects right on the nose.

AUDIO TECHNIQUES

There are three methods of sound pick-up: (1) by microphones, (2) by records, and (3) by sound film. All three may be employed on one program. For example: The program might open with a fanfare pick-up from a record; as the main title flashes on the screen an announcer (not seen) speaks into a microphone, giving the sponsor's plug and perhaps even reading the whole title, the names of the cast, and the credits; and over this the audio engineer picks up background music from a record. The play opens with a mood picture of rain beating on a window pane; the sound-effects man gives out with the sounds of rain and howling wind, which are picked up by the sound-effects microphone; the actors on the set are cued to start their dialogue, which is picked up by the boom mike; the story cuts back to some earlier period by means of motion picture sound films; then, back again to live action.

This is only one of many combinations of audio technique. It has been enumerated in order to bring out the important fact that television sound falls into two main divisions: (1) sound used for *factual* reasons, and (2) sound used for *emotional* reasons.

1. *Microphone Pick-up*

Microphones are used in television to pick up the following sounds:

a. Dialogue and Sounds on the Set

These are picked up almost entirely by the boom mike, which hangs at the end of a long telescopic arm, mounted on a high, movable pedestal. The boom man can retract or extend the boom, can swing it over a wide arc, and can orient or "gun" the microphone toward any point. In this way the microphone can be brought to any pick-up location within its radius. The playing area must therefore be planned, as to width and depth, with the reach of the mike boom in mind. If this reach is exceeded or, as noted before, the distribution of characters makes it necessary, concealed microphones will have to be used.

The present-day boom stand is a hand-me-down from motion picture studios and is unsuited to television production because of the floor space it takes up. It so happens that the boom mike is almost always needed in close proximity to the playing area and, what is more, jammed in close to the cameras. Invariably the producer needs to move the camera to the exact spot occupied by the bulky pedestal of the boom.

Wireless microphones are now in use which give exceptionally fine results. These microphones are sufficiently small so that they are composed of two boxes approximately the size of large packs of cigarettes. These are secreted on the artist's person and the microphone approximately the size of a half-dollar is hung under the lapel or in an ornament on a dress. The artist has complete freedom of movement and the microphone is always as close to the artist as is his own voice. The microphone boom, pedestal and man necessary to operate it are removed from the limited studio floor space.

b. Off-screen Sound Effects

As indicated on page 78, section (f), sound effects are best produced on equipment designed for the purpose by specially trained personnel and in a specially built studio (Plate II).

c. Announcing

The pick-up of announcements is subject to wide variation, dependent upon the nature of the program and the practice in the studio. The announcer may appear before the camera, or the voice alone may be used.

The announcer may be picked up by either the boom mike or a fixed announce mike. An excellent arrangement from a production viewpoint is a portable announce stand, complete with lights, background (arranged so that it can be changed), and microphone. Equipment of this sort will save a great deal of set-up time for the production crew.

d. Voice-over Narration

This technique may be used for a number of useful purposes. It consists of an off-screen voice "over" the picture, which may be live or film. The voice may be used either for commentary on the action being pictured, as in a sports broadcast, or for narrative purposes to accompany action on the screen. On a commercial or factual sequence, voice-over narration may be employed to describe products, demonstrated methods, scientific phenomena, and the like. When this technique is used imaginatively, dramatic and supernatural effects can be achieved. It is sometimes possible for the narrator to take his cues directly from the action on the set—that is, when the microphone can be placed so that he has a clear view of the action. In the case of narration with film, it is necessary for the narrator to work in front of a viewing monitor and take his cues from the picture tube. It should go without saying that voice-over narration should be neatly timed to the action.

e. Off-Screen Music

Live background music, where the musicians are not included in the picture, is picked up by microphones set up for the purpose.

f. Remote Pick-up

Various types of microphones are required to meet varying conditions. This is a technical problem and not within the province of the program department personnel. The producer should go over the location with the engineers and work out with them the way the pick-up can be handled.

2. Recordings

Records constitute a useful source of sound origination. Ordinary phonograph records are one large source of supply. Also, transcription libraries may be purchased from a number of suppliers in a wide range of classical, popular, and mood music, fanfares, bridges, and sound effects. The advantage in using these transcriptions is that the station does not have to do anything about clearance for the use of any of the music included in the service.

Phonograph records which run at 45 r.p.m. have entered the field of transcription where the ordinary phonograph records were run at 78 r.p.m. and transcriptions at 33⅓ r.p.m. It is safe to assume that 45 r.p.m. will become a standard for the record industry; for household as well as studio use. It is now important that studio equipments be capable of variable speeds so that no recorded material of any kind will be eliminated from potential use.

If the studio is equipped with recording apparatus the program department can put it to a number of uses. The producer can make recordings of music, speech, or sound effects for special uses on productions. Records can be cut of parts or all of a program for study and personnel training purposes or for auditions.

The tape recorder is another form of recording which may be used. It has the merit of low cost, portability, and simplicity. The producer will find many ways of using the tape recorder; for instance, in filming special events or material to be integrated with live production, the desired sounds, background noises, and even on-the-spot commentary can be picked up by the tape recorder. These are then played back and timed with the program when it is prepared for televising.

3. Sound Film

The third and last source or method of sound pick-up is from motion picture film. Ordinarily the picture and the sound are used together, but it will be useful for the producer to know that there are sound-film libraries which carry an extensive supply of sound track. Their stock covers music, sound effects, animal noises, and many unusual items sometimes not available on records. The sound track is printed on regular motion picture film and can be run through the projector in time with the action. For further information regarding the use of film, refer to Chapter IX.

THE CREATIVE USE OF SOUND

Many sounds have symbolic meaning and are often more effective than words in creating emotional response. Sounds may be used to interpret action, to strengthen a mood, or to establish locale; they may be used to heighten comparisons or point up contrasts, to effect transitions and to bridge time gaps. They may be produced on sound effects equipment, they may be picked up from recordings, or they may be produced as live-music effects.

Sound used in this way has the effect of unifying the program and knitting the various elements together. It is a useful device in strengthening continuity. It can be used also as a time-saving device or as a running gag. With it a piece of business important to a plot or perhaps a factual demonstration is not only seen but heard by the audience so that the relationship of action and sound are firmly established. Subsequent repetition of the sound alone or of a small portion of the action will make it unnecessary to repeat the action visually; in fact, the dramatic or comedy effect of the situation may thus be heightened.

It has been noted before that the ear is more susceptible to emotional response than is the eye, for the reason that we tend to associate the sounds we hear with past experiences. This accounts for the extensive use of mood music as an accompaniment to motion pictures. When such music is skillfully handled, the audience is unaware of the fact that they are being moved quite as much by the associations which the music conjures up as by the action on the screen or the spoken words. This points the way to the potentialities of mood music in television.

Nevertheless music adds a potent element of appeal—so much so that it forms the backbone of television programming. It should be employed for mood effects whenever its use is fitting and practical. For the low-budget program there is an ample supply of recorded music which, if tastefully selected, will adequately serve the purpose. With a more elastic budget (and a more benevolent Petrillo) live music can be used with greater effectiveness.

Straight musical programs usually require that the musicians be included in the picture. This sometimes presents pick-up difficulties in maintaining the proper balance between soloists and the accompanying orchestra. It is often necessary to provide separate microphones for the orchestra.

When live music is used for backgrounds and bridges, the conductor should be provided with a monitor or viewing set in order that he may view the production and cue the music properly. The ideal condition is to have such music originate in a separate music studio. This removes a considerable amount of confusion from the studio where the cameras, scenery, lights, and other equipment are, and the production can be better controlled.

Much of television sound is produced by the action caught by the cameras and is picked up by the microphones on the set. This is called *synchronous* (or more commonly "sync") sound. *Off-screen sound,* however, affords the greatest opportunity for the imaginative powers of the producer. At present only the crudest beginnings of the development of an acceptable television sound technique are in evidence. The field is wide open for the creative work of imaginative minds—pioneering minds which will not be content with carrying over the outworn conventions of radio and motion pictures but will develop techniques and forms that are specifically designed for television.

Chapter VI

~~~~~~

TELEVISION WRITING

WE ARE concerned here with writing specifically for television. We shall assume that those for whom this chapter is written have learned how to express what they think and feel in word pictures that will arouse *similar states* in the minds of others. We shall also assume that they have thoughts and feelings that are worthy of expression. From this as a point of departure we can pass directly to the problems that confront all who write for television, be they playwrights or factual writers.

Fortunately television is a stimulating medium. It gives the writer an opportunity to express himself in a satisfying way, for here is an instrument as responsive as the console of a mighty organ, a medium as plastic as sculptor's clay and as expressive as a painter's palette. For the writer who has an awareness of life, television provides a satisfying means of self-expression. What more could he ask than the opportunity which television affords of bringing his creative work, his thoughts, and his reactions to life into the lives of millions of others; what greater satisfaction than to bring pleasure, comfort, and relief from boredom into those lives?

The television writer occupies a place akin to that of the composer of music. His works, if they are worthy, stimulate the interpretive powers of other artists, and through their talents his compositions are enriched and brought to life. Through their interpretation, the mood pictures which flowed from his pen are projected into the minds and hearts of his audience. The writer creates. The player interprets. The audience responds, and thus the cycle is completed.

This cycle aspect of television has significance for the writer. He who writes for the printed page reaches his audience without the help (or hindrance) of a middleman who interprets his meanings. He can do more or less as he pleases, in the hope that there will be some who can interpret his fine phrases for themselves. The television writer, however, must keep uppermost in his mind to *write only that which can be played*—only that which has significance to the eye and the ear. Furthermore, as the words flow from his mind to the paper, they must be judged not as they appear on the page but *in the form of pictures and sounds*. This does not rule out the noble phrase, but it does mean that as it is being written it must ring in the writer's ear as it will come from the speaker on the television set, and he must see its visual form as it will look on the screen. In the graphic words of Victor Borge, the television writer should be able to "hear how it's going to look and see how it's going to sound."

The television writer, therefore, is not one who sits in an ivory tower and writes as he pleases. He is a composer who sets down notes for others to play—notes so conceived and so ordered that they can be interpreted and given meaning *as interrelated pictures and sounds*.

The writer's personal approach to the medium is of prime importance. He should constantly keep in mind that the members of his audience are not in a theater but in their homes, and that television plays an intimate part in family life. For this reason all its manifestations must be tailored to fit the pattern of life *in the home*. Being the most sensitive of the communications media television becomes an integral part of living— of realistic living which to some will mean glorious adventure, to others dull monotony, to still others grim actuality.

When people leave their homes or their "four walls of lonesomeness" in search of entertainment, they want to escape from reality for a few blissful hours; they want something in contrast to the routine of home life. They want to get out of themselves and project their hopes and dreams into the lives of others. They choose what suits their taste or lack of it and ask only to be amused or amazed; anything goes and the more of it the better. They have paid for a trip to a dream world and a chance to forget their troubles. Hence they are quite willing to accept situations, characterizations, and glamorizations that would be repugnant, tawdry, or downright silly to them in the reality of their homes.

Television, on the other hand, though it affords entertainment and a means of taking imaginative flight, is tied closely into the business of actual living and in the very place where that living goes on. Since the audience, at the time of the broadcast, is surrounded by all the evidences of realistic existence, the factors governing picture and sound treatment are dictated by the mental and emotional states that prevail in the home.

This prescribes quite a different set of specifications from those which apply to the wonderland of the cinema or the theater.

Television in the home must be colored more truthfully with reality. Not that there is any limit to the flights of fancy that are possible; nevertheless, these imaginative excursions should not be seasoned beyond digestibility in the place where people face from hour to hour all the realities of laughter and tears. Many relished dishes of cinema fare are ptomaine poison in the home. The television writer must be a wise and clever chef.

THE APPROACH

Misconceptions arise from the loosely made statement that television is a visual medium. To be sure, it is visual, but its pictures are not an end in themselves. Television is visual only in the sense that pictures supply that portion of the effect which can best be produced by visual means.

This dualism of television demands that picture and sound aid and abet each other. Each must contribute something that is lacking in the other. There are instances, of course, when either one may carry the effect alone for a considerable period of time, but in the main the one must complement the other—must find completeness in association with the other.

The television writer should have a type of mind that can *preview all that he writes*. In one corner of his brain there should be a television set on which his word pictures take visual form and from which his mind's ear receives the sounds. He will then realize that the vital aspect of television writing is to create situations and effects that are not just picture *and* sound but a truly artistic blending of the two, and to produce effects and arouse responses that could be achieved in no other way.

The motion picture theater is a classroom in which the television writer can learn much. Many techniques and devices of the cinema are directly applicable. Many cannot be used at all. Technical differences between the two media account for some of the disparity. The difference between audience reaction in the theater and in the home account for still more, as has already been pointed out. The most important differences, however, are often completely neglected or thoughtlessly regarded, to wit, the *intimacy* of television, the closeness of its contact with the *one* individual or the *small* family group sitting at home, and the inappropriateness of extravaganza.

In radio this intimacy is not so complete; here the listener is reached through only one of his senses, and mental pictures are produced only in proportion to the individual's ability to visualize. Nevertheless the radio listener will conjure up pictures that are formed directly out of his own life experience, and these images will be completely satisfying to him—he will have no quarrel with his own visualization. That is one of the great attributes of radio. And, by the same token, it can easily constitute a weakness of television if the visualization is not acceptable to the audience.

The writer will do well to study the essential nature of television and scrupulously avoid imitating radio, the motion picture, or the theater, for *an imitation is something less than the real thing*. The television writer must *write for television*. This means that he will capitalize on its intimacy, its ability to make much out of little, its effectiveness in delicate shading and subtle nuance, its genuineness and sincerity. He will do well never to forget that his characters are not separated from his audience by rows of seats but are in the same room with them. He will take advantage of this intimacy and, rather than attempt to impress his audience with super-duper spectacles or mesmerize them with theatrical artificialities, he will build situations and develop characterizations that are suitable as an intimate part of normal living.

Television writing is not merely a matter of filling screen time with pictures to go along with the sound; it is a *fusion of two essential ingredients*, each so dependent upon the other that the omission of a word or a bit of action is felt as a loss. Where a shrug of the shoulders or the flicker of a facial expression means more than words, it should not be diluted by needless dialogue; where words alone are more effective, pointless action should not be used. The writer should be continually aware of the fact that he is writing *action and reaction* as well as words.

Whereas the radio writer has only words and sounds as implements, the television writer has in addition the visual appearance and the movements of his subject matter. For this reason *the picture should carry as much as possible of the story. The amount of dialogue should be held' to the minimum needed to supplement the picture.* If the words are complete in themselves, it will not be necessary for the audience to follow the picture and their attention will wander away.

WRITING CONTINUITY

Television continuity consists of a progression of related elements or sequences so arranged and integrated as to arrive at a climax, which it should reach through a succession of related steps.

The writing of television continuity, whether it be for the individual program or for the broadcast day, involves the weighing of program elements for their relative importance or their contribution to the main effect and then the arrangement of these in coherent order. *Coherence* is needed to hold the program together. *Flow* is essential for it to arrive at the climax. Lacking either of these elements, a television program will fall apart or bog down and become static.

1. *Continuity in the Individual Program*

The individual program is an entity in itself and must find its own resolution. It must have a beginning, a middle, and an end. It must have its own flavor, and everything in it must contribute in greater or less degree to its appeal. The pace may be slow or fast, but *there must be progression.*

The writer will tend to fall under the spell of his own words as they are written, paragraph by paragraph; this and that bit may indeed be pretty good, but unless they form good continuity they have been a waste of paper and perspiration. The audience will rebel at being shoved from one attraction to another, but they can be led on and on if cleverly handled. That is the function of continuity.

The capable writer keeps his eye on the flow from one situation or idea to the next, balances his key situations, and builds interest or sustains suspense right up to the climax with just the right amount of crescendo. He knows that the program, whether it be educational or entertaining, must be so constructed that the tension of interest or suspense is maintained throughout. If he can previsualize as he writes, if he can be the author and the audience at one and the same time, he is fortunate; if he is not so endowed he must develop that ability.

2. *Continuity for the Broadcast Day*

The writer of continuity for the broadcast day faces the same problems as he does in preparing the program segment, but with a vengeance. Here his solution of these problems is made difficult by the strange jumble of program fare that somehow or other must be put together. He must suddenly force the audience to jump from Bach to bock, from pharmaceuticals to farm forums, from soap to hope, and back to soap again. Pity him—and the audience.

How can he do this? Only by constructing transitions that will ease the audience over some of the humps. But it can be done to a fairly satisfactory or at least acceptable degree. Each sponsor and each producer will be interested primarily in his particular segment of the broadcast. It is up to the continuity writer to win their co-operation in devising transitions that will hold the audience during the station break and lead them smoothly into the next program.

The writer must make the expenditure profitable for the sponsor who is footing the bill. Without the sponsor's advertising budget the public would be deprived, not only of singing commercials, but of the best in entertainment. The writer's most important consideration is to make the commercial or the factual slant palatable to the audience and productive for the sponsor in actual sales or good will.

The radio commercial writer has only to reach the ear. The listener has only to listen or shut out the sound, which interferes not at all with any bodily movement or any other activities, including homework. But the television "looker-listener" (did the Greeks have a word for it?) cannot pursue other activities while he is "looklistening" (or would it be "eyearing"?). Therefore, if the television writer is to justify the cost of presenting the commercial visually, he must create treatments that will insure looking as well as listening. If the budget is such that he can make full use of the potentialities of the medium he is indeed fortunate, but more often than not he is forced to a compromise, and it is here that he must rely on ingenuity and good construction.

The commercial continuity writer will bear in mind that the mere physical appearance of a product is not the important thing to feature, except in such instances as package identification. The most effective appeal is based on the *benefits of ownership or use*. The advertiser is not selling *things* or *services*, but comforts, security, happiness, health, glamour, and all the fundamental things of life that accrue through the elimination of B.O. and regular doses of YENOLAB spelled backwards.

CONTINUITY DEVICES

The purpose of continuity is to achieve a transitional flow from one element to the next and to maintain tension of interest. A succession of musical numbers, played one after another without any transitional link to compensate for the change in key or tempo, does not produce a pleasing effect. A succession of unrelated pictures does not hold the attention, for there is no flow of thought. *Continuity demands that each picture and each sound be a preparation for the ones to follow.*

Various continuity devices may be employed. The following, though not by any means complete, are the more important ones with which the writer should be familiar:

1) *The announcer, the emcee, or the moderator* may be used as in radio to introduce the various program units and to act as the bridge connecting them. In certain instances, notably the musical, variety, or personality program, it is a useful device though certainly far from novel.

2) *The narrator* who carries the thread of the story or supplies historical, interpretive, or corollary remarks is frequently used to supply continuity. He may be seen, or his voice only may be used.

3) *The storyteller* may be used in the same way, and he may be one of the cast if desired.

4) *Picture and sound symbolism* afford the most artistic means of obtaining effective continuity. For example, some visual symbol representing the essence of the theme can be used in the opening title sequence, repeated as the piece progresses, and/or used in the end title. It may be a "running" symbol or an intercut shot that points up the adjacent scenes— for instance, a hand reaching out to turn on a bedside lamp to light the face of a clock, in order to indicate a sleepless night; a picture of tired, dragging feet; a shot of a speeding train accompanied by the oft-used but always good sound effects, for the purpose of lending excitement to the hero's return to save the farm.

5) *The montage* consists of a series of pictures or sounds assembled in juxtaposition in such a manner that they evoke emotional response through the power of suggestion. It is a motion picture technique (often misused) which lends itself to television, though in a limited degree since it must be built "on the fly." It is a useful form of dramatic expression for the reason that the audience creates its own response. Although the long, complex montage which either takes the action out of the studio or else is a series of cut-backs to previous action must always be put on film, there are many instances where the device may be used in live television.

One of the common uses of montage is in plot exposition. For example, a character is relating the incidents leading up to a certain situation, and, rather than hold the camera on him throughout a long monotonous monologue, a series of rapidly intercut scenes is used to picturize the action and/or his reactions to it. It is much more dramatic and interesting than a long display of surface emotions on the face of the actor.

Another common application is in showing cause and effect. Suppose it is a talk on safe driving. The inevitable results of reckless driving can be put over with stronger impact by a montage of quick dissolves and intercuts of speeding cars, screeching brakes, mangled wrecks, and ambulances and operating tables than by the speaker's words alone. The montage is a useful device in explaining how things work or are put together; in fact, it is one of the best ways of making a factual program exciting.

6) *Intercutting* has already been mentioned, but it is such a useful continuity device that it warrants further study. One of the most dramatically powerful techniques of television and the cinema is the *juxtaposition of action and reaction*. All too frequently their interdependence is disregarded. The tendency is to hold the camera on action, whereas reaction is usually the more important of the two. In a dramatic sense, the audience is much more interested in what *results* from action than in the action itself; they are more deeply moved by the reaction on the face of the man receiving the death sentence than they are in the stern expression of the judge, hence by intercutting the judge's pronouncement of the sentence with flashes to the convicted man, his wife, the murdered man's wife, the district attorney, and the spectators a more dramatic feeling is obtained.

Intercutting is also effective in pointing up the essence of a situation by quick flashes to something that parallels or opposes it. If the intercut scenes are themselves given continuity, they can form a contrapuntal theme.

As in the case of the montage, the value of intercutting arises from the fact that the audience is drawn into the situation and contributes its own emotional reaction.

7) Superimposure is still another device for obtaining continuity through dramatic impact. It is the "stream of consciousness" technique most commonly employed, and it may be either visual or aural. Childhood memories, a sweetheart's face, and some poignant situation permeate the mind of the dying man, and over the shot of his face the scenes flitting through his mind are superimposed. By so doing it is possible to reduce the amount of dialogue to a point where it is dramatically strong, because the superimposed scenes force the audience to supply it. That, regardless of the device, is drama in the highest sense—inducing the audience to round out a situation for themselves rather than actually giving them the complete lines; making them really live it and put it into their own words.

Visual continuity in television is a knotty problem for the writer and may well be an impossible one for the producer unless the writer has made it practical from a production standpoint. In motion pictures the cutter, as he is called, can take separate scenes and with the aid of optical printing put them together in smooth transition. In live television this "cutting" must be done in the control room as the show is being broadcast. The writer therefore must use transitional devices that are producible. He must know what the cameras and microphones can and cannot do. In many instances it will be well for him to sketch a floor plan of the setting or go so far as to make a small working model.

If the entire production is "live," the writer must pay particular attention to the mechanics of camera, microphone, and light manipulation; otherwise he may create traffic jams on the studio floor. Often by the introduction of a film sequence an impossible bit of studio routine can be overcome, as in the case of time needed for costume changes or the shifting of props or actors from set to set.

BASIC PRINCIPLES

The ten basic principles of composition outlined in Chapter III are also the writer's foundation stones in program construction. It is not enough that there be capable talent and direction; if the script is not built on solid ground, it will fall apart.

It should not be necessary to elaborate to any great extent on the application of these principles. Obviously there must be unity, variety, and harmony. The importance of balance is self-evident. The value of rhythm, however, is not so manifest, yet it is essential to good continuity. It is, in fact, one of the most important considerations in television.

1. Rhythm

We have already alluded to the rhythmic nature of life and noted how the rise and fall of cadences in music and speech contribute form, clarity, and beauty. Television continuity derives the same virtues from rhythm when it is used with finesse. The writer initiates rhythm in the structure of his word patterns by giving his characters lines which inspire rhythmic utterance. He establishes rhythm, good or bad, in the action he motivates. He predetermines to a considerable extent, the rhythmic patterns which the producer can create with the camera.

As to the latter, the potent quality of rhythm in camera cuts, changes of camera angle, scale, and direction of movement should be thoroughly appreciated by the writer. His script, if written in the light of such knowledge, will give the producer an opportunity to achieve notable results. Certainly continuity made up of scenes of the same length, always from the same camera angle, and with no change in the size of the subject or the direction of its movement could hardly be called distinguished. The capable writer will work these rhythms into his script.

2. Pace

Pace and rhythm are interrelated. The speed at which a rhythmic pattern moves and the variety introduced through change of pace have a tremendous effect on audience attention. Pace is also a factor in the quality of mood which the scene induces.

The television writer must realize that he is writing for a definite time block. In a factual program the amount of subject matter must be such that, in the time scheduled, it can be paced at a rate that allows it to be understood and enjoyed.

In the dramatic program pace and mood are closely linked. Each scene has a pace that best suits its mood. Change of pace is in itself a dramatic effect. The success of the producer in achieving proper pace will depend largely on the writer's handling of the problem. In live television this is made difficult, at times, by the limitations of continuous production. Bits of action or business often slow down the camera cuts. The writer must therefore watch the movements of his characters and the mechanics of production. When there is any doubt in his mind as to the pace at which a scene can be played, he should work it out on a floor plan or scale model.

A moment's consideration will expose the problems which the writer and producer must solve. In a given amount of time there is a definite limit to the amount of action that can be presented visually in good continuity; it takes just so long for a movement to be completed, and in most instances if a movement is started it must be finished. This means that the writer must motivate only such action as fits the situation and the time factor. In radio the pace is limited only by the intelligibility of speech; in motion pictures pace is controllable almost at will in the cutting room, and scenes can be re-shot if necessary. In television, however, the producer is limited by the necessity of continuous production, and if the writer has not written within the limits of the medium there is not much that can be done about it.

3. *Proportion, Emphasis, and Dominance*

Regardless of the type of program, if it is not built around a dominant theme it will produce a scattered effect and leave the audience wandering around trying to find out what it is all about. A balanced proportioning of the separate elements and the relative emphasis placed on each will correct this condition. Just as in pictorial composition each shape or line has its own power of attraction, so too in the writing, each phrase, each thought, and each situation has an interest-holding value. It is the writer's function to evaluate, apportion, and arrange the various units or sections of the program so as to lift the interest and pace here and there and to build always toward a climax.

4. *Application of the Ten Principles*

The fundamental principles of program construction which have just been outlined are the nearest approach to rules that can be laid down for the television writer. Let him shun like the plague the purveyor of formulae—he who says to do it thus and so, and he who hands out rules. There are none—except the ones which the talented writer will break, to his eternal glory. Even basic principles elude capture in ironclad bonds. The writer must adapt them to his own uses and abilities.

They will be used for the most part unconsciously, having become a part of the writer's working equipment. They can be used consciously, however, during the polishing and rewriting stage. After a script has been worked up "in the rough" it should be subjected to the test of detached analysis. The writer will find that it pays to apply the ten principles of composition, one at a time, to his script; it will bring weaknesses to light and show him how to correct them. Through repeated use in this way, the basic principles of program construction will bed themselves in the background of his mind and guide him unconsciously in all his writing.

TELEVISION PLAYWRITING

Since television is a co-operative activity, the script is only the first link in a long chain of efforts forged out of the contributions of many minds, talents, and skills. The author is first of all writing for the actor and the producer. If he succeeds in stimulating them he may succeed in reaching the audience. To reach this first objective he must make his meanings clear; the characters must be sharply etched; situations and plot development must be well defined; and, finally, his script must be so arranged that dialogue and business can be read easily and clearly. Before taking up the details of play construction let us become familiar with the form of the television script.

1. *Stages of Development*

There are three types of script. More explicitly, there are three stages through which the play script may pass: (a) the scenario; (b) the manuscript; and (c) the production script.

The *scenario* describes the play in outline form but with sufficient detail as to setting, characterization, action, and plot development to enable the reader to form a good impression of what the piece will be like in final form; the *manuscript* is complete as to dialogue and such stage directions as are necessary to indicate action and outline the mechanics of production, but it leaves the details of these matters of production to be worked out by the producer; the *production script* is complete in every detail and does not reach its final stage until the last rehearsal has brought all the necessary cues, warnings, and production directions to light.

The primary function of the scenario is to simplify the play so that it may be analyzed for what it really is when stripped of its trimmings. In this form it is useful to those who may buy or produce it, because its possibilities can be evaluated quickly and clearly. But, even more important, it is useful to the author, because he can subject the piece to more detached analysis at this stage than when he comes to write the complete dialogue. If the scenario clicks, he then goes on to write either the complete manuscript or the production script, depending on his qualifications and whether he is a free-lance or a staff writer. If he is not thoroughly versed in the mechanical side of play producing, he should leave camera instructions and the actual details of production to those who know. In any event the writer should remember that he is only one of a team and should leave something for the others to contribute.

As an example of script treatment, suppose we take the situation used in Chapter III to illustrate the visual method of planning. We have thus far only the bare skeleton of a dramatic situation: A drunken father breaks into the quiet of his home and so frightens a small child that she runs from the room; crossing the street in her panic, she is run over by a truck; on being brought back to the room she dies. Not much of a story, to be sure. A temperance speaker might take it and develop a preachment on the curse of drink. But suppose we add motivation, conflict, and human values. Let us establish a *conflict* between the father and the little girl and develop this as the one weakness in an otherwise decent sort of person. Such a conflict might result from a number of causes, but let us say that the little girl is actually not his daughter though she had been brought up as such; it turns out that she is the child of an older daughter who died when she was born. It is further shown that the father had so bitterly opposed the marriage of his daughter that he had driven her out of the home; for this reason the father could never take the child into his heart. Here we have motivation for a conflict. Let's see what might be done with it and set it up in the three stages of script development.

a. The Scenario

Form of the Scenario

(Date
Author's name
Address and
Telephone number)

FORGIVENESS

Scenario for a Television Play

by

(Author's name)

A chapter in the life of a family which
might have taken place anywhere at any time

Characters

A Mother, middle-aged, patient, and understanding. Has character.
Mary, a sweet child of ten. She has few lines but must be a good little actress.
John, a boy of twelve.
Luke, an older son. About twenty-four and dependable.
James, the father, stern, relentless, and unforgiving.
Ruth, a daughter now dead.
Steve, a no-account, in his late twenties.

Sets Required

1. A comfortable and charming living room, furnished in the manner of a lower-middle-class family.
2. A dingy boardinghouse room.
3. A corner of a cabinetmaker's workshop.

Film Footage Required

A sequence, to be specially filmed, showing the scene of an accident on a residential city street. A huge truck has just injured a small child.

Sequence 1.   Set 1.

A living room, charmingly furnished in the manner of a lower-middle-class family. There is an upstage door and a window at stage left through which afternoon sun is streaming.

The Mother is seated on a sofa, surrounded by her mending. Mary and John are reading and talking casually. Mary is stretched out on the floor with a story book and her doll. The Mother keeps looking anxiously at the mantel clock, though trying not to show her concern. It is obvious that the life of the family revolves around Mary, whom they all adore—especially twelve-year-old John. Luke comes home from work.

Mary plants the plot with a question: "Mother, why doesn't Daddy like me?" . . . Mother tries at first to gloss over the fact, but the child persists. Finally the Mother asks John to bring a picture from the table, where he is dawdling over his homework. She says to Mary: "Listen to me, my child; you had to know this some day; I wanted to wait until you were a little older, but there is a reason why you must hear it today . . . This is a picture of your mother."

Mary had always thought it was a picture of an older sister who had died . . . Mother explains poignantly that the child's mother died when she was born; there was "a reason" why they brought the little girl up as their own . . . She tells the child about her mother . . . how she was trusting and full of sweetness . . . how she fell in love with a man who deserted her . . . "He was not nice to your mother, Mary, and Daddy told her she must not see him, but you see, my dear, love does strange things; Ruth thought she could make your father a better man." DISSOLVE to . . .

Sequence 2.   Set 2.

A dingy room with a disorderly bed; clothes thrown about; a table littered with cigarette butts and racing forms.

A man is nervously throwing himself around; he grabs up a racing form, dumps a small amount of money out on the table, and is counting it when a knock comes at the door . . . Ruth enters and there is a strained, contrasting dialogue between them over his gambling; Ruth is sweet and you can see she is throwing herself away on a worthless though fascinating man (older and worldly wise) . . . She tells him her father has forbidden her to see him any more; Steve puts on his act . . . He tells her he has "just one more little job to do," then he will be able to take her away and give her everything she wants; he promises to reform . . . She is happy and leaves to go to her father.

Sequence 3. Set 3.

A corner of a cabinetmaker's shop. There is a workbench at which the Father is occupied as the scene opens.

This is a short, bitter scene in which the Father displays unrelenting qualities . . . To him right is right, and there are no two ways about it . . . Ruth pleads with him to believe, as she does, in Steve; she finally flares up and, with the unreasonable bitterness of youth, vows she will go away with Steve . . . The Father tells her to "go then" and may she never set foot in "his" house again.

Sequence 4. Set 1.

"So, my dear, your mother went away with him. For a long time we heard nothing, and then one day a letter came; it was from a hospital, and it said your mother had died when you were born. We went and brought you home. Your father had gotten into trouble and they had sent him to jail for ten years." She goes on to tell how they moved away and came here to live. The Father never has been able to get over it; that is why he has sometimes been strange; Mary reminds him of the daughter whom he had loved; he still tries to justify his sending her away . . . It comes out that Steve has been released; he has traced them, and only today Father encountered him; they are together now . . . She keeps looking at the clock and occasionally goes to the window to look out . . . Then she sees him coming; they wait for his entrance—not knowing what to expect . . . He opens the door and stands there in a state of fury; nothing is said for a moment; then Mary thinking in her sweet way to soften him, moves toward him with, "You're not my daddy any more, but I love you just . . ." (the Father, cutting in) . . . "Get out of my sight," and he makes as if to strike her; Luke goes to the Father and remonstrates with him; Mary rushes, terror-stricken, out of the room. The scene is near its end; Mother goes to the window and sees the child is about to cross the street; she sends John to go after her . . . Turning toward her husband, she says: "She is our own flesh and blood. There is no evil in her heart. But there is evil and hate in yours, James." The screech of brakes is heard. Luke, who is near the window, looks out and starts for the door as the scene is CUT to . . .

Sequence 5. Film.

A street, a huge truck, a gathering crowd. Mary is lying injured and John is kneeling beside her. There are the usual street overtones and people are asking who it is and how it happened. All of this is background for Luke's few, tense words as he picks Mary up to carry her into the house.

Sequence 6. Set 1.

Luke places Mary's limp form on the sofa. The Mother kneels by her; there is little if any dialogue; focus keeps coming back to Mary's face . . . Will the eyes open? They do, of course, and her first words are: "Where is grandfather? I didn't finish telling him" . . . A close-up of him shows his inward conflict; finally he goes to the child . . . "You didn't let me—finish— grandfather—I love you—just the—same—." Her eyes close. SLOW DIS- SOLVE to big close-up of story book and doll, just as she left it on the floor.

As it has worked out, we have ended up with something of a tear- jerker; the drunken father idea which we started with dropped out along the way, because it gave more scope in character development to build an uncontrollable internal conflict. By this change he could be made stronger; furthermore, by having him drive Mary out of the house rather than merely frighten her, it was possible to develop a "tag line" for the ending and give the ending to her.

We are leaving these steps just as they have evolved and are not changing the scenario to agree with later revisions. In this way it will show how a finished play may grow out of the merest germ of an idea— some chance remark that is overheard, some figment of the imagination, or something encountered in the day's experiences.

In Chapter III we needed a situation that could be given visual treat- ment as a means of explaining how to apply the basic forms of compo- sition; we thought it would require five characters to demonstrate all the basic forms; some dramatic situation involving conflict was needed . . . Well—why not a drunken father breaking into a peaceful domestic scene? . . . Yes, and have him frighten a little girl, and have her run out on the street and get run over. When later it came to the selection of material to use as an example of script treatment, we thought: Why not tie in the visual treatment in Chapter III and in this way present a complete and connected example of development—an acorn-to-oak sort of thing?

That is how many authors work; some germ of an idea will pop up out of nowhere; it will be planted, cultivated, pruned, pulled up by the roots, and started over again. They find that the scenario method saves time and produces work of more distinction, because if they have not analyzed the framework for what it really is they are apt to hang beautifully written dialogue on badly built plot structures.

b. The Manuscript
The general form of the television manuscript follows the format used for motion picture manuscripts: Picture directions and camera cues are written on the left of the page; audio directions, sound effects, music cues, and dialogue are placed on the right. The page is thus divided into two main columns: the one on the left, headed "Picture" or "Video," has in it all the video information needed; the one on the right, headed "Sound" or "Audio," contains all audio information as well as the dialogue.

So many things can happen (and mishappen) during production that it is essential to have the script arranged for quick, clear reading. Dialogue should be double-spaced, but not the video or audio instructions, which should be brief and explicit. The names of characters should be in full caps. Instructions to them as to playing the lines should be in parentheses at the right and not capitalized. All other audio instructions should be in full caps. On the left, the video side, the author's description of action and locale should be in lower case, single-spaced; but standard camera instructions such as PAN, TILT, and DOLLY IN and control room terms like FADE IN should be in full caps. The pages should be numbered in both the upper and lower right-hand corners for quick handling during rehearsal.

In a manuscript the author should not include any more camera instructions or production detail than is necessary to bring out the possibilities of the play. For one thing, it obscures the dramatic qualities of the piece, and, for another, it gives the producer a lot of work to do in crossing stuff out so that he can treat it in his own way (that's gratitude for you).

There should be a title page giving the name of the piece, a word or a sentence classifying it, the author's name, and his address in case he is not a staff writer. The approximate running time should also be given. If it is an adaptation, or if it is copyrighted, complete information of this kind should also appear on the title page.

Page one should list the cast, with brief descriptions of each member's age and type; the number of sets and their description should be given; any special motion picture footage or stills should be described, as well as any special effects or properties. If the script has been accepted and scheduled for rehearsal, the manuscript should contain complete lists and descriptions of properties, music, and sound effects.

Form of the Manuscript

FORGIVENESS

(page) 1

Picture	Sound

TITLE SEQUENCE:

(If the author has any good ideas for this, they may be outlined here.)

SUITABLE MUSIC: SOMETHING THAT CAN WELL BE TAKEN OUT ON THE OPENING OF THE FIRST SCENE.

Set 1. LIVING ROOM

Open on a CU of Mary on the floor with doll, reading story book. DOLLY BACK to take in Mother on sofa surrounded by her mending. At logical point, continue DOLLY to take in Luke as he sits.

MARY

(After some little business to establish the scene.) Mother, the o-g-r-e . . . What is that, Mother?

MOTHER

That's an ogre, Mary child—a cruel man who frightens children.

MARY

Well, this ogre wasn't really and truly cruel, 'cause he wanted to be good inside.

(More)   (page) 1

Picture	Sound
	MOTHER Yes, dear, there are some men . . . (with implied meaning) . . . who are kind inside, though it doesn't show through. Always look for the good inside of people, Mary child.
	MARY Yes, mother. (She hears whistling off-stage.) Luke's home, I guess.
Luke enters with evening paper in his hand.	**LUKE** (To mother) Hi-ya, beautiful.
	MOTHER Hello, Luke.
	LUKE (To Mary, with affectionate whack) Hi, adorable.
	MARY (ad libs as Luke sits)
	MOTHER (glancing at clock) I wish James would get here. (She goes to window.)

(page) 3

Picture	Sound
John is now seen at a table near window, doing his homework.	**JOHN** Mom, if A has six apples and B has twelve, how many does B have to give to A so they both will have the same number? **MOTHER** (trying to do it on her fingers) You'll have to wait till your father gets here, John. I've no head for figures. (She goes back to her mending.) **MARY** Isn't daddy at his shop this afternoon? **MOTHER** No, he . . . is seeing a man. **MARY** (going to mother) Mother, . . . why doesn't daddy like me?

(More)   (page) 3

This is sufficient to show the set-up of the manuscript and the amount of detail included. Playing directions should be descriptive of the characterization the author has in mind, and action not apparent in the dialogue should be given if it is important to plot development.

The audience must be told at the very beginning who and what the characters are. The author must remember that the audience knows nothing about his brain children and will not be interested in them unless they are *made interesting in the first few minutes.* Supporting characters should be typed by their first few lines; main roles can be developed at will, but they should be given revealing lines as soon as possible. First and last impressions are the ones that remain.

Another point to be kept in mind is that the audience at first is interested more in the characters *as people* than it is in the plot. Plot exposition, therefore, should not be carried very far until the characters have been established. This may be done in a matter of seconds, but it is unwise to force the audience to absorb a new idea and get acquainted with new people all at once. Also, at the first entrance of each character the audience should not be left to wonder about his importance. Note that Luke's entrance is heralded by his off-stage whistling and by Mary's "Luke is home, I guess." The eyes of the audience will instinctively go to the door. It is a good idea to begin building the characterization of each important character before his entrance and to prepare the audience for it.

Various devices may be used to introduce the theme of the play and the players. In the instance cited we have made use of the dolly-back. Starting with a close-up of Mary, the camera dollies back to take in the mother. This is held as a two-shot until the mother has been established, the camera angle being such that the door through which Luke is to enter is included. During his breezy entrance the dolly-back is resumed until we have a three-shot. This gives enough head room for the mother's rise, and as she moves to the window the camera pans with her, revealing John for the first time. He is immediately given lines. As it now stands, all four characters have been established, as well as the character of the living room; the audience knows who the people are and has some idea of how they live. Plot development may now begin, and from this point on the camera work should be intimate.

c. The Production Script

A smooth television production requires clock-work co-ordination of the duties of all who are involved—the producer, who directs the cameramen from the control room; the stage manager, on the studio floor; the video engineer, who manipulates the channels and makes the cuts, fades, and dissolves; the audio engineer, who controls the sound; and the lighting director, who controls the lighting effects. All must function in unison. To make this possible—to insure perfect co-ordination—each of the foregoing individuals must have a copy of the script. On it he will mark in his own way the particular notations that apply to his operations.

The ideal condition would be a standardized form of production script that could be used throughout the industry. This perhaps is asking for the moon. Each producer will have his own ideas and think they are the best, but the basic requirements of the production script are the same everywhere. They are: clarity; quick readability; and a set-up that helps to prevent mistakes.

The form recommended here achieves these ends. It is based on the fact that there are four principal people using the script during production—the producer, the technical director, the video engineer, and the audio engineer—each one following a different set of cues but all of them requiring the other cues at times. It is set up so that the producer finds all his cues in the first column at the left; next to this there is a column giving the video engineer all his channel switching cues; the audio engineer uses the sound or audio column at the right. This separation of the picture column into two parts makes for easier and quicker reading by the producer and video engineer. Furthermore, the video engineer's cues are close to the audio column, and he can pencil-mark his cuts to specific words clearly because of this proximity. Names of characters are lined up at the edge of the audio column (instead of in the center of it), thus minimizing eye travel.

Form of the Production Script

FORGIVENESS

(page) 1

(Station, date, time of broadcast and producer)

Video	Audio

[Note: The tie-in with the outgoing program should be given here. Title sequences may take many forms; we are showing the script set-up for a filmslide title and a voice-over announcement.]

Video	Audio
TITLE 1 FADE IN	FANFARE—DROP TO BG LEVEL
The WXYZ	
Tele-Theater presents . . .	ANNOUNCER—(off camera)
	"The WXYZ Tele-Theater presents . . .

(More)   (page) 1

Video	Audio
TITLE 2 DISS.	
FORGIVENESS	. . . Forgiveness."
by	
(author's name)	MUSIC UP FULL—
TITLE 3 DISS.	(give selection)
featuring	
(names of leading players)	
TITLE 4 DISS.	
with	
(names of supporting players)	
FADE OUT #	FADE OUT MUSIC ON CUE
Set 1 LIVING ROOM	
#1 CU of Mary. FADE IN #1	MARY (on cue)
CUE Mary and start DOLLY BACK to take in Mother & door. (___ " lens)	Mother, the . . . o-g-r-e . . . What is that, mother?
HOLD DOLLY.	MOTHER
	That's an ogre, Mary child—a cruel man who frightens children.

Video	Audio

READY #2 for two-shot of
John & Mother.
(___ ″ lens)

MARY

Well, this ogre wasn't really and
truly bad, 'cause he tried to be
good inside.

MOTHER

Yes, dear, there are some men
. . . who are kind inside, though
it doesn't show through. Always
look for the good inside of people,
Mary child.

CUE Luke to whistle.

OFF-STAGE WHISTLING BG
FOR MARY'S LINE

MARY

Yes, Mother. (after brief pause)
Luke's home, I guess.

Luke enters.

LUKE

(to mother) Hi-ya, beautiful.

MOTHER

DOLLY BACK to
take in Luke's
chair.

Hello, Luke.

LUKE

(to Mary, with affectionate
whack) Hi, adorable.

MARY

(ad libs as Luke sits)

(More)

Video	Audio
WATCH for Mother's rise.	**MOTHER** (glancing at the clock) I wish James would get here. (She goes to window.)
#2 two-shot of John & Mother. } TAKE #2	**JOHN** Mom, if A has six apples and B has twelve, how many does B have to give A so they both will have the same number?
	MOTHER (trying to do it on her fingers) . . . You'll have to wait till your father gets here. I've no head for figures.
PAN with her as she sits to take in Mary.	
READY # 3 on Luke in wing chair with paper. (___ " lens)	**MARY** Isn't Daddy at his shop this afternoon?
	MOTHER No, he . . . is seeing a man.
DOLLY IN with Mary to tight two-shot.	**MARY** (going to mother) Mother, . why doesn't Daddy like me?
READY #1 on Mother taking in John at table. (___ " lens)	**MOTHER** Why, darling, he does like you. He loves you, as we all do. (She looks toward Luke.)

Video	Audio
#3 MCU of Luke. TAKE #3	**LUKE** (making a this-is-*it* gesture toward mother)
#1 MS of Mother and John. } TAKE #1 READY #3 (___ " lens)	**MOTHER** (looking at John, as he looks up) John, bring Ruth's picture here . . . Mary child, listen to what I am going to tell you. You had to know some day. I wanted to wait till you were older, but there is a reason why you must hear it today . . . This, dear, is a picture of your mother . . . She died when you were born, and we have brought you up as our own little girl because . . . well, because of the way your grandfather took it.
#2 two-shot of mother & Mary; favor Mary. } TAKE #2	
#3 BCU of Mary. TAKE #3	**MARY** Then daddy isn't my daddy?
	MOTHER (off camera) No, dear. Your father . . . went away.
	MARY Oh . . . Then . . .
#2 two-shot of mother and Mary. } TAKE #2 BREAK #1 and **3** to Steve's room.	**MOTHER** (taking Mary in her arms) Then James and I are your grandpa and grandma, and he loves you too, but. . . . (etc.)

(More)   (page) 5

Here an important point comes to light and brings out the value to the writer of knowing production routine and the possibilities of television continuity in order to make full use of its potentials. It was our intention, when writing the scenario, to go directly from the living-room scene to Steve's room; to make a direct cut from the mother's last line, "You see, your trusting mother thought she could make your father over into a better man." But when we came to write the actual script it became clear that a transitional scene was needed in order to have Ruth presented on the screen before Steve. During the above lines the audience is thinking more about Mary's mother (whom they have not yet seen) than about the child's father. Cutting directly to Steve in his room and then having Ruth enter, though this would be acceptable, would force the audience to reverse its thinking. Furthermore, by inserting a short scene showing Ruth knocking at a closed door we introduce an element of suspense, for in that brief moment before the door opens it will be possible to show the audience that Ruth is a sweet, lovable girl and to make them wonder what Steve will be like when he opens the door.

From this it should be clear that the writer must guard against focusing his attention on the *words* he writes; instead, he must keep the *flow of pictures* constantly in mind, for the order in which scenes are presented and their juxtaposition are the two most vital factors in visual continuity. So let's get back to the play and work out this new transition. Note: We pick the scene up where we left off.

(page) 6

Video	Audio
#2 two-shot of mother and Mary. $\Big\}$ TAKE #2 BREAK #1 to hallway. BREAK #3 to Steve's room.	MOTHER (taking Mary in her arms) Then James and I are your grandpa and grandma, and he loves you too, but it has been hard for him to forget about what your mother did. She was gentle and loving and she fell in love with a man who was not . . . who was not

(More)   (page) 6

Video	Audio

good. He was not nice to your mother, Mary, and James—your granddaddy—told her she must not see him. But you see, my child, love does strange things and she was very young. Your trusting mother thought she could make your father over into a better man.

Video	Audio
Set 2. HALLWAY	TIME ( ) ....
#1 MS of door and stair rail. Ruth walks into picture. (" lens) } DISS. #1	**RUTH** (hesitating at the door before knocking)
DOLLY IN a bit on the air.	**STEVE—OFF CAMERA** (after second knock) Who is it?
BREAK #2 to cabinet shop. MCU of father at bench. (" lens)	**RUTH** It's me, Steve. (After he opens door) (tentatively) Hello, Steve.
	STEVE I thought I told you never to come here.
	RUTH But I had to talk to you, Steve.
	STEVE Okay, come on in.

(More)

Video	Audio
Set 3. STEVE'S ROOM	TIME ( ) ....
#3 med. two-shot. TAKE #3 WATCH for her cross.	**RUTH** (still in the hall) It will be all right, won't it, darling?
PAN with her.	**STEVE** Sure. What do you want?
TIGHTEN UP; favor her. READY #1 CU of Steve. (" lens)	**RUTH** (picking up Racing Form) (innocently) What's this, Steve?
	STEVE That's racing dope, Baby. I've got a hot tip today in the fifth.
	RUTH That's what I came to talk to you about. Steve, darling. . . . (etc.)
	(page) 8

Take note that before the end of a scene, when there is to be a shift to another set, the producer must have a cue in his script reminding him to shift one or more of the cameras. For instance, at the end of the first scene the mother's lines are all taken on one camera; as soon as this camera is on the air, the producer cues the other two cameras to move into position for the ensuing scenes—assuming a three-camera studio set-up. In this case, just as soon as camera number two is on the air, camera number one can break to the hallway set, and camera number three to Steve's room. Note also that, since most cameras are equipped with turret lenses, the lens to be used for each camera set-up should be indicated on the script.

It will also be noted that all camera switches (cuts, fades, and dissolves) are made to stand out on the page by *underscoring lines that connect columns one and two*. This makes it easier for the producer and technical director to follow, and gives an idea of the speed at which the switches are coming. Also, by the dotting or ruling across the page to indicate *change of set* it is possible to see at a glance how long a scene has to run. Furthermore, throughout the script certain strategic points are used for writing in the *running time*. Notice too that the script should be marked with pencil to indicate the exact word or action for a channel switch. The first column should also include any cues which the producer must give to the stage manager or the lighting engineer, both of whom of course will have copies of the script.

When there is to be a switch from studio to film, there must be a warning cue for the projectionist and a cue for the technical director on the exact second for punching in the projector, allowing time for it to come up to speed, so as to bring the picture in at the proper point.

The manuscript and the production script are separate and distinct, because they perform separate functions. The former is often used as the production script by marking it up with pencil notations. Unfortunately these notations have a way of getting into a hen-track condition, and it is a wise safeguard against production blunders to have the production script clearly typed after all the cues have been finally set. The form of script suggested here may be used with equal success for any type of program.

2. *Adaptations*

There is much good material that can be adapted to television. As a matter of fact, it has been proved over and over again in radio and motion pictures that the presentation of familiar material in new clothes is welcomed by the audience. Often a new medium brings out facets of enjoyment that are a distinct improvement. Certainly television offers countless opportunities for bringing the best of the world's literature and drama to vast numbers of homes.

To the uninitiated it may appear that adaptations are an easy way out of the problem of digging up program material. Actually it is often more difficult to write a good adaptation than to create a new play, and in any event it calls for knowledge and skill. There is the ever present danger of taking over—hook, line, and sinker—material that is unsuited to television. High selectivity and a thorough conception of the potentialities and limitations of the television medium are essential.

In adaptations, as a general method of procedure it is best for the writer to put the essence of the thing he is adapting into scenario form as the first step; then to determine how it can be most effectively treated as television entertainment; next to select those parts of the original that can be carried over intact; and finally to round these out with his own writing, adhering of course to the original work in feeling and basic fact.

If the material is copyrighted, a release must be obtained from the author, his agent, or the one who holds the rights.

3. *Creative Writing*

It is trite to trot out the old saw that all the world's a stage. Nevertheless it is certainly true for the writer of plays, for all about him people are playing parts in the drama, the comedy, the tragedy of life. It is from their performances, either seen, heard, or imagined, that the playwright gets his story ideas, characterizations, and plots. He has only to look about him for material. But he must be sensitive to all that goes on around him and so responsively tuned as to react emotionally himself, if he is to arouse emotional response in others.

It is this connecting link of emotion that holds the secret of the successful television play. The author who is moved by the drama of life and uses well the tools of his craft—plot, action, dialogue, and characterization—achieves a state of *rapport* with his audience. As one of the greatest teachers of the drama, George P. Baker, puts it:

"From emotions to emotions" is the formula for any good play. To paraphrase a principle of geometry, "A play is the shortest distance from emotions to emotions." The emotions to be reached are those of the audience. The emotions conveyed are those of the people on the stage or of the dramatist as he watched (or conceived) the people represented. Just herein lies the importance of action for the dramatist: it is the quickest means of arousing emotions in an audience. Which is more popular with the masses, the man of action or the thinker? The world at large believes, and rightly that, as a rule, "Actions speak louder than words."

Comparatively few people . . . are capable of sustained attention when their emotions are not called upon. . . . We may arouse emotion in an audience by mere physical action; by physical action that develops the story, illustrates character, or does both; by mental rather than physical action, if clearly and accurately conveyed; and even by inaction, if characterization and dialogue by means of other figures are of a high order.

In drama, undoubtedly the strongest immediate appeal to the general public is action. Yet if a dramatist is to communicate with his audience as he
wishes, command of dialogue is indispensable. The permanent value of a play,
however, rests on its characterization. Characterization focusses attention. It
is the chief means of creating in an audience sympathy for the subject or the
people of the play . . . If the character utters phrases which an audience
recognizes instantly as characteristic of his supposed type, there is special
satisfaction to the audience in such recognition.

All that has been said comes to this. Know your characters so intimately that
you can move, think, and feel with them. . . . See that they are properly
introduced . . . that they are clearly and convincingly presented.[1]

Reduced to its simplest terms the writing of a television play consists
in: selecting a plot involving situations and characterizations touching
the interests and experiences of the average person; giving the characters lines and actions that are natural and clearly related to the plot
development; sharply defining the relationship between each of the
characters, and making it clear how each character is affected by the
conflict; using economy in words, and choosing words that fit the plot,
enrich the dialogue, and motivate the action; using economy in the
number of characters; and finally maintaining progression—a striving
forward—in interest or suspense.

The wise writer will not overwrite; he will leave something to the
audience. He will weigh every word and every picture for the immediate effect they will produce and for what they will contribute to the
plot development and the continuity. His sentence structure will be
simple and direct, so that the meaning may be instantly grasped. His
phrases will be conversational rather than literary. Neither his words
nor his pictures will dilute each other by their own completeness; each
will lean on the other for support. His lines will leave no room for misinterpretation and thus will be "hard for an actor to spoil." His writing
will have style, distinction, and charm. His characters will be *personae
gratae* in the home, offending neither race nor creed.

OTHER PROGRAM TYPES

Practically everything that has been said thus far in this chapter is
applicable to the writing of any type of program, even down to the spot
commercial. They must all have structure and continuity. They must all

[1] *Dramatic Technique,* Houghton Mifflin Company, Boston, 1919.

have a central theme, an objective, and a way of getting there. They must all be the product of a skilled craftsman.

1. *Audience Participation Programs*

The audience participation program consisting of gags, stunts, or questions involves more than the selection of bigger and better ways of getting laughs; it calls for skillful timing, pacing, and routing; it requires well-chosen contrast and emphasis, as in the juxtaposition of opposites to achieve the ridiculous; above all, it demands showmanship. This type of program, which must bear all the earmarks of spontaneity, actually requires careful preplanning and writing of a kind that not too many people can do. The gags or stunts themselves are relatively easy to think up, but to work them out and put them together in a show that will at one and the same time move at the proper pace and come out "on the nose" requires skill.

The script for this sort of show is merely an outline, but it must contain all the guiding elements of production routine. Naturally it must give the order of events, but more particularly it must give the controls which the producer and the emcee can rely on in building the gags and moving the show along on schedule; it must make provision for things that may happen unexpectedly, such as a stunt bogging down or going sour and having to be played short, and conversely for spontaneous situation developments that consume time but are too good to pass up.

The script should specify the musical selections that are to be used throughout, should indicate whether the music is live or recorded, and should furnish the audio engineer with all the information he needs. It should include a complete list of properties and any special effects or set-ups.

The actual planning and writing is done ordinarily either by the emcee, the producer, or one or both of them in collaboration with the continuity writer. A typical script for an audience participation program is shown on page 137.

2. *The Factual Program*

The factual program must be dramatized if the interest of the audience is to be captured and held. By that is meant, not necessarily actual dramatization, but treatment with an emotional basis for winning the interest of the audience. That may be found in the desire, which most people have, to know as much as the other fellow, to keep up with the Joneses, to be in fashion. The writer can make an educational subject attractive by sugar-coating it with a form of presentation that lifts it out of the category of the lecture and arouses a lively interest. It is not enough, however, to make it entertaining; it must have some meaning, some value or benefit to the viewer; it must pay off directly in economic, social, or personal improvement. The strongest appeal is to the universal desire for health, wealth, and happiness.

The writer of factual programs is apt to make the false assumption that his audience will have the same interest in the subject that he has. He is usually in danger, too, of crediting them with either much more or far less knowledge of the subject than they possess. The best approach is to start with the familiar and by comparison or analogy move to the less known or the unknown. Continuity. Flow. Progression. Call it what you like; there must be a smooth transition from one thought to the next, as well as a lively forging ahead of interest.

Television, fortunately, supplies the stimulus of visual interest. The writer will therefore capitalize on the fact that "a picture is worth ten thousands words" and lean heavily on the picture to carry the story. He will take advantage of television's effectiveness in *explanation through demonstration*. He will build on the recognized fact that *visual motion arouses emotion*. He will use fewer words, because much that is seen will be self-explanatory.

The pictorial devices that may be employed are practically endless. In the how-to-do-it and how-it-works type of program, working models and cut-aways, pictures showing cause and effect, slow motion, animation, microphotography, and many other visual aids may be used. The writer will do well to study the techniques developed during the war in the military training and orientation films. Here the art of visual education has been raised to a high point and, what is more, the methods have been tested and proved. He will also study the better documentary films for the technique employed there in reaching the audience through their emotions and making them *feel* the subject as well as think about it.

The factual program that presents only sterile fact will have little or no appeal, but, if it takes into account the interest that people have *in* *people* and is built around a personality, it is certain to appeal to many. It matters not whether the subject is the atomic bomb or how to swing a golf club, it will interest more people if it is humanized. This, on second thought, should be made conditional on ruling out the usual interview technique, than which there is nothing more deadly, except when an outstanding personality is being presented.

The dramatization of factual material is highly advantageous but at the same time tricky. It is valuable as a means of holding audience attention, but this attention is quickly lost if the dramatization is not convincing. The dragging-in-by-the-heels of irrelevant material or the sudden injection of dramatic incident that contributes little else than confusion are things to be avoided. The audience may be slow in their ability to absorb the subject matter of a dramatized factual program, but they are self-appointed critics of dramatic presentation and are quick at dial turning.

Chapter VII

~~~~~~

DIRECTING AND PRODUCING

ALL that has been said thus far—in fact, everything about program construction and production—applies to the work of the producer, the master mind who co-ordinates the activities of all who are involved in the program. As stated previously, he is variously referred to as the producer, the director, or the production director. In some stations the producer handles the job alone; in others he has the help of an assistant producer and an assistant director. In the latter case he supervises the entire production from the selection of material and talent to the final performance, but turns the direction of the talent and other matters over to his assistants. For the sake of simplicity we shall make no division of these functions but treat them as the work of one individual known as the *producer*. Let us see what his job involves.

First, the producer analyzes the program assignment for its television possibilities. He may originate the idea for the program himself, even going so far as to do part or all of the writing. Having analyzed the script, he works out an over-all treatment. He *televisualizes* the production. At this stage his mind is focused not on details but on the broad treatment—the essence of the production. He is planning his approach and crystallizing his ideas. This is an important stage, for his decisions at this point will determine to a large extent the over-all reaction of the audience to the program.

The producer then begins to work out details. He has a general picture in his mind of the whole production—the setting, the talent, and the feeling of the show. Either through the talent director or by himself, he selects the cast and schedules rehearsals. The mechanics of production now begin to evolve, and the planning of sets is begun. Collaborating with the scenic designer, the set builder, and the property man, he works out all these details completely. He sees to the matter of costumes and special make-up. If there are any motion pictures or stills to be prepared, he contacts the photographic section. He confers with the musical director regarding the music to be used on the program, and musicians are engaged. In the meantime rehearsals are going on.

Production details have by this time jelled sufficiently for him to call a meeting with the members of the technical staff. He gives them complete information to enable them to plan the production from their end. He arranges with them for any special set-ups that are required and for making any experiments that involve the use of cameras or other equipment. In a truly co-operative spirit, these two main divisions of the production staff correlate their activities and their combined contributions, to the end that each is given a fair chance to do a good job with a minimum of conflict and a maximum of teamwork.

Finally, after the last camera rehearsal, he puts the show on the air and takes the consequences. It has been pretty much his show; but the wise producer will never forget that if it has turned out well and pulled a good rating it is only because of the teamwork that has gone hand in hand with his own personal contribution. If he is a man of the right sort he will always rate his own triumphs by the success he is able to bring to others, for *the essence of television program production is teamwork.*

From the foregoing sketchy outline of a television producer's many duties it becomes evident that he must needs be a person possessing many talents. He should have a facile mind, coupled with a personality that will enable him to handle people under tension. He should be a perfectionist, but a practical one. He should have a capacity for detail and a tremendous capacity for work. He should be a showman.

PRODUCING A SIMPLE VARIETY PROGRAM

Rather than attempt an abstract discussion of program production, we shall consider concrete examples and thus be able to treat the many problems which face the producer in a way that will give them more meaning. We shall start with a fairly simple problem—the producing of a short musical variety show—and, without attempting to cover all aspects of producing, shall endeavor to bring out the framework of the whole operation.

Let us say the producer has been assigned a period of time to fill with a variety program. It may be necessary for him to choose the talent, or this may already have been chosen by the advertising agency or the program planning board.

1. *The Program Idea*

In network stations it is the usual procedure to assign a prepared program, but in the smaller stations the producer may have to work up the entire show. In this event he may start with a basic idea and then find the talent; or he may work the other way around, evolving the idea out of the material at hand. Regardless of the method, the program must be *built* and not thrown together without structure or form.

The tendency in the musical variety program is to follow the line of least resistance and to give an announcer a few inept lines to introduce each number. But the air is too full of this sort of mediocrity to attract much of an audience for the sponsor's dollars. Furthermore, the public is becoming more and more selective. Being creatures of habit, people tend to follow the same programs week after week. They are held to those programs because each one is built to a pattern and supplies some special and consistent type of entertainment. They remember them for the pattern or for the personality around which they are built. But even a famous name is not enough to overcome the handicap of a hodgepodge structure.

The reason, then, for building around a program idea or central theme is to create unity and progression and to tie the program together and move it along to a climax. Each musical number of a variety show comes to a definite ending; it is an entity in itself. Therefore, without continuity, the program comes to as many endings as there are numbers, and the audience is apt to switch to another station unless some device is used to carry the interest along.

Apart from the basic idea or theme, the program should have *structure*, and this is the producer's first consideration. Structure is created through the control of balance, pace, proportion, and emphasis. It is achieved by arranging the numbers so that each unit of the program leads smoothly to the next. A time-tested structural scheme is: to open with an attention-getting number; to build the body of the program around some central theme, moving it along with varied interest and change of pace and giving the audience occasional periods of rest; and to end on the strongest possible note.

2. *Planning the Production*

The producer now has the material and the format of his show. He has worked closely with the musical director, and between them all matters pertaining to music clearances and scores for the musicians have been attended to. The show has been roughly timed, and consideration has been given to cutting or stretching the material when it is put into rehearsal. If this last item is overlooked in the planning stage, valuable time will be lost in rehearsal should it develop (as it usually does) that the numbers selected cause the program to run much over or under the time limit. Rehearsal is no time for a frantic search for numbers that can be substituted; the producer should have prepared for such a contingency.

Until the show is rehearsed it is difficult to estimate the exact running time. Therefore it is a good plan to write the continuity a trifle on the long side, provided that known cuts of varying length can be used to pull the show down to the scheduled playing time. If the show happens to run a little short it is an easy matter to stretch it out; it is easier to stretch it without having this become apparent than it is to make up time. It is a good idea for the producer to set up a running schedule showing the time at which each number must finish in order to bring the show out on the nose. Thus when the show is on the air he can cue whoever carries the continuity to speed up or slow down.

The next step is to work out the visual treatment. Up to this point the producer has developed only a radio show; now come the many problems of picturization and production mechanics. Until he has become so experienced that he can think out spontaneously all the problems of staging, lighting, pick-up, and camera work, it will be better for him to work it out on paper. Understand that we are speaking now of the producer's own problem of picturization; he is not up to the point yet where he can turn his ideas over to the other members of the production staff.

Each producer will evolve a method that works satisfactorily for him. For the benefit of the beginner or the producer who finds it difficult to previsualize, we shall describe a helpful method.

3. *A Method of Production Planning*

The producer is faced with three main problems: (1) the size and general treatment of sets; (2) the arrangement of the sets in the studio; and (3) the mechanics of cameras, mikes, and lights. Not everyone can visualize space and proportion or camera angles. The following method will aid the producer in working out set arrangements and the disposition of players and in preplanning camera work, thereby saving precious rehearsal time:

Graph paper is available in sheets 18 x 24 inches, ruled with light lines in half-inch squares. These lines are for the purpose of establishing scale. If the half-inch spaces represent one-foot divisions, then the whole block covers a ploying area 36 x 48 feet; if they represent two-foot divisions, the total area of the block would be 72 x 96 feet. For our purposes we shall let each half inch of graph paper represent one foot of studio floor space.

Next prepare or have made a quantity of scale-model flats to represent the standard scenery that is used by the television studio. If they are made according to the sketches in Figure 23, they will represent, on the scale we have chosen, flats of two and four feet in width, respectively, each ten feet high.

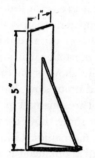 

FIG. 23. REAR VIEW OF MODEL FLATS.

Cut from some durable material, about three-sixteenths of an inch thick, a supply of the standard properties used in the studio—tables, chairs, sofas, pianos, and other ordinary furnishings. Make them to a scale of half an inch to the foot, and let the shape be merely a simplified version of the floor area covered by each of the pieces. Label them clearly.

Now make a supply of domino-shaped blocks, cut from the same material, to represent the players. Make the supply ample, because more than one may be needed for each player. A person standing occupies a floor space approximately one by two feet. Hence, make the dominoes one-half by one inch. One used alone will represent a player standing. Two may be used side by side for a person sitting, and three end-to-end for someone lying down.

From a sheet of celluloid cut a triangle to represent the angle of vision of the lens or lenses in each camera. It is convenient to have

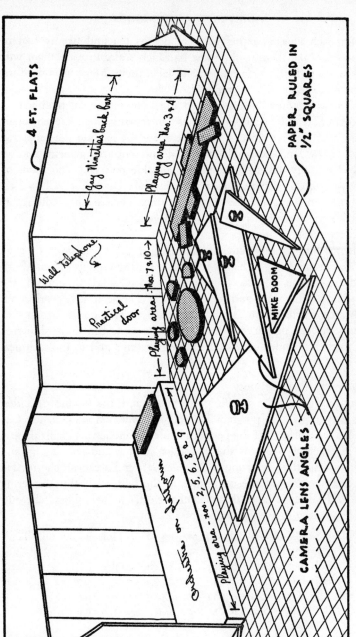

4 FT. FLATS

Gay Nineties Back Bar

Playing area - Nos. 3 & 4

Wall Telephone

Practical door

Playing area - Nos. 7 & 10

2, 5, 6, 8, 9

Playing area - nos.

Playing area

PAPER RULED IN
½" SQUARES

MIKE BOOM

60

CAMERA LENS ANGLES

FIG. 24. SHOWING HOW TO USE SCALE MODELS IN PRODUCTION PLANNING. BASED ON AN
ACTUAL PROGRAM PRODUCED BY R. J. GOULD AT WRGB.

two for each lens, to represent focal depths ten and twenty feet respectively. Make them to the same half-inch scale. Provide them with small knobs to facilitate handling, and label them. Make a similar form to represent the mike boom pedestal.

The producer now is equipped to work out the actual treatment of his program idea. By setting up scenery on the ruled paper, each square representing a square foot of floor space, and by moving the properties and players around, he is able to try out different arrangements and see clearly how they will work in production. He may make notations on the walls and occasionally do a repapering job. Using the celluloid triangles he can work out the camera routine. The sketch of the set-up shown on the foregoing page will give a general idea of the usefulness of this type of preplanning.

The method of production planning just described saves time all around. For one thing, it makes it possible for the producer to cut down on rehearsal time, because there will be fewer snarls to unravel; the disposition of characters and camera shots can be accurately worked out in advance. Furthermore, it affords a much quicker and more satisfactory way for the producer to transmit his ideas to the scenic designer, stage manager, cameramen, and lighting director and to the technical staff.

4. *Planning the Continuity*

Continuing with the specific problem at hand, the producer decides, let us say, to give the program a nostalgic flavor and set it in the Gay Nineties in a barroom of the period. He uses an orchestra, a male quartet (one member of which is the bartender), a boy-and-girl singing and dancing team (the boy is one of the quartet), and a cancan chorus. He gives the handling of the continuity to the bartender, thus centering much of the show around that area of the set. He makes a sketchy outline of the order of events, something like this:

No. 1.   Title sequence—orchestra playing "Hot Time in the Old Town Tonight."
No. 2.   Full shot of the orchestra finishing the number.
No. 3.   Bartender—a few opening lines. Breaks into a verse of "Tavern in The Town." Quartet on chorus. Next verse by lead.
No. 4.   Bartender—"Sidewalks of New York." Quartet chorus.
No. 5.   Orchestra number.
No. 6.   Boy and girl—"Strolling through the Park." Dance routine. Play in front of orchestra.
No. 7.   Solo at table—"After the Ball." Quartet chorus.

No. 8. Boy and girl—"Charm." Play in front of orchestra.
No. 9. Cancan chorus—"Ta-ra-ra Boom-de-ay." Orchestra. Dance routine.
No. 10. Bartender at telephone—quick sign-off. Orchestra BG.
No. 11. End title—orchestra up full.

With this rough scheme as a pattern, the producer now works out his continuity and the mechanics of production as shown in Figure 21. He decides to what extent he will use the bartender as an announcer—the producer can be unimaginative and have the bartender simply introduce each number, or he can devise some entertaining continuity scheme. He arranges and rearranges the routine of the show until it flows with a lively pattern of picture and sound. As pointed out previously, this is the important stage of program planning—the concept stage, during which he puts himself in the position of the audience and previews the show. The scale model method will help him to previsualize and will also make it easier for him to explain the details of production to the key members of the production staff.

5. Production Co-ordination

The producer's concern now is to co-ordinate the production and set deadlines for the completion of all preparations. These are his next steps: He works out the treatment of the sets with the scenic artist. He prepares property and costume lists. He discusses lighting effects with the lighting director. He confers with the technical staff and explains the production in complete detail, so that they may plan their end of it and be prepared for any complications in sound pick-up or any unusual engineering problems.

Audition and rehearsal dates are scheduled, and a deadline is established for the completion of sets, properties, and costumes. A sufficient number of copies of the script are typed, and they are marked up with cues by the producer in conference with the video and audio engineers and the stage manager. This mark-up of the script will not be final until after rehearsals, and it is sometimes necessary to have the script retyped just before going on the air, in order to avoid production blunders through misinterpretation of illegible cues.

6. Casting

Casting for television presents numerous difficulties, for the player must have well-nigh everything—a pleasant voice, ability to act and memorize, an attractive screen presence, and above all a feeling for the medium. Assuming all these things, the producer still has many problems to solve: He must select a cast of actors who play well together; a group of artists who will work together for the good of the production as a whole; a group of individuals who will complement each other and lend variety and contrast in both picture and sound. Let us consider the last item for a moment.

Take the case of the male quartet. Pictorially the problem is to achieve variety. The same four faces are to be held on the screen for a considerable length of time. If the players are all of the same facial type and all the same height, the pictures will be monotonous. The producer therefore should *cast for variety and contrast in physical appearance.* If the supply of talent does not make this possible, he may have to depend on make-up in obtaining visual variety.

The producer in casting the show, should also guard against monotony of sound quality and *select voices that establish a pattern of pleasing variety and contrast.* He will keep in mind the fact that voices are typed and that a voice often suggests more or less definite physical characteristics, and he will strengthen this relationship in costuming and make-up and avoid the incongruous except for an intentional comedy effect.

In the case of new talent, auditioning should always be done on camera and mike. It is the only safe way, for the reason that both camera and microphone magnify mannerisms and bring out qualities that are not apparent in the flesh. By casting on camera the producer can often suggest improvements in technique on which the talent can work prior to rehearsal.

At the time of casting, the producer should let the musicians know what he wants in the way of effects and the feeling he is after. By so doing he will save time and avoid frayed nerves during rehearsal; by knowing in advance what is desired of them the artists will be able to make the necessary preparations and as a result will turn in a better performance.

As a final step in casting, the producer should see to it that all the preparatory details of costuming are attended to; that copies of the music are in the proper hands; and that the cast is given *written instructions* regarding the time for rehearsals and the make-up time for the performance.

7. Rehearsing

There are three kinds of rehearsal, each of which has a particular function. First in order comes the *dry rehearsal,* as it is called. This is carried on without cameras or mikes and is continued until the cast is familiar with the lines and business. Its function is to bring the players as close as possible to a finished performance without involving the entire production staff.

The second type is the *technical rehearsal*. Its purpose is to give the production staff an opportunity to work out all the mechanics of production. The lighting director is shown the principal and supplementary playing areas which he is to light; the audio engineer is given the pick-up routine and a chance to prepare for unusual or difficult set-ups; the video engineer is given an opportunity to iron out any complex visual situations; the cameramen are schooled in the camera routine; and the stage manager is instructed regarding the handling of properties, talent, and special effects. In the case of a complex production, the technical rehearsal is preceded by a run-through with stand-ins, so as not to tie up an expensive cast.

When the mechanics have been pretty well smoothed out, the *camera rehearsals* may start. Before attempting a complete rehearsal it is important to take the cast through all the *key situations*, cleaning up each one before going on to the next. The producer should show each member of the cast where he is to play, if necessary marking the floor with chalk. He should rehearse them all thoroughly in orientation to the cameras, mikes, and lights.

The individual actors and the band may be seeing the sets and each other for the first time; therefore the producer's first move should be to familiarize them with the production and show them how their various acts are to be integrated. For instance, in the case at hand, with the entire production crew present, he will start with the orchestra in position and have them play the opening number. He will go through the transition to the bartender, and then, jumping to the end of the second quartet number, he will rehearse the shift back to the orchestra. Next, he will run through the transition from the orchestra to the song-and-dance act, and so on through the whole show until everyone is familiar with the routine. Thus he can go into camera rehearsal with some assurance that the many people involved have a clear idea of the key situations and difficult shifts, and he can then use the precious rehearsal time for polishing the production. This is an extremely important point and one to which some producers pay little attention; often they use up valuable rehearsal time in a hectic unsnarling of tangles and in frenzied half thinking, whereas it should all have been worked out before the camera rehearsals started. The worst of it is, in such cases the show, the talent, the station personnel, and the audience all suffer.

8. *The Telecast*

After the final rehearsal and before going on the air, the producer should attempt few if any further instructions to the cast, provided they are to go on the air within a few minutes. At this stage they are all strung up and are not in any condition to remember what he says. New instructions at this point will only confuse them. But he will go over the show carefully in his own mind and will make final checks with the video and audio engineers and his stage manager, making sure that the pages of all scripts are in order and that last-minute cues are clearly understood. A few minutes before air time, he will check with the stage manager to make sure that everyone is "standing by."

When his show hits the air, the producer must watch two things closely —the camera and stage directions which he gives, and the running time of the show. The audio operation is now out of his hands. If he has a capable video engineer and the proper cues have been established, that part of the operation too will be off his shoulders. But a variety show is more apt to be ad-libbed as to picture editing, and he probably will call the cuts, fades, and dissolves, at the same time directing the cameramen through their headphones.

With it all he must be alert and articulate, even if he is not exactly calm and placid. His phone cues to cameramen and stage manager should be given clearly and sufficiently in advance to make them possible of execution. He must keep ahead of the show in setting up camera shots and at the same time keep an eye on each picture that is on the air. He must be ready for any contingency and have an immediate answer. Some of his camera shots may not go as expected, and the players may jump their lines or deviate from rehearsal business; hence he must be flexible enough to make split-second decisions as the situations arise. Often these unexpected happenings can be capitalized on and turned to advantage, thus producing better visual continuity than he had planned. But as a general rule he should not depart from his pre-arranged plan, even in minor details; if there are any changes, they should never be made in any way that will upset the co-ordination of the other members of the staff.

As to timing, he will try to keep a few seconds ahead of his schedule, because it is a relatively easy matter to stretch the show at the end; this is preferable to running late, because it is difficult to make up time without having it noticeable to the audience.

9. The Play-Back and Post-Mortems

The producer is not by any means through with the show after its flight along the air waves. There are matters to be attended to in connection with station routine, and there are the inevitable post-mortems. He will, of course, have the good sense to thank his cast and the production crew for their contribution; he will give credit where credit is due, for he will not forget that the success of the show accrued through their efforts as well as his own. If he is wise, he will scrutinize any failures or shortcomings on his own part in casting or direction, and will profit by the experience in future shows.

There is a certain amount of clerical routine for the producer to supervise or attend to himself. A complete copy of the script, with all corrections showing exactly how the show went on the air, should be signed by him and turned over to the program manager. This should be accompanied by a list of the cast, the music, the properties, and everything necessary to give a complete record of the show for the accounting department and the station files. Any sketches, photographs, or movies made for the production should be put in final shape for future reference; some day someone is likely to need this information, either for reference or use in another broadcast.

A picture and sound *film transcription* contributes much to the advancement of the art. It is the fulfillment of the prayer, "Oh wad some power the giftie gie us to see oursel's as ithers see us." Without it there are only the vagaries of untrustworthy memory to aid in post-mortem review of the program. With a sound-film play-back, however, the cast and production staff can subject their work to the kind of critical analysis that makes for improvement; the players can see and hear themselves and profit thereby; the producer can really watch the show in a detached way for the first time, for during production he was under too much strain; the cameramen who have never seen more than their own individual camera pictures can benefit tremendously by seeing how their work is integrated into the pictorial continuity; the lighting director and the engineers can study their effects, and find ways to improve their techniques. With the aid of a film transcription the producer has only to point out rough spots or faulty technique, and the responsible parties can see and hear their mistakes for themselves. This makes for a much more effective and less personal critical approach than can ever be achieved without the visual and aural evidence.

These are some of the things a producer has to do in putting on a program, but only some of them. Thus far we have sketched only the routine of producing, in order that the duties and responsibilities of the producer would be understood before taking up the details of production and the fundamental principles which guide it. We shall now consider these matters as they apply to another type of program, somewhat more complicated than a variety show but less complex than the television play.

PRODUCING THE AUDIENCE PARTICIPATION PROGRAM

The appeal of the audience participation program stems from the fact that to most people it is funny to see *someone else* slip on a banana peel. Everyone enjoys seeing others make fools of themselves, and some are not averse to playing the part. Anything can—and usually does—happen on this type of program.

Its success depends on: spontaneity and pace; a clever emcee; luck in choosing good contestants; a nice balance of focus between the performance of the contestants and the personality of the emcee; and, finally, the use of stunts that are visual. This type of program is a natural for television because of its immediacy; the home audience in effect becomes part of the studio audience.

Since it is almost entirely ad-libbed and since contestants picked at random are unpredictable and the unexpected always happens, it is not an easy type of program to produce. It must be shot "off the cuff," and it is hard to control. While the show is on the air the producer, sitting up in the control room, with no very effective means of communication with the emcee, is often in the position of the spectator at a dog fight; he would like to put a stop to the whole thing, but he cannot.

There are, however, ways and means of control. They consist of adequate preplanning and a system of cues to use while on the air. Let us consider then the matter of setting the program up so that there is some element of control.

1. *Preplanning the Program*

Although the audience participation program may take a number of different forms, the format is essentially the same in all of them. A master of ceremonies first warms up the studio audience; he picks the contestants or those who are to take part in stunts; he brings them before the cameras and puts them through their paces, with or without the aid of assistants; he takes advantage of all the breaks that come along and "washes out" the contestants quickly if they are duds.

The whole show rests on the emcee's shoulders; he must carry the continuity and build the situations. To do this he must play to the studio audience and put himself over; yet he must not appear to be the whole show, for the home audience is equally interested in the performance of the participants. Hence it is essential that a nice balance be maintained between the two. This can only be achieved by perfect co-ordination between the producer and the emcee and by skillful co-ordination of the entire production staff.

The very nature of this type of program—its unrehearsed spontaneity—accounts for both its charm and its problems. To keep it informal, gay, lively, and natural while at the same time catching good pictures and sound—on the fly—is the producer's principal headache. He will need fewer aspirin tablets if he takes enough precaution in planning.

2. The Format

First of all, the situation must be visual. If the material offered is not interesting visually or cannot be made so by the way the emcee or quiz master handles the contestants, the producer should insist on other material that is. Having selected the material, he should go into a huddle with himself and devise a structural routine, applying the same principles of balance, variety, change of pace, and climax that are used in building any other program. The principle of opening fast and building to a climax is especially applicable here.

3. Rough Timing

With the main routine established, the producer should check the timing and make sure that there is enough elasticity in the transitions to permit stretching or speeding up. These time controls should be thoroughly understood by everyone involved, so that they may be applied smoothly during the broadcast. A running schedule should be worked out showing the time at which each situation must start and finish to bring the show out "on the nose."

4. Picturization

Next comes the problem of picturization. For developing a visual treatment, the method illustrated on page 33 will be found helpful. It will enable the producer to work out the placement of contestants, the handling of properties, and the camera routine; it will also be helpful in preparing the floor plan, which is the first step in picturization. Figure 25 shows a floor plan that proved satisfactory for a series of thirteen broadcasts. A feature worthy of note is the integration of a portion of the studio audience; this made it possible to include their reactions and thus add interest to the visual continuity.

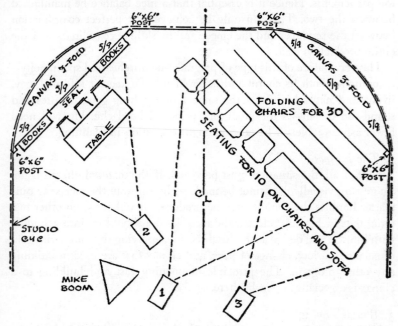

Fig. 25. Floor Plan for a Series of Audience Participation Programs, Youth Wants to Know.

Having worked up such a floor plan, with the aid of scale-model players and props and the use of the celluloid camera field triangles, the producer works out his key shots and the scheme of moving properties into and out of the playing area. This is important in a show where the stunts involve property set-ups, because there are sure to be stage waits and awkward situations if the handling of properties and contestants is not carefully planned.

5. *The Production Script*

Up to this point the script has been merely a list of the stunts in the order in which they are to be played. The next move is to crystallize the routine into a schedule of *known quantities*. It will be only a skeleton, but all cues and controls that can be definitely established should be put in the form of a production script. In the following example it should be noted that the opening and closing are set up *exactly as they will be played*. Although the body of the program may be ad-libbed, *nothing should be left to chance in the opening or closing.*

Example of Production Script

December 5, 1954   YOUTH WANTS TO KNOW
1:00-1:30 PM EST   —page one—

Video	Audio	Music Theme
	FIRST TEENAGER— (question) SECOND TEENAGER— (question) THIRD TEENAGER— (question)	
FADE IN: Camera 1 on title plaque	ANNOUNCER: The National Broadcasting Company presents YOUTH WANTS TO KNOW . . . the unrehearsed, spontaneous questions of *today's* young people!	Music Theme Theme: FADE OUT
DISSOLVE to Camera 2 CU of McCormick	MODERATOR: Hello, I'm Steve McCormick, welcoming you to another session of YOUTH WANTS TO KNOW, founded and produced by Theodore Granik. . . . What is now Austria was inhabited by the Celts in Caesar's time, when the first Roman Legions marched northward over the Brenner Pass. From that time to the present Austria and its people have played a key role in the history of the world. Today on YOUTH WANTS TO KNOW we are pleased to have the head of the Austrian government,	

Video	Audio	Music Theme
CUT to Camera 3 CU Dr. J. Raab	now in our country on a state visit by invitation of President Eisenhower— the Chancellor of the Federal Republic of Austria, Dr. Julius Raab. . . . Welcome to "YOUTH WANTS TO KNOW", Dr. Raab. (Dr. Raab responds).	
CUT to Camera 1 CU Dr. E. Buresch	To assist us today, we have invited Dr. Eugen Buresch, Director of the Austrian Information Service. . . .	
CUT to Camera 2 LS of the group of youngsters. PAN along their faces. Frame the first girl and PAN up with her as she rises.	The youngsters who participate in our program, under the auspices of the American Legion, are ready with their questions. Let's ask this young (lady, man) to start.	
CUT to Camera 2 three shot of Raab, McCormick, Buresch	CLOSING MODERATOR: I wish we had more time for questions, but we must end today's discussion. Thank you *Chancellor Julius Raab, of the Federal Republic of Austria.* . . . and our thanks to you Dr. Buresch.	
CUT to Camera 1 CU of McCormick	MODER. CONT'D. Next week, we'll have as our guest of YOUTH WANTS TO KNOW, *Seaborn P. Collins, National Commander of the American Legion* . . . . . and now, this is Steve McCormick speaking for Theodore Granik and bidding you goodbye.	

Video	Audio	Music Theme
CUT to Camera 3 LS of the group of youngsters. PAN along faces.	ANNOUNCER: The questions you have just heard asked by the youngsters are entirely their own, and do not necessarily reflect the opinions of the American Legion, YOUTH WANTS TO KNOW, or the National Broadcasting Company.	
	ANNCR. CONT'D. Would you like to submit a question and have it answered by the guest speaker on YOUTH WANTS TO KNOW? . . . . If your entry is chosen as the most provocative timely Question of the Week, the producer of YOUTH WANTS TO KNOW,	
DISSOLVE to Camera 2 CU of books and pan along them.	in cooperation with the editors of the *Enclyclopedia Americana,* America's first and oldest encyclopedia . . . will award you a thirty volume set of the *Encyclopedia Americana* . . . and name your local radio or television station the Americana Station of the Week.	
CUT to Camera 1 flip-card with information	To participate, simply mail your question, together with the name of your station to: YOUTH WANTS TO KNOW . . . NBC . . . Washington 8, D. C. In case of duplicate entries, the one bearing the earliest postmark will be chosen. Contest entries should be postmarked no later than Thursday of each week.	
CUT to Camera 3 CU flip cards "Ransdell Inc. etc.	ANNCR. CONT'D. For reprints of today's discussion on YOUTH WANTS TO KNOW, send ten cents to Ransdell, Inc., Printers and Publishers, Washington 18, D. C.	Music closing

Video	Audio	Music Theme
DISSOLVE to Camera 2 on title plaque	You have been listening to YOUTH WANTS TO KNOW, founded by it's producer, Theodore Granik. This program of YOUTH WANTS TO KNOW was presented by	
	ANNCR. CONT'D. the National Broadcasting Company in cooperation with the National Public Relations Division of the American Legion.	
Super Telop Credits		
	Technical Direction by: Directed by: This program came to you from———	FADE OUT music closing
FADE OUT telop FADE OUT Camera 2		

THE END

This is the producer's plan of action. Naturally when he gets the show in rehearsal there will be modifications; some of the camera routine will not work out as expected, but he is in a position now to discuss his plan with the other members of the production staff.

6. Production Conferences

The producer should bear in mind, when outlining his plans for handling a production, that the other members of the production staff cannot read his mind. He should have the matter so completely in hand that he can make everything clear to them. The floor plan and copies of the production script are given to the emcee, the stage manager, the musical director, and the engineers, and all matters pertaining to production are now thoroughly discussed. The design of the set will be worked out with the scenic artist. Properties and costumes will be arranged for. A rehearsal schedule will be set.

7. Rehearsal

Though it might appear out of place to hold a rehearsal for a spontaneous show, this is the surest way of achieving spontaneity. In the type of program under discussion it is absolutely essential to try out the stunts and run through the mechanics of production. This is done by using stand-ins for the contestants. The emcee should take them through the stunts in order to work out the stage positions and playing areas, as well as the handling of properties, and to determine the probable running time of each stunt. Playing areas and the locations of important property set-ups should be marked on the floor with chalk to insure repetition of the camera shots rehearsed.

This run-through will afford the video and audio engineers an opportunity to mark up their scripts and work out their routine. The stage manager will gain a clear understanding of his cues and how he is to handle properties, and so on. Having gone through the routine with stand-ins, the emcee is now in a position to go into the show knowing where and how he is going to play the contestants, and thus he can deliver a more spontaneous performance.

8. Technique

It must be obvious that, although the appeal of this type of program is its spontaneity, it will lose in effectiveness if the visual continuity is not convincing. The action is fast and difficult for the cameramen to catch from the most effective angles and for the boom man to follow with the microphone. It behooves the producer, therefore, to train the emcee in the technique of playing to the cameras, lights, and microphones and of guiding the contestants to do likewise. Business that may seem good to those on the studio floor may be impossible from a camera standpoint.

An important consideration is the orientation of the home audience. With cuts coming from three or more cameras, each at a different angle, it is easy to confuse the audience if the camera angles are not well planned to maintain the orientation of the viewers. A good rule to follow on this type of stunt show is to keep the shots so tight that it will not be necessary to make too many cuts and, when a cut is made to a big close-up, to be sure that it has meaning and adds to the enjoyment of the action. The audience should be entirely unconscious of the camera technique, the sole purpose of which should be to intensify and clarify the action.

Whereas in a play with slower pace it is necessary to speed up the cuts in order to create emotional tension, in this type of show it is better to let the action develop on *one well-composed camera shot* that shows everything clearly than to create confusion by too many cuts. Then, too, it often happens that, while a big close-up is being held on a bit of business, one of the contestants will do something worth catching that the close-up camera misses. We do not mean to imply that close-ups are to be avoided; we are only pointing out that in the off-the-cuff show they are hard to handle.

Other matters in which the emcee may have to be schooled are: keeping the contestants from "covering" each other; keeping them from wandering out of the camera field; and keeping the action within the focal depth of the lenses.

Referring to the floor plan on page 134, it will be noted that the contestants are all placed in one section of the bleachers. This makes it possible for the producer, who knows where they are coming from, to get one of the cameras in position for their entrances and exits. Furthermore, if they are all on one side, while camera number two is following them to and from their seats the props can be moved in or out at stage left without being seen on the screen.

The producer will have to exercise control over the direction and speed of all movement. In general, motion is easier to follow in tight shots when it is somewhat slower than normal. It should be realized that all movements in close-ups are more noticeable on the screen than in actual life; the confining boundaries of the screen seem to exaggerate both the speed and the breadth of such close-up movement, and the motions must be carefully paced. In close-ups involving hand movements, particularly if the hands enter or leave the screen, the movements should be controlled and rhythmic; otherwise they will be confusing.

The emcee should know that the *strongest movement is in a direction toward the camera.* He should also know the relative values of the body positions: (1) squarely facing the camera is the strongest; (2) three-quarter view is medium strong; (3) side view is weak. He should make use of these facts in handling the contestants before the camera; for instance, if he wants to "give" the scene to a contestant, he (the emcee) will turn sideways; then when he turns back in full view the emphasis on him will be stronger.

A spirit of complete co-operation must exist between the producer and the master of ceremonies or quiz master in the audience participation program, for they both have strong roles to play and it is only through perfect co-ordination of effort that a good production can be obtained.

9. *On the Air*

There is little to be added to what has already been said regarding the producer's duties while on the air, other than that on an ad-libbed show it sometimes happens that things are said and done that should not be allowed on the air. It is the producer's responsibility to prevent these things from being broadcast if he can.

On a quiz show he may have to have the answers to certain questions verified to pacify a contestant. He should do everything in his power to establish and hold good will. The producer is also responsible for the studio audience; it is important that they tell others they had a good time, so there will be a good turnout for the next show and an ample supply of contestants. He will see to it, therefore, that they are courteously handled and that after the broadcast they are thanked for coming. And he will vigorously follow up any untoward incidents.

PRODUCING THE MUSICAL PROGRAM

The problems of producing a musical program are as varied as the nature of music and the manner of presentation. Musical programs come in all shapes and sizes and are directed toward as many targets as there are classes of audiences. Some like it hot, some like it cold with long hair. Some like to see the musicians; some like just to listen. But there is one common ground on which all musical programs meet: music is universally enjoyed and will be accepted in larger doses than any other form of entertainment. There is also a common ground on which the requirements of producing musical programs meet: the main appeal is to the ear, and visualization must be of such a nature that the eye appeal is in harmony with the ear appeal. Let us pursue this last element.

1. Visualization of Music

The visual presentation of musical programs may take many forms. Certainly nothing could hold more of a challenge for the producer—a challenge to his inventiveness in devising novel and interesting ways of handling visual continuity; a challenge to his imagination in creating visual images for the wealth of the world's music; a challenge to his craftsmanship in bringing these images to the screen as an added facet in the enjoyment of much-loved music.

The general classifications into which musical visualization may fall are as follows:

a) *Direct presentation,* which brings the musicians before the camera and broadcasts a straight telephotographic picture.

b) *Interpretive presentation,* which translates the musical story or mood into representative images, either natural or imaginative.

c) *Abstract expressionism,* which translates the subjective form of the music into abstract visual forms.

2. Visualization Techniques

From the standpoint of production problems, these three categories cover practically every trick in the producer's book, plus many that are yet to be dreamed up. Many of the problems are common to all types of programs, and the approach to them is treated elsewhere. We shall therefore touch only upon the special techniques peculiar to the three main forms of musical presentation listed above.

a. Direct Presentation.

This form of treatment is by far the most common and in any but skilled hands by far the safest, for it is completely objective and does not tax the imagination. The singer is seen in the facial acrobatics of singing (let us hope she is telegenic); the pianist's hands are caught from many angles as they wander idly over the keys; the orchestra is spread out on the screen like codfish drying in the sun; the operatic tenor titillates his avoirdupois and struts pompously along the chorus line. Well, perhaps it is not quite so bad as that, but these illustrations indicate the all-too-usual, unimaginative approach and point the way to a possible and practical solution of the problem here.

A well-televised musical program, whether it consists of soloists and an orchestra, a hillbilly band, or grand opera, calls for a blending of production talents that frequently mix about as well as oil and water and are seldom found coursing through the veins of one person. These talents are: (a) an extensive musical knowledge; (b) skill in musical direction; (c) showmanship in presentation. The first two are apt to go hand in hand, but showmanship is a special gift of the gods that enables a select few to instinctively create audience appeal, even though they may split an occasional infinitive.

The solution, if the paragon cannot be found, would seem to be to combine the efforts of two people: (1) a musical director capable of handling the musical end of the production; and (2) a musical program producer who is a good showman and at the same time will be able to divert the efforts of the musical director and the musicians (who are naturally interested in music for music's sake) into channels of thinking that attach prime importance to entertainment value.

The producer in televising a musical program faces many problems which are peculiar to this type of show. They are principally visual, though some are problems having to do with sound—for example, the difficulty of maintaining good pick-up when soloists and an orchestra are included in the same picture and the microphones cannot be placed to good advantage without being seen. The motion picture industry has spent years and a great deal of money trying to solve this problem and still finds it better in most cases to record picture and sound separately.

The problems of pictorial continuity are complicated by the fact that musicians as a class are not trained to act and that therefore they cannot be shoved around as actors are in arranging pictorial compositions. Many musicians are good performers and catch on quickly to the technique of television. The producer must school those who are not adept in camera and light orientation. He should rehearse them in their stage positions and movements and in pantomimic expression.

Many singers tend to weave or sway with the music, and they must be broken of this habit, for otherwise they drive a cameraman out of his mind and are annoying to watch. Solo violinists have the same little trick, which is all to the good on the concert platform but not in television. To make matters worse, some of them wave their violins around in a manner that is disturbing in close-ups. The producer should give all soloists using hand instruments a routine of postures and position, and rehearse it thoroughly with them, in order to be able to plan his camera work and be reasonably sure of getting good shots.

As an instance of the importance of instrument orientation we may cite the accordion, the guitar, the cello, or any instrument which presents a flat surface to the camera. Since these are almost always highly polished surfaces, they will "kick" light so strongly as to cause "blooming" on the screen if they are held at certain angles with relation to the lights. It is only by careful positioning in rehearsal that this condition can be remedied. In this connection, any instrument owned by the station should be dull-finished.

The handling of musical comedy and operatic programs from a televising standpoint differs little from a dramatic show involving a number of people playing in front of scenery. The camera and lighting technique is practically identical. There is, however, a very definite requirement in editing—and this holds true of any musical program: the *camera cuts should be executed in rhythm with the music, or in synchronism with its phrasing.*

b. Interpretive Presentation

This form of musical presentation does not show the musicians themselves, but it makes use of natural phenomena to interpret either the objective meaning or the subjective feeling of the music. This simply means, when taken out of highfalutin language, that the story or the mood of the music is interpreted visually by the use of recognizable natural images. Such images may be produced by live action in the rhythm and tempo of the music, such as pantomime or the dance, or by means of rhythmically edited motion picture footage drawn from the wealth of library material available. The possibilities here are practically endless and are limited only by the budget and the imagination of the producer.

An outstanding example of what can be done in the field of fantasy through the use of both natural and supernatural imagery is the Disney opus FANTASIA. The great music of the world can be given imaginative interpretation in countless ways and in all conceivable manners from the sublime to the ridiculous. One has only to recall the old silent "flickers" to visualize the possibilities of comic and corny interpretation.

Symphonic music in particular lends itself to the relatively simple technique of editing stock motion picture footage to the music. To do this it is only necessary for the producer: (a) to outline the visual continuity suggested by the music; (b) to time each scene in seconds with a stop watch; (c) to reduce this to feet of film, figuring one and one-half feet of 35mm film per second or six-tenths of a foot of 16mm film per second; and (d) to have the film cutter edit the film, putting in optical effects—fades, lap dissolves, and so forth—where indicated.

Interpretive films of this sort, either in color or in black and white, if capably executed, can be used over and over again, for it is a well-recognized fact that musical favorites can be repeated ad infinitum.

c. Abstract Expressionism

Music itself is abstract, and it follows that abstract visualization is definitely in keeping here. To many music lovers it has more appeal than the use of naturalistic forms. The color organ is a case in point. The weird, ever changing shapes produced by the kaleidoscope are fascinating to watch, particularly when they are timed to music, as in W. C. Eddy's novel equipment. Certainly this is a fruitful field for further tillage.

PRODUCING FACTUAL PROGRAMS

Since it is not the purpose of this book to discuss program material except as it presents specific production problems, we shall not go into the details of producing the wide variety of factual programs which may be broadcast. By and large, the problems which accompany a factual program are no different from those of any other program. What difference there is results principally from the producer's attitude toward the program and the way he approaches it.

The philosophy in back of the program, the psychology used in slanting it toward the audience, and the showmanship that goes into the production are the three most important considerations. The reader is referred to the section in Chapter VI on writing factual programs, in which much of the philosophy is discussed in detail; these factors apply equally to the producing. As pointed out there, factual material should be given an emotional basis, and the appeal should be made to the universal desire for health, wealth, and happiness.

News, sports, special events, and remote pick-ups of public happenings are reportorial in nature. Their function is to show the audience what, where, when, why, and to whom a thing happened. The problems of the producer center around matters of selection and clarity of presentation. In any news event or public happening there are trivia which dilute that which is interesting or important. It is the producer's function to discriminate, giving the audience only the concentrated essence.

CUES

This seems as good a time as any to cover the matter of cueing. It is more or less of a science, in itself and an important one in television because of its complexity. As concerns the players, cues may originate from light signals, from viewing monitors, or from hand signals thrown by the stage manager.

The cameras themselves are equipped with red signal lights. When a camera's red light is on, it means that this camera is on the air. Additionally, a series of individually controlled lighted numbers are mounted on the cameras so that when the red light goes off the number lights up, indicating to the performer which camera has gone on the air so that he may make the transition gracefully from the camera on which he was to the camera on which he is.

The stage manager gives the players cues during the broadcast by a system of hand signals, and the producer is in constant communication with him by means of headphones. Although practice varies somewhat, the hand cues given below are almost universally used.

Stand by. As a warning that a cue is about to be given, the arm is raised and kept poised until . . .

Cue . . . the cue is given by bringing the arm down and pointing with the index finger at the person waiting for the signal. Sometimes the stage manager cannot be in a position visible to the player, and he will then "throw" the cue to someone else in the studio, who will in turn give the cue to the player.

Applause. The hands are raised and held as one would when about to begin clapping. At the proper time, the person giving the cue starts to clap. To sustain the applause he turns both palms upward and moves the hands vigorously with a "come on" motion.

Silence. To stop laughter and applause, or to maintain quiet, the finger is brought to the lip in the common "hush" gesture; this is followed by spreading the arms out with palms pushing downward.

Speed up. If the program is running behind schedule or if any of the players are not maintaining pace, the producer will ask the stage manager for a speed-up. The cue to the player consists of moving the index finger in a circle, as if following the hands of a clock. The speed at which the finger is moved indicates how much more to speed up the pace.

Slow down. The slow-down cue is a stretching gesture, in which the two hands are moved away from each other with the fingers held as if they were stretching something. If the pace is only a little too fast the hands will not be moved very far apart, but if it is much too fast the hands are stretched wide.

On the nose. If the program is running on schedule, the players are so informed by a signal that is both expressive and welcome. The index finger points to the tip of the nose.

Tighten up. It happens frequently in television that players tend to work too far apart for camera composition. The signal to pull them closer together is made by raising the hands vertically, palms facing each other, and moving the hands closer.

Open up. If the players are bunched too close, or if someone is covering the action, the opposite gesture is used; the palms are turned outward and the hands moved apart.

Upstage or downstage. If a player is working too near or too far from the camera, the two hands are used in a "go-away" or a "come hither" gesture. This cue frequently has to be used with dancers and specialty acts; in both these cases there is a tendency to use too deep a field.

Play to the camera. Very often a player forgets to be camera-wise and turns too far away from the camera. The corrective cue is to bring the hands up as if they held the player's head and to give it a turn in the proper direction. This may be immediately followed by pointing to the camera.

Play to the lights. If a shadow is being cast on a player's face, as often happens, the stage manager or assistant gestures toward the light source and wipes his hand over his face. He may follow this, if necessary, by gestures indicating the proper direction for the player to move.

More, or less, volume. If more volume is desired, the arm is extended with the palm upward and the hand is moved up and down at a speed indicating the increase desired. To reduce volume the palm is turned downward and the hand is moved up and down.

O.K. When everything is all right, the common gesture of the index finger and thumb in a circle is used. This signal is used in conjunction with all cues indicating a change, as a sign that the condition has been corrected.

Cut. This cue is executed by a cutting-the-throat movement of the finger or hand across the neck. If the producer wishes to stop dialogue or action, he tells the stage manager what is to be cut. If, for instance, the show is behind enough to necessitate a cut of a complete number, the stage manager will throw a pointing cue to the proper person, followed by the cut cue. He will then cue the person who is to pick up the continuity. At the end of the show it may be necessary to cut a number and . . .

Play the theme. This cue is given to the musical conductor; it is made by forming a T with the index fingers.

Sign off. If there is no theme music and the producer finds it necessary to cut something at the end, a cue may be given the announcer to sign the show off. The usual cue is followed by an immediate gesture with the same hand as if something long were being pulled out of the mouth.

Chapter VIII

~~~~~~

PRODUCING THE PLAY

THUS far we have covered most of the producer's duties. They are so multitudinous and there are so many things he has to know that we have endeavored to bring them out a few at a time as they applied to the two types of programs that have been considered. With this as a groundwork we can move on to the producer's most complex assignment—the television play.

Since the case method is most explanatory and since we have already worked up a play script, we shall take as our example the play FORGIVE-NESS which was partially outlined in Chapter VI.

The producer's first step, *televisualizing* the script, is covered in Chapter III under the heading, "A Visual Method of Planning." The example used happens to be the crude form out of which the script of FORGIVE-NESS grew; it differs from the final treatment in some details, but the method has been completely described and will not be repeated here.

We shall assume then that the producer has worked out a visual treatment and a production pattern; that he has planned the mechanics of the production, and that set construction is under way; that he has lived the play over and over in his mind and has formed a definite approach to his handling of it; furthermore, that he has decided on the feeling, the flavor, the color he intends to bring out and has set a definite goal to be reached; and, finally, that he has cast the show with regard for balance, variety and contrast in type, physical proportions, and voice. If all these steps have been taken he is ready to put the show into rehearsal. If he has neglected any of them, placing a blind trust in some guardian angel, the production will suffer.

1. *The Line Rehearsal*

At the first meeting with the cast the producer should fully describe the play and what he wants to get out of it. Any play is open to a number of interpretations. Characterizations are subject to wide variation. Having decided how he wants to type the dramatic form of the play and what he wishes in characterization, he must get his ideas across to to the cast. If this is not done right at the beginning—if scripts have been handed out and the actors have begun to form their own interpretations —the producer may have much to undo. At the same time, the producer must not rob a capable actor of his own contribution in character development. It is simply a matter of harmonizing the objectives of the producer with the efforts of the talent, so that all may work toward the same end.

Methods will vary as to how the producer goes about this stage of directing. In a capable producer's hands, the best method is for him to read through the play, either completely or merely as to key situations, discussing treatment and characterizations with the cast as he goes along; then to have a table reading, in which the cast begins to develop the feeling desired and the producer starts to set the pace and rhythmic pattern. This method has the decided advantage of taking *essentials first,* that is to say, setting the over-all feeling, bringing out motivations of conflict and action, etching characterizations, and establishing what the characters are thinking and feeling. It is advisable to make this a *discussion* of the play rather than a rehearsal. On this safe foundation, line rehearsals may begin.

In the first line run-through the producer should work on dialogue and interpretation and not attempt to rehearse business. It is confusing to a cast to be asked to learn business along with characterization and dialogue. Furthermore, action must be the product of motivation, and until the meaning and significance of the lines have been established the action will be unnatural and mechanical.

During this period the producer will find out how successfully he has cast the talent; he will discover who are the capable actors and which ones need special handling. It is wise to concentrate on the weaker players at this time and bring them along as fast as possible, because if they are allowed to lag it will hold back the production in the polishing stage. A director can usually tell in the first line rehearsal which players are weak, and if he feels that they will require a lot of coaching it is best to take them individually, rather than to embarrass them with criticism and repeated coaching in the presence of the cast.

At this reading the director should bring out the key situations and discuss the plot outline. He will himself have analyzed the dialogue for the important lines in plot development and characterization. It is a good plan to have the actors, at this point, underscore these particular lines; it will help them to grasp the structure as a whole when memorizing their own parts and also to give these important lines the proper emphasis.

There are as many ways of directing as there are directors, and no formula has ever been devised for the best method. As a matter of fact, the method and approach will vary also with the type of play and the type of actor. In general, the function of the director is to stimulate and guide; to direct but not dictate; to control but not dominate—in other words, to bring out the best the cast can give and, above all, to inspire them into giving. To do this he must win their confidence and respect and must make the project a truly co-operative experience.

As the players are reading and as their contribution to the various roles begins to bring the play to life, the producer, while forging ahead with his preconceived plan, should remain plastic and quick to grasp new—and perhaps better—twists in situation and interpretation. He will follow the lines visually and on his script make marginal notes of scene composition, camera cuts, action, and business, revamping and improving his original conception. Where necessary he will make revisions in the script. At this stage he will have to play a dual role, that of director and audience, for the production is still in a malleable state and the actors have not settled into their parts; the die is not permanently cast, and he can shape it into whatever form he desires. This formative period is by all odds the most important, for "as the twig is bent, so grows the tree."

A final and important step in the line rehearsal is to see that all scripts are marked alike as to changes and special instructions. Then— and this is essential—before the next rehearsal the actors should *learn their lines*. Nothing slows up production more than the actor who tries to walk through a part leaning on his script. The producer should be very firm about this matter.

2. The Walk-through Rehearsal

Each main division in the directing of a television play should center around a specific objective. In this way the matter at hand can be crystallized into something like its final shape, and each step can be made definite. To be sure, the final objective is a good production, but this can only be arrived at by approaching it through well-defined routes of travel.

The second stage of progress is the walk-through rehearsal. Its objectives are: (a) to familiarize the cast with the scheme of picturization; (b) to school them in their placement in the various playing areas; (c) to rehearse business; (d) to set the mechanics of the production in so far as it applies to the talent. The director should take a scene at a time and put the cast first through the key situations, explaining how he will treat them pictorially, and then put the cast through the whole business in the scene. He must make the cast *camera-conscious;* they must be made to realize that, whereas they are seeing the entire set and all the characters, the audience will see only those portions framed by the camera field which the producer selects. They must be schooled to so dispose themselves as to make this possible.

In this rehearsal it is better to rehearse only those lines which lead up to or involve business or important movement, and to work on each situation until it has jelled. Since the objective of the walk-through is physical, the emphasis should be entirely on stage position, grouping, movement, and business, with little attention being given to characterization. The chances are a hundred to one that the cast is not yet up in their lines, regardless of the producer's entreaties, but even with that handicap the net effect of this rehearsal will be that the actors will begin to *associate lines with movement.*

This correlation of dialogue and movement constitutes one of the most troublesome problems for the producer. His direction of this aspect should be explicit; otherwise it will not be possible to get good picture continuity. If, for instance, an actor is directed to rise on a particular word and the video engineer has a switch cue to another camera on that word, the sequence will be gummed up if the actor forgets to rise.

Actors who are not adept at television acting must be trained in the technique of continuous orientation to three mechanical devices: the cameras, the microphones, and the lights. They must be shown how to adapt their creative work to these apparently restricting contraptions. The producer may have to demonstrate how to play to the cameras and yet not appear to be doing so. He must stress the importance of space relationship and playing within a given area, no matter how restricted it seems to the actors. He should have them *memorize body positions and movements* as carefully as the lines and *associate* the two. They must be schooled in the speed of movements, particularly across the screen in tight shots.

No cameras are used in the walk-through, which will be carried on in a rehearsal room without the aid of sets or properties. It is a good idea, however, to have all hand props there—or something that closely simulates them—in order for the actors to become familiar with the handling and disposition of these props and to develop this familiarity into a fixed pattern.

The producer will now have an opportunity to check his original plan of picturization and modify it where necessary. It will help him—and the cast too—if he uses some means of indicating where the cameras are going to work. Dummy cameras equipped with ground-glass optical finders and mounted on light rolling pedestals are the ideal arrangement and highly advantageous. If equipment of this sort is not available, an ordinary chair turned with its back to the stage will do to represent a camera. As the producer sets the grouping or business, he can go from one camera location to another and with the aid of a finder, or a piece of black cardboard having a three-by-four-inch opening, he can form a fairly accurate idea of how the shots will look on the camera. As a matter of fact, the more accurately the producer is able to rough out his camera shots at this stage and during the dry rehearsals to follow, the more time can be put into refinement and polishing during the camera rehearsals, for the cast will have been rehearsed in positions and movements that will require little alteration when put on the cameras.

3. *The Dry Rehearsal*

Up to this point the producer has taken the play through the roughing-out stage. Now comes the development period, in which without scenery or equipment the bulk of the directing is carried out. This is continued until the cast is up to the point of a finished performance so far as they are concerned. During this period the producer should mentally perform all the functions of the production crew; that is to say, he should visualize his camera shots and editing routine, at the same time remaining alert to audio problems.

Since the producer is not actually seeing his production on the screen, there is danger that he will direct the play as if it were a stage or radio presentation rather than television. For this reason he must train himself (as well as the players) to see *screen pictures and to play for the medium*. The dry rehearsal should actually be television.

This is still the creative stage. The production is plastic and radical changes can yet be made. He is alone with his cast and not under the strain of control-room tension. Now is the time for him to get in his best work.

A sensible and purposeful order of procedure is as essential in directing rehearsals as in anything else. The producer should not attempt to accomplish everything all at once; he should have a working plan, built on the principle of taking first things first and working out major problems one at a time. There are many slips between the rehearsal and the performance, and the producer who works without a plan of procedure is apt to be caught with his slips showing.

In the line rehearsal the play has been brought through the roughing-out stage. The dry rehearsal should be marked by three distinct phases—distinct in the sense that they are concentrated on individually, though sometimes in parallel. They are as follows:

1. The Molding Phase

a) Key situations are made clear to the cast and rehearsed until they have jelled.

b) Characterizations are etched, and the relationship of one character to another is definitely set. By having these factors fixed early in the rehearsals the cast will make more rapid progress in their roles.

c) The essence of the dialogue is brought out and the last drop of meaning is squeezed out of the lines. Often this can best be accomplished by group discussion—talking over the situation and trying to find out how one would react to the given situation in real life; tracing antecedent influences; studying psychological factors; charting the relation of each character to the conflict.

d) Dialogue and movement are made to complement each other. The motivation of all movement and business is clarified. It is helpful in directing movement and business to have a few run-throughs in which the actors go through their movements, giving only the cues for movement and not the complete dialogue. The ideal condition would be for them to perform in pantomime, for then the producer could properly evaluate the movement.

e) The moods of the various scenes are developed, and the players are specifically rehearsed in the relationship of their roles to the moods.

2. The Refining Phase

   a) The play takes shape, and the rough edges are smoothed off.

   b) Lines are given shading, and attention is focused on intensifying the drama inherent in the plot and the situation.

   c) Pace and build are now established.

   d) Emotional factors are enriched.

   e) Continuity is refined.

3. The Polishing Phase

At this stage the producer should, as far as he is able, put himself in the position of the audience. He should let the performance run through without interruption and should observe it critically. He will look for little things—little bits that are out of harmony, or distracting, or irrelevant and better thrown out. He will look particularly for small movements and gestures that are out of character or draw the attention from something important. He will watch placement and movement for "covering" and bad focus.

As a final step the producer should apply the finishing touches to emphasis, pace, and rhythm. As a matter of fact, it is only at this point that it is possible to manipulate the rhythm of the performance. During earlier rehearsals the pace and rhythm of individual scenes should be set, but the producer should reserve the refinement of the rhythmic pattern for the very end.

4. *The Camera Rehearsal*

The general routine of rehearsing with the cameras is described on page 131. There is little to add here, except the rather obvious statement that the complexities of dramatic production require that a considerable amount of time be spent in camera rehearsal.

Considering that a Broadway play is in rehearsal for weeks and then has an out-of-town try-out, the amount of time that can be allotted to camera rehearsal in television seems all too short. That is why it is essential that the producer shall *televisualize* the play—even before it goes into dry rehearsal. Then, if sufficient work and intelligent planning have gone into the production, much valuable time is saved in camera rehearsal, which ties up equipment and personnel.

Though the manner of working and the methods used in directing a play are as varied as human nature, the guiding principles are the same. As brought out in Chapter III, they are the principles that underlie all the arts. In planning the treatment and in selecting the cast, the producer will have been guided by considerations of unity, balance, harmony, and the other fundamentals of composition. Let us see how to apply these in directing the dry rehearsals.

BASIC PRINCIPLES OF PLAY DIRECTING

1. *Unity*

In molding the performance the director must achieve unity throughout. Since any characterization is open to many different interpretations, it is up to him to guide the development of the several characters in the play so as to form a unified pattern. He must not allow an actor to fall out of character, even for an instant, for it breaks up the feeling of unity. If the piece is high comedy, everything about it—every gesture, every inflection—should be played in that manner; for instance, the director must guard against the tendency many actors have of slipping into farce when playing high comedy.

In the example under consideration, the play FORGIVENESS might easily take on the flavor of the drippy soap opera. If the producer wants it that way, all right; but if he is after serious, straightforward drama he must avoid lapses into the sickly sentimental by directing the cast into channels of restraint and dignified naturalness.

2. *Variety*

The producer should work variety into every element of the production—variety in voice quality, in pitch, in pace, in rhythm; variety in movement, both in speed and direction; variety in grouping and stage dressing; variety in body position and in gesture. Yet all must be bound closely together to form a unified whole, for *variety without unity is chaos.*

To cite only one instance of the controlled use of variety, take pace and pitch in dialogue. We have a long scene between two persons. Obviously if the pace and pitch of both are alike the scenes will be monotonous. Hence we introduce changes of pace throughout the scene; we give one of the players a characteristic manner of speech that sets him off from the other; we pace his lines and/or pitch his voice in a distinctive manner. In this way we achieve not only variety but also stronger characterization. In developing the picturization of scenes between two people the producer should inject variety in gesture and body position;

if movement on the part of the players is illogical, he may create variety through camera movement and composition.

3. Harmony

Since harmony is the adaptation of parts to each other, and since lack of harmony produces discord, every detail of the play must be scrutinized and any discordant notes stricken out. Harmony involves coherence. It demands that a close relationship exist between the several parts of the play, between the characters, and between the situations. It demands that one thing lead logically to the next; that the characters act and react in ways that fit the situation or the mood. It demands flow and smooth continuity.

4. Balance

Balance involves the relationship of parts in respect to force or weight. The producer must obtain balance not only in picturization (discussed fully in Chapter III) but in sound pattern and characterization as well. A scene may easily be thrown out of balance by the overplaying of one of the characters. It may be made monotonous by the continuous or excessive use of equal balance, that is to say, equal focus on two characters. Informal balance, in which one character is placed in counterpoise with one or more other characters of graded strength, is more interesting.

5. Rhythm

In speaking of the value of rhythm in the television play it is difficult to avoid the use of extravagant superlatives, for it is all-important, since rhythm is so deeply rooted in our life processes.

In directing a play the producer should determine the basic rhythm of the piece, and he should exercise every means at his command to develop this. It is so elusive a thing, however, that not until he has brought the production to the polishing stage can he do much about it except to work toward it during the development stage of rehearsing. He should work for rhythm in the delivery of lines, in movement, in pictorial arrangement, and in editing the camera shots. He should weave these separate but interrelated rhythms into a pattern tying the whole production together.

Through the use and control of rhythm the producer can invest the production with qualities that will have a powerful effect on the audience, for rhythm contributes a pulsing beat that sustains interest and vitalizes the continuity. It is essential in characterization; each general character type, each race, each locale has its characteristic rhythm. Emotional states are reflected in particular rhythms; hence this quality is useful in establishing mood.

a. Rhythm Control

As to the application and control of rhythm, *the dominant character in each scene should set the rhythm.* The other characters should be directed to play to this lead. There is then some opportunity for control, and the device will help to build the leading character. For instance, in our play specimen the mother would set the rhythm in the first scene —a gentle rhythm at first, to give the illusion of peaceful domesticity, building up in poignancy to the end; in the next scene between the child's mother and her worthless lover, the rhythm should be hesitant and faltering; and in the scene between the stern father and the daughter a relentless, heavy beat should be set by the father.

b. Rhythm in Transitions

Careful attention to rhythm is necessary in producing smooth transitions from scene to scene, because usually the rhythm changes and it is desirable not to have the change sharply felt. This can be done by modulating the rhythm at the time of the shift of scene. For example, at the end of Scene I the mother is telling Mary about her mother, Ruth, and at this point there is a dissolve to Ruth as she is about to knock on Steve's door. To effect a smooth, dramatic transition, the director can have the mother modulate the rhythm of her lines as she nears the dissolve; then he will gauge the length of the pause before Ruth knocks on Steve's door, so that it ties into the cadence of the foregoing lines; and finally he will have Ruth modulate her first lines to complete the transition.

c. Rhythm in Movement

Rhythm is of the greatest importance where movement is involved. Everyone is conscious of this aspect of movement through association with the dance, the movements of certain sports, and the simple act of walking. The producer should give special attention to rhythm as follows in situations involving movement:

1) Keep all movement over lines in rhythm with the mood of the scene. The mother, for instance, is mending in the first scene, which opens on a tranquil note. At this point her hand movements as she sews

should be leisurely, but after Luke's entrance, as she glances anxiously at the clock and says, "I wish James would get here," her hands should reflect her emotional state. Rhythm of movement can be effective in heightening mood, as in the tapping of a finger or the swinging of a leg during a dramatic pause. But the beat of the rhythm should be in harmony with the mood.

2) In close-ups, be particularly careful to avoid jerky, unrhythmic movements. The eye is quickly distracted by movement or action of any kind, especially in a close-up. Let us say that a hand is to be brought into the picture field to pick some object up and take it out. The audience should be prepared for the entrance of the hand, either by a line or a pause; the hand should be brought in at a rhythmic speed; and it should linger momentarily at the object before taking it out. The whole maneuver should be in rhythm. This may seem like too small a detail to bother with; but the producer must realize that good television is made up of countless small details brilliantly and thoughtfully executed.

3) Watch the rhythm of such movements as rising, sitting, turning; entrances and exits; the opening and closing of doors; the handling of properties; even the muscular movements of the face in big close-ups. If anyone doubts the importance of rhythm in muscle-twitching and eye-blinking, let him study the technique of the more finished actors in movie close-ups.

The application of rhythm to pictorial arrangement has been fully covered in Chapter III and will not be touched upon here. Its function in the technique of video and audio continuity was discussed in Chapters IV and V.

6. Pace

Having established the basic rhythm of a play and the rhythmic pattern of each scene as dictated by its mood content, the producer should control the *pacing* of dialogue and movement and see that it is in keeping with that pattern. Change of pace arouses interest. Increase of pace is a device in building. Decrease of pace, though its immediate effect is to diminish intensity, is also a means of building, for, in order to build, a relatively lower level must first be established.

Since pace and rhythm are interdependent, the producer should watch to see that there is no change in the basic rhythm of the play as changes of pace occur. The audience should be continually conscious of the basic rhythm through its recurrence, and changes of pace should but amplify this condition. The producer should plot in his mind (or even graphically on paper) the main build of the play and work out the changes of pace and pitch within this guiding structure.

a. Plotting the Main Build

We shall include in this discussion matters affecting not only *pace* but also *proportion* and *pitch,* because they all contribute to the build.

Obviously the graphic pattern of the main build in a tragedy would be noticeably different from that in a farce. All plays, however, have one common characteristic—they reach their highest level in the main climax, at or near the end; also, as the play progresses, the low points become shorter and never so low as at the opening, and the minor climaxes become longer and greater.

Using our play as an example, the build might be plotted as follows:

Title Sequence. Use as title music something in three-four tempo in the manner of *Valse Triste.* Fade it out as the big close-up of the child's book and doll come on the screen.

Sequence 1. Living Room. Have Mary start at once to read, *sotto voce,* and continue until the dolly-back has included the mother. Pace her reading in the slow rhythm of the music.

Maintain a leisurely, measured beat, unchanged through Luke's entrance. Let him lift the pitch, however.

Now gradually build to Mary's line, "Mother, why doesn't daddy like me?" Drop abruptly, but have the mother build again as she is telling Mary that her mother is dead, and make Mary's line, "Then Daddy isn't my daddy?" a minor climax. Drop again slightly and hold a measured tempo up to and through the dissolve to Ruth's scene with Steve.

Sequence 2. Steve's Room. In this scene establish a faltering rhythm, and build to the clash over Steve's gambling, but do not make it a big build. Then give the remainder of the scene to Steve and have him carry it at a slightly higher pitch and faster pace than has been used before, in order to form a contrast with what follows immediately.

Sequence 3. Cabinet Shop. This is the father's scene, and he should sustain a relentless, heavy rhythm, the climactic point coming on Ruth's flare-up when she says she is going away with Steve. The father has the last line and forms the transition to the mother's lines in the next scene.

Sequence 4. Living Room. There are two minor climaxes in this scene. The second one, which comes at the very end, should be the sharper and higher of the two. Open on the heavy rhythm of the preceding scene. The mother is finishing the story of Mary's parentage and is trying to explain to Mary why her grandfather treats her coldly. During this long speech have her lift gradually and introduce a suspense rhythm, building up to the climactic entrance of the father, terminating in a minor climax (higher than any before) as Mary rushes in terror out of the room. Drop sharply and build again to a sharp, high peak as the screech of brakes is heard.

Sequence 5. Street Scene. This is a short scene, with little dialogue, and should be played low throughout. The sparse dialogue should be handled in a tentative, tense rhythm, filled out by traffic sounds and some "walla-walla" from the curious who have gathered.

Sequence 6. Living Room. The rhythm and pace of this scene must be handled with precision. The tentative, tense quality of the last scene should be carried over and given increasing tension, reaching the main climax as Mary gives her last faltering lines and her eyelids close. For the denouement, the stricken father reaches out lovingly to stroke her hair, as the *Valse Triste* theme fades in, and the picture dissolves to Mary's story book and doll. The rhythm of the music, therefore, should form the basic rhythm of the dialogue and movement throughout this scene, and the mood of the whole performance should be resolved in the concluding music.

7. *Proportion*

We have just seen how proportion enters into plotting the main build of a play. It is also a factor in other details of directing. Though the writer has set the broad proportions of the play and has proportioned the length of scenes and characterizations, the producer should not hesitate to change these things if he can improve the production. He does have direct control of the proportioning of movement, gestures, business, sound effects, and especially the proportions of his scenes as he builds continuity. If he is an artist—a good showman—he will know what is meant by that most intangible of all things to define, *good proportions.* Hosts of people will be able to tell him when the proportions are bad; only an inward voice can tell him how to make them good.

8. *Emphasis.*

No other one thing will give the producer more concern, more worry, more nervous breakdowns than the control of emphasis. It is a major problem and an important one. The producer must weave a variegated pattern of emphasis in the delivery of lines, in gestures, in the body positions and movements of his actors; he must control the emphasis of characters and of properties that is created by lighting and by sharpness of camera focus. The producer is literally surrounded by pitfalls of emphasis.

The deepest pit into which the unwary (and the careless) can fall is in the use of overemphasis. It is a mark of mediocrity in both actor and director if this is tolerated, and it should be avoided except when used for a good and sufficient reason. Overemphasis, like overplaying, is an indication that two important factors have not been taken into account, to wit, *breadth* and *sacrifice*.

Breadth demands a wide range of emphasis and interest. *One of the best ways of achieving breadth is through sacrifice* of all but the essential qualities of a situation or a characterization. Through the sacrifice of interest and intensity at the beginning of a scene, it is possible to build a climax; through the sacrifice of some of the qualities a character might display, the qualities essential to the situation are made more potent.

By plotting the main build of a play, the producer can see the main contours of emphasis; he can see the high and low points within which he must work in controlling emphasis of dialogue and action from moment to moment. Let us consider some of the more important ways of obtaining and controlling emphasis.

a. Emphasis in Dialogue

The basic requirements of good dialogue are that it have clarity, expressiveness, and a rhythmic cadence in harmony with the mood. Variety of emphasis is one of the ways of obtaining this. The richness and vitality of the dialogue will naturally be dependent upon the sensitivity, responsiveness, and acting ability of the cast, but the burden of control falls on the producer, if for no other reason than that an actor can treat a line in many different ways.

The producer should sense the important words in a line and see that they are given just the right amount of emphasis; furthermore, he must instinctively feel the balance of emphasis between characters playing against each other. In the line reading and in coaching individual players it is a good idea to have the actor underscore the important words to be stressed.

Words, phrases, and sentences may be given emphasis in many different ways: (1) by a change in volume, in pace, and in pitch; (2) by a change in voice quality; (3) by a dramatic pause; (4) by a break in rhythm; (5) by inflection; and (6) by the use of the "throw-away" line or phrase.

The producer should bear in mind that the audience will not catch all the words and may even lose many of the lines. It is essential, therefore, that the important words be emphasized and the important lines pointed.

b. Emphasis in Movement

It is equally essential that the audience notice important movement. To achieve this, *movement should be used with a purpose* and kept carefully under control. The eye is quick to observe movement and to follow it. The mind readily becomes interested in movement, so much in fact, that it may even blank out dialogue if the visual attraction is strong enough. This means that the producer must carefully watch the balance of emphasis between picture and sound. As a general rule, lines and movement for the purpose of emphasis should be used *separately*, for they tend to cancel each other out.

An important line may be pointed by putting movement before it. In the same way, a *movement* may be given emphasis by having it come *after a line*.

There are two kinds of movement: those which are motivated by the lines or are essential to the plot and the characterization; and movements of a purely technical nature, such as those which must be made in order to get good picturization. The producer must be on guard lest these two become confused and the emphasis diluted. It frequently happens, when dealing with three or more characters in a long sequence, that in order to get variety in camera shots it is necessary to move the characters around arbitrarily. When this is done, the producer must avoid having such arbitrary movement assume emphatic value.

c. Emphatic Values of Movement

In order for the producer to control emphasis in movement, he must know the values of the different kinds of movement. He should realize that all movement has a definite value in the sense of attracting or holding attention. We shall therefore speak of movements as being either strong or weak.

1) A movement toward the camera is strong; one away from it is weak.

2) Vertical movement is stronger than horizontal.

3) Diagonal movement is the strongest of all.

4) Upward movement is stronger than downward; hence, rising is stronger than sitting down; a hand up-flung or a lifting of the chin is stronger than the corresponding downward movement.

5) Movement from the right to the left of the picture is stronger than from left to right, the direction of reading.

6) Movement that enters the field and stops is stronger than that which continues on out.

7) An extended movement which changes direction is stronger than one which continues in the same line.

8) Movement is made stronger by opposition and by isolation.

9) The emphatic body movements are: (a) a turn toward the camera; (b) a rise; (c) a movement or a gesture which employs a diagonal; (d) a pointing gesture with either the hand or a property; (e) a lifting of the chin or eyelids; and (f) a straightening up or moving forward. "Opening-up" gestures are strong, contracting gestures weak.

10) A cross is stronger in front of another actor than behind him.

11) Movement on another's lines is weaker than that in which the actor moves on his own lines.

12) Movement on lines is given greatest emphasis by having the actor *point* his line with a gesture or small movement, then *start* to execute the movement, *arrest* it for the delivery or the start of the line, and finally complete both line and movement with vigor.

13) Movement of actors toward each other is stronger than away.

14) Movement is weakened by repetition.

15) Movement is strengthened by contrast, as, for instance, in the nervous, jerky twitching of the accused in contrast with the stability of the judge and jury.

A final word about movement used for emphasis: *Watch the relative strength of all movements and gestures; give them strength or weakness in proportion to the emphasis inherent in the line, situation, or characterization; develop variety of emphasis; avoid overemphasis.*

9. Dominance

Dominance or principality must be present in every aspect of a play, in order that the audience may know the relative importance of the various characters, situations, ideas, and moods. The producer must so direct the cast and organize the production that some single idea, or theme, or mood is dominant; furthermore, every scene must be dominated to a greater or lesser degree by one of the characters. It must be clear to the audience who is carrying the ball. But this does not mean that this should be monotonously obvious, for the fifty-yard run is more dramatic if the player is at times opposed or covered by others, or even lost for a time in the melee.

Since the emotional interest in a play centers around a conflict, the audience must be clear about the relation of each character to the conflict and to the other characters. To achieve this clarity, the producer must pay particular attention to the relative importance of all the elements involved. His means at hand are to be found in the control of emphasis in dialogue and in the application of the principles of pictorial composition. Here are a few of the ways in which a scene may be "given" to one of the characters:

1) Supporting characters may underplay.

2) The leading character may "point" his own lines by a pause, gesture, movement, change of pace or pitch, and so on.

3) A character may dominate a scene through body position. A full front view of the body and/or the face is stronger than a three-quarter view; a three-quarter view is stronger than a profile; a back view may be strong or weak, depending on how it is used. Hence in a three-shot it is possible to give the scene to any one of the three characters by merely changing the orientation of the faces to the camera.

4) A scene can be given to any character by means of the pictorial composition. Through the application of the principles outlined in Chapter III, any unit of the composition may be given principality.

10. Continuity

The burden of creating continuity rests squarely on the producer's shoulders. Out of the warp and weft and tangled skeins of many colors he must weave a fabric of interesting design. Out of confusion he must create order. Out of a jumble of interesting sights and sounds he must select only those which will flow together in a logical and pleasing progression. He is an editor, with cameras and microphones for his reporters; they will report all that appears before them, and from it he must choose only that which is good, that which is pertinent to the story, and that which has meaning for the audience.

PICTURIZATION AND COMPOSITION

The basic problem and the ultimate objective of picturization is to present the visual concept of the story, and to direct the attention of the audience to those parts of the continuously flowing picture which are essential to its understanding and enjoyment. Obviously the pictures will be made up of many elements, some of them competing for attention; it is the producer's function to take the audience figuratively by the hand and point to those things which he wants them to see. The method by which he accomplishes this is divided into three distinct steps:

1. *Procedure in Planning Picturization*

a) Determine the emotional content of the scene or sequence; its inherent mood; its pictorial relation to adjacent scenes in the continuity; its relation to the main build of the play.

b) Apply to the key situations the principles of pictorial composition, outlined in Chapter III, as follows:

1) Select the fundamental form or combination of forms that best expresses the feeling of the scene, on the basis of whether its essential qualities indicate equality of interest, opposition, climax, concentration, and so forth. This is as important as the gestures the actors use to give meaning to their lines; for, if the abstract form of the picture is inappropriate to the emotional content, no amount of "emoting" on the part of the actors will make it right.

2) Apply the *psychology of line, mass, and form* to the compositional scheme as regards placement, grouping, and movement of figures in such a manner that the mood content of the sequence is definitely felt.

3) *Arrange the composition with regard to focus of interest*—decide whether it is to be held on one character or to flow from one to another.

4) Check these compositional arrangements for their *practicability* in camera work, mike pick-up, and lighting.

c) Direct the actors to work within this pictorial pattern, while at the same time giving their own individual visual performance.

Not until the producer has analyzed all the foregoing factors and has composed the sequence in the light of such analysis is he ready to direct the players in individual picturization. This phase of planning the picturization should take place while the producer is alone with the script.

Though the steps we have outlined may seem too laborious—too detailed and cumbersome—for practical use, it should be borne in mind that the capable producer goes through all of them consciously and unconsciously drawing upon his fund of experience, his training, and his talents. The less capable producer, therefore, as well as the student, can well afford the laborious effort of analytical, detailed planning.

2. Factors in Composition

From the producer's point of view, the technique of pictorial composition is used not alone as a means of obtaining pleasing arrangements but also as a means of telling the story and giving it emotional impact. In creating picturization and applying the techniques of composition, the producer assumes the function of a creative artist—a painter of pictures. Not that he must let his hair grow long and his morals short, as with the artists usually pictured on stage and screen; but as the artist whose work is worthy of recognition really is—a man of keen perception, possessing strong powers of analysis, high critical standards, and exacting selectivity, all under the disciplined control of common sense. Let us pursue this generalization and give it practical significance.

a. Psychological Factors

The human mind has definite habits of association. These associations are based on the psychological experiences of existence. Certain lines, masses, and forms elicit definite emotional responses: the horizontal line is associated with sleep or death; the mass of the cathedral spire with uplift and spirituality; the form of the square with equality and honesty. Certain shapes have become symbolic: the cross with sacrifice; the triangle with unity; the circle with continuity. Certain forms have been woven into a universal language: a man is as "straight as an arrow"; as "fat as a hog"; as "sleek as a leopard." Out of the primitive struggle for existence, certain actions and movements have taken on definite associations; the slinking movements of the cat; the clenching of the fist; the encirclement of protecting arms.

b. Physical Factors

The human eye in examining a picture has certain physical habits and preferences resulting from the manner in which it is used in day-to-day living. It is sensitive to conditions of unbalance, for it is by this sensitivity of the eye that its owner has kept from falling. It is accustomed to reading from left to right; hence it tends to enter a picture from the left, and move from left to right. It resists looking long at the exact center of things. It likes to move continuously; hence it resists looking fixedly at one point for any considerable length of time. It tends to follow lines and to form imaginary lines along points of accent. It follows contours; hence the edge of a shape is important. The eye goes first to the strongest contrast of light and dark, or of color, then on to the next, and so on; hence it is possible to control the route of travel by controlling the contrasts. In much the same way, it goes first to the hardest edges; hence the eye can be directed through control of the quality of the edge of all shapes. It is strongly attracted by movement and never tires of it if given an occasional rest. In following a sustained movement across the field, it tends to "lead" the movement, apparently in an effort to know where the object is going.

Out of these known facts concerning the habits of mind and eye the producer can derive a useful set of postulates to aid him in working out compositions.

c. Postulates

1) All other things being equal, a figure will dominate if it is noticeably higher in the composition than the others.

2) A figure at the bottom will dominate if its posture is in contrast with the others or if it is isolated, as, for example, a figure seated or lying prone while the others are all standing.

3) Looking or gazing up is a stronger attitude than looking down.

4) A figure in the foreground is normally stronger than one in a background or upstage position, though an upstage position is much the stronger of the two if it is arranged as such and if the other actors "give" the scene.

5) A figure can be made dominant in any part of the field:

   a) By having the other figures assume relatively weaker body positions.

   b) By having the other figures look at it or move toward it.

   c) By transitional lines leading to it. These lines may be either actual or the imaginary lines formed by the placement of the players. The eye will form lines of travel from one player to the next.

   d) By repetition. A figure is made stronger by placing another just behind it, or by having it stand near a strong vertical shape, such as a pillar, a tall chair, or a door.

1. Dominance by position.

2. Dominance by contrast.

2. Dominance by isolation.

3. Dominance by attitude.

4. Dominance in foreground.

4. Dominance in background.

FIG. 26. ILLUSTRATING POINTS 1 THROUGH 4.

e) By comparison. A figure will stand out in a large group if its position, posture, physical appearance, or movement is different from the rest. The eye is quick to spot anything that differs from the norm.

f) By contrast of light and dark; placing a light figure against a dark background, and vice versa; also, by contrast of color.

6) The exact center of a picture is a weak position unless there are strong lines of concentration. It is better not to put the dominant figure there.

7) In a one-shot (head and shoulder) the strongest position is with the body full front and a little to the right of center, and with the head turned slightly to the (picture) left. If the head is turned the other way the picture is thrown out of balance; it is badly out of balance if at the same time the person looks fixedly out of the field to the right (see Figure 17, page 41).

8) A single figure is made stronger by means of comparison; that is to say, by introducing a comparatively weaker figure. If the weaker figure plays a little nearer the camera and is seen in a three-quarter back view, thus definitely "giving" the scene, the other figure will be made very strong.

9) Head and shoulder two-shots should be used sparingly. They are hard to compose and monotonously repetitious, principally because the hands cannot be brought into play.

10) In a two-shot where the scene is equally shared, the focus can be diffused by giving both figures body positions of equal or similar strength; by the use of diagonal line structure; or by alternating the focus through change of position. Shared scenes are ones in which both characters have dialogue of about equal importance. If one of them, as the scene progresses, becomes more important through the implications of the plot, the other characters should be directed to "give" the scene compositionally, that is, by assuming a weaker body or picture field position.

From the foregoing it should be clear that posture, gesture, and movement are vitally important elements in picturization. It should also be apparent that it is principally through the control of these three factors that dominance and emphasis are controlled. We have only to recall the old silent movies to realize the extent to which posture, gesture, and movement can be completely expressive. This form of picturization, without the use of dialogue, we call pantomime. Let us see how it may

5a. Dominance by body position.

5b. Dominance by head position.

5c. Dominance by transitional lines.

5d. Dominance by repetition.

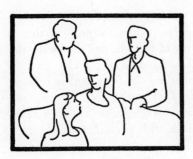

6. Weakness in exact center.

8. Dominance by comparison.

FIG. 27. ILLUSTRATING POINTS 5, 6, AND 8.

be employed as a means of enriching and vitalizing television picturization.

PANTOMIME AND ITS VALUE

Although we are dealing at the moment with producing a television play, and are exploring the many factors with which the producer must deal when a play is in rehearsal, it should be pointed out that all these considerations are applicable to any type of program where the participants can be given direction. Hence the matter of pantomime should not be confined to this one application.

The value of pantomime in vitalizing a television play derives from its potency in *visual dramatization*. The producer who neglects or underrates this aspect of television is not making proper use of the medium. He might better be devoting his attention to radio, for the first essential of the television play is that the emotional impact be visual as well as aural; furthermore, many of the emotional elements and many of the subtle shadings of character can be expressed only by visual means.

We are speaking of the use of pantomime not in an isolated sense (not as a "dumb show" as the dictionary describes it) but as a means of giving visual effectiveness to all action and dialogue. We are using it in the sense of gestures, postures, attitudes, and mannerisms in performing business, that are used as a "plusage" to give added expression and vitality.

1. Pantomime in Characterization

Every characterization can be given pantomimic expression that is suggested by the type of play, the nature of the role, and the locale, the period, and the personality traits and background of the character. In real life people are typed by their mannerisms—by the way they perform simple acts: the way they walk, or stand, or enter a room—by the way they handle things: their coats and hats, the telephone, a book, a newspaper. We associate certain mannerisms with particular social strata, locales, or emotional states.

It follows, therefore, that, if at the very beginning of a play each character is given individualistic pantomimic expression, the audience will form a quicker understanding of the nature of the play and the characters portrayed. Furthermore, if these visual symbols are skillfully used throughout in proportion to the demands of the action and the dialogue, the performance will be greatly enriched. The producer should continually search for bits of pantomime that will strengthen and vitalize each characterization.

These are the touches that bring a character to life. They are the magnets that hold the visual attention of the audience. They are the ways by which realism is achieved and dialogue is given clarity. If the actors themselves do not develop sufficient pantomimic expression, the producer should supply it. As a matter of fact the greater part must come from his direction anyway, because in composing continuity and working out camera shots the producer frequently introduces business for purely technical reasons. These pieces of extraneous business can be given motivation, or at least be made to appear logical, if they are executed not as isolated acts but rather as an extension of, or a carryover from, some bits of pantomime that have been "planted" or made a part of the character's manner of playing.

2. Pantomime in Business

Every piece of business, aside from that which has just been mentioned, should be motivated and have dramatic value. It should be expressive of the dialogue and the mood of the situation; it should be in absolute harmony with every element of the play; it should be in spirit with the locale and the atmosphere. There should be an apparent reason for its use, and the way in which it is executed should be in keeping with the established characterization. It should be performed, not just as a piece of business indicated in the script, but as a form of pantomimic expression as important in its manner of execution as the subtle shading of a line of dialogue.

The producer should rehearse business until it is executed with precision and finesse. This must be done not only because business executed in an awkward, fumbling manner is mediocre but because all business consumes time, and "time is of the essence." What is more, it should be executed in rhythm with the flow of the dialogue or the basic rhythm of the scene; otherwise disharmony will result. By all means it must be executed with regard to camera orientation and lighting, in order that it will go over visually and not be missed by the audience.

The amount of business which should be used will depend on the type of play and the factors involved in each situation. Certain generalizations can be made regarding different classifications:

a. In Serious Drama

In the play FORGIVENESS, which we have used as an example of script writing and directing, business and pantomimic expression should be used with restraint; its sole purpose should be to give conviction and sincerity to the conflict and the people involved. The main action is clearly indicated by the plot; therefore business and pantomime should be confined principally to the development of the characterization.

Thus it may be established as a basic principle that pantomimic expression should be underplayed. This is particularly necessary in dramatic presentations, but it applies in varying degree to all television acting because the medium magnifies all gestures and mannerisms.

b. In Farce

In the farce we have a condition that is quite the reverse; the whole thing revolves around situation, and business may legitimately be carried to an absurd degree. Farce deals with the ridiculous situation; with outlandish goings-on; with laugh-provoking satire. Farcical business is broad and often exaggerated to the point of burlesque. It is paced rapidly, for the audience is not supposed to think about its lack of logic, and the timing must be precise.

c. In Mystery and Horror Plays

The thriller-diller mystery or horror play is also much concerned with situation. Here business and pantomimic expression are in definite keeping with suspense, and they are expressive of the character types usually associated with such plays. Pantomimic action may be effectively used: (1) to direct or misdirect suspicion; (2) to throw the audience off the track or lead them on; (3) to heighten suspense and make the customers wonder what is going to happen next. In melodramatic situations the producer should watch carefully to see that the business is performed with stark realism and is not executed with farcical exaggeration.

d. In Comedy

Probably no clearer example of the value of pantomimic expression in comedy could be thought of than the much-used *double take*. Also, this may be used as an example of the necessity for proper pace and accurate timing.

Much use can be made of pantomime and business in comedy, but it must be handled with precision and a high degree of showmanship; it can be pretty awful in the hands of the novice. A skilled craftsman like Charlie Chaplin can make pantomime vastly more expressive than words. His work and the technique of other great comedians should be an inspiration to the television producer.

3. *Pantomime in Dialogue and Story Development*

Pantomimic expression is the essence of effective screen technique; without it dialogue is nothing more than words and voice tones. The work of the better motion picture players, particularly in some of the French films, may well be studied with regard to the use of pantomimic expression in adding visual dramatization to dialogue. Not that these film techniques can be taken over here *in toto*, for television demands more restraint; but they may be used as a guide.

Probably the most contributive aspect of visual dramatization through pantomime is the focusing of attention on the picture and the minimizing of wordage which it makes possible. When it is realized that visual attention is more difficult to hold than aural, the importance of pantomimic expression becomes apparent.

Another valuable application is in showing *reaction*. A character can give outward expression to his thoughts and reactions by the mere use of gestures and posture, thereby adding vitality to dialogue and clarity to plot exposition.

The complex nature of television play directing and the many problems of production place a limit on the amount of dramatic work that can be written into a week's broadcasting. But dramatic entertainment rates high in audience preference and is a necessary part of balanced programming. It is not a simple undertaking, especially for a new, undeveloped organization; but as the art progresses, as writers, actors and producers learn to use it, the rawness will diminish, the failures and flops will be less frequent, the aping of other media will vanish, and the television play will come into its own.

Chapter IX

~~~~~~

MOTION PICTURES AND FILM INTEGRATION

THERE have been countless discussions between the proponents of radio, stage, and motion pictures as to which medium is most closely allied with television and from which one television derives the greatest heritage. The argument is as unending as it is pointless. Since television admittedly stems from all three, is it not more to the point to accept the heritage without bickering and to take with gratitude all that each has to offer?

Certainly the motion picture industry has developed many techniques that are adaptable to television—some without modification, others requiring some change. Barring the cameras, much of the equipment is identical. The sound is picked up in the same way. In a given scene the acting technique, the manner of directing, and the general method of production are similar. Only in the matter of continuous production do we find a striking difference in methods.

THE USES OF MOTION PICTURE FILM

In addition to furnishing a complete program of entertainment, motion pictures have other uses. In the form of shorts running anywhere from three to ten minutes, they are a godsend to the television program department when used to break up a complicated program schedule and give the production crew a few minutes off the air to make changes in studio set-ups. For the coverage of news, sports, and special events, motion pictures serve as an auxiliary to the television cameras. Many events are unsuited to direct remote pick-up, either because of the time at which they take place or because of the nature of the event. When recorded on film they can be broadcast during the good viewing hours. Some events are broken up by long or monotonous periods devoid of action and are much improved by editing. Others are of such a nature that the interest is scattered over too large an area for the ordinary remote pick-up equipment to cover effectively.

As a matter of fact, a better job of reporting and a more showmanlike presentation can be achieved in certain types of pick-up simply because the material can be *edited and shown in well-planned continuity*. A prize fight is a type of sports event that can be televised in its entirety, because here the interest is sustained throughout. The same is true in a wrestling match, or bone-crushers' ballet as it is so aptly called. These and many other events are grist for the television mill exactly as they occur. The television cameras make it possible for every viewer to have a fifty-dollar ringside seat with no parking problem and without leaving that favorite chair. But events which in themselves do not possess natural continuity are more interesting when presented on well-edited film, and what is lost through the lack of immediacy can be offset by showmanship in presentation.

Another use to which films may be put in television is in adding variety to live studio origination. Integrated sequences recorded on motion picture film make it possible to introduce scenes that could not be set up in the studio. Many programs require or are greatly enriched by sequences that are impossible to produce except by the integration of film. These are too numerous to list completely, but the following examples may be cited:

1) *Title backgrounds.* One of the most interesting techniques in the making of opening and closing titles is accomplished by the superimposure of the title wordage over a live-action background. Frequently this can be done by picking up the action on one of the studio cameras and superimposing the title scanned in one of the projection cameras. There are times, however, when this is not practical, and the action must be recorded on motion picture film. The background material may be some characteristic bit from the studio production (made during rehearsal); it may be a piece of stock footage obtained from a film library; or it may consist of footage shot by the studio camera crew.

2) *Mood scenes.* Waves beating against a stern and rockbound shore, drifting clouds, wind-lashed trees, and other phenomena of nature are useful in establishing moods.

3) *Time lapses and transitions.* Often it is desirable to denote the passage of time or a transition from one situation to another. Also, there are times in studio production when a few moments are needed for a costume change or the shifting of scenery, props, or cameras. All these

situations can be effectively taken care of by film sequences or by loops (short runs of film with the ends cemented together to form a loop that will run continuously through the projector).

4) *Antecedent or paralleling action.* Situations in a play which took place at some previous time or which parallel the action being portrayed lend themselves to the film technique. A character may be describing some previous event pertinent to the plot or a sequence of happenings which motivated his actions. As he relates the story it is effective to dissolve from a shot of him to a film sequence picturizing the events. In a commercial program demonstrating the virtues of a manufactured product, it is possible by the integration of film footage to take the audience into the factory and show them how wonderfully well the product is made.

5) *Historical background.* Stock footage from film libraries, of which there is a vast amount, can occasionally be used to establish the historical background of some element of a program. Isolated shots and complete sequences of this sort are particularly useful in period plays. Sometimes they are best when used with voice-over narration, though occasionally the sound track can be used.

6) *Variety of locale.* Specially prepared film makes it possible to add interesting touches of variety and increased substance to many a television play by extending the action to locales that cannot be presented in the studio.

7) *Close-ups.* In live studio production it frequently develops that a bit of pertinent action cannot be caught in close-up because of the impossibility of getting a camera into proper position. Suppose, for example, that it is important to the plot to show some slight act or piece of business such as the pressing of a call button, the throwing of a switch, or a hand surreptitiously reaching for a gun in a desk drawer. If it is not possible to maneuver the camera into position, the shot can be made on film during rehearsal and cued into the production. It is even possible to use the live sound over the film, provided there are no unusual synchronizing problems.

Since motion picture film plays such an important part in television programming, it is necessary for the producer to have a good working knowledge of film techniques. At one time or another almost any member of the program staff may be called upon to handle film in some way. We shall attempt to cover, in an elementary fashion, the things which the program staff need to know about the making of motion pictures and the handling of film.

THE HANDLING AND INTEGRATING OF FILM

Let us first outline the production mechanics of tying a motion picture sequence into a live show. We shall assume that at a certain point in the production the script calls for a switch from studio to film with voice-over narration. The film is either obtained from some source of supply or shot especially for the occasion. It is then timed so that its running time equals that covered by the narrative. It is threaded into the projector and everything is in readiness for rehearsal.

The narrator is seated before a microphone and a viewing monitor in order that he may view the film and cue his narration. The live action begins, and as it nears the point of switching over to film, the video engineer is on the alert for the cue to press the projector starting button. It takes just so many seconds for the projector to come up to speed and bring the picture on the screen. If, for instance, the required time is eleven seconds, he presses the starting button that much in advance of the time for the film to come up on the line monitor. When the narrator sees the film come up on his monitor or is cued by the producer he begins his narration. As he nears the end, the producer gives a warning cue to the studio and then a cue to start the live action. If everything has gone properly the sequence is set.

1. *Film Timing*

Motion picture sound film runs through the projector at a rate of twenty-four frames per second. Television, however, operates at *thirty* pictures per second. This rate is due to the fact that television operates on electric current which alternates its direction sixty times a second, and because the scanning apparatus requires two scannings of each picture frame. Hence thirty pictures are completely scanned each second. We need not go into the technical means of overcoming this apparent discrepancy. It is only necessary to remember that in timing film it should be figured at the rate of *twenty-four-frames per second.*

Both 35mm and 16mm sound film run at the same camera and projection speed in terms of picture frames *but not in feet of film* per second.

Note that 35mm film runs at the rate of 90 feet per minute; 16mm at 36 feet per minute. Therefore, in timing film it is only necessary to measure the film or count the number of frames to determine the running time of a given length of film. Mechanical counters can be purchased and should be standard equipment in a television studio. These counters show the footage of film running through them, and with a tabular chart it is a simple matter to convert this into minutes and seconds. Lacking a mechanical counter, an index can be marked out on the editing table. For 35mm, figure 1½ feet per second; for 16mm figure 6/10 of a foot.

For marking up the film itself to show where splices are to be made, red china-marking crayons are used. The marks should be made lightly; otherwise the crayon grease will come off in the film gate of the projector.

2. Leaders and Starting Marks

After the film has been cut to the proper length and the various shots have been spliced together, a *leader* should be spliced on the front end. This is a length of blank film long enough to thread the projector for starting. As already noted, it takes a projector a certain number of seconds to get up to speed after the starting button has been pressed. When the exact number of seconds is known, the number of feet and frames can be calculated. By measuring back from the first frame of the picture, a starting mark can be indicated with the grease pencil. The word "start" is written and the frame lines are marked. The projectionist in threading the projector puts this start mark at the film gate, and if it has been accurately laid out the picture will come up at the right time. Obviously the distance will be different for 35mm and 16mm film. It is helpful to have these distances marked on the rewind table.

Since one roll of film looks like any other, it is important to use identification marks on each film leader as well as on the container. The leader should be marked (preferably with ink) to show what the film is and what production it is to be used on. The can should be marked and stored in the vault and a card record kept for future reference, provided the film is to be preserved.

Some productions call for a number of film runs separated by live pick-up. These can be put on one reel with the proper amount of leader spliced between each run of film. If the studio pick-up is of short duration the blank leader can be cut to length and the projector need not be stopped. But if the period is too long a short run of leader may be used. As soon as one section of film has been run the projectionist will thread the next start mark into position.

3. Film Suitable for Television

The basic requirement for television film is that the definition and contrast range be suitable for transmission. In the present state of the art, night scenes are not suitable because of edge flare. We may say in general, therefore, that scenes that are dark or run to large areas of black around the outside of the picture field will not televise well. Pictures containing a large amount of small detail, as in long shots, lose most of their effectiveness. Medium shots and close-ups with a nice range of middle grays, a few accents of light (but not brilliant white), and a few spots of dark (approaching black) are the general specifications for film suitable for televising. In ordering prints it is sometimes advisable to specify that they be made one or two printing points lighter than for theater projection.

It is possible to televise either negative or positive film. Negative can be reversed in the system and shown as positive film. This feature is often a decided advantage, because it means that the time required for making prints can be eliminated. One of the advantages of using positive film, however, is that the various shots can be balanced up in density in the process of printing. This will equalize variations caused by irregularities in camera exposure.

Color film is quite as satisfactory for television as black and white, provided the contrast range is right. The light and medium blues tend to wash out and for this reason scenic shots are not usually desirable. Many kodachrome films of travel and exploration are acceptable with a little editing to eliminate the shots which would not show up well.

This is perhaps as good a place as any to point out that some film stock is highly inflammable. Ordinarily it is well to assume that 35mm film is in that category, though it can be obtained in safety (slow-burning) film. Smoking should never be permitted in the room where inflammable film (with a nitrate base) is being handled, and such film should be stored in fireproof vaults approved by the insurance underwriters. The ordinary 16mm film is safe as regards fire hazard, since it is made of "safety" or acetate stock. "Safety film" is always so marked along the edge.

At this point mention should also be made of the relative merits of 35mm and 16mm film. The picture quality obtained with the larger film is considerably better, as might be expected. With the larger area it is possible to produce more components in the picture field. Also, the accuracy of projection is greater with 35mm, for the reason that the clearances in the projector gate and pull-down mechanism are about the same for each size. Hence in a 16mm projector the errors in alignment are greater. It takes a keen eye, however, to notice any great difference on the television screen, and the average person will find 16mm pictures satisfactory. But the job of editing is much easier with 35mm, and the balance would swing heavily in its favor were it not for the economy of 16mm film as regards the cost of equipment and production.

FILM EDITING

Editing is a problem of building continuity. We have considered the many aspects of continuity in various chapters of this book and shall concern ourselves now only with the mechanics of putting film shots together. We shall assume that the studio is equipped with the necessary rewind stands, splicers, and viewers.

The film to be edited is in rolls as it came from the processing laboratory. The shots are probably not in sequence, and the job of editing consists in cutting each one to the proper length and splicing them all together into the desired continuity. If the film is to be used with voice-over narration which has already been written, the film will be cut to the script. If the script has not been prepared, the film may be edited and a timing schedule set up in the following manner:

Scene	1. Shot of billboard advertising the event	Time—4 seconds	
	2. Line-up at the ticket window	" 3	"
	3. Shot of toothless old-timer	" 4	"
	4. Shots of grandstand, crowds along the rail, and sipping cool drinks at the clubhouse	" 12	"
	5. Shot of the $2 window	" 4	"
	6. Shot of the $100 window	" 3	"
	7. Shot of the tote board	" 5	"
	8. Medium shot in the paddock	" 10	"
	9. Close-up of the favorite	" 6	"
	10. The parade to the post	" 11	"

(and continuing in this manner)

With a schedule of this sort the narration can be written and timed with a stop watch to fit the picture.

Film splicing should be done carefully, with the use of the proper film cement. The splice should be allowed a few seconds to set before its removal from the splicer. When properly made it will be impossible to pull the splice apart even in the most vigorous testing. The cutting table should be kept clean and free of dust, and after the film has been edited it should be thoroughly cleaned before its projection, in order to remove particles of dust and pieces of emulsion. If this is not done, the film will be scratched in the projector. The cleaning may be done by running the film through a soft cloth dampened with carbon tetrachloride. In cutting negative, cloth gloves should always be worn.

A PRIMER ON FILM PRODUCTION

Motion pictures play such an important part in television programming that a basic knowledge of how they are produced is desirable. All who are concerned with television programs will be better equipped for their work if they have an insight into the problems and techniques of film making. Lacking this knowledge they will be apt to use faulty judgment in the purchase of films or in film production by station personnel.

The price range of a picture in the open market may be almost anything, depending upon (a) the way the script is written, (b) the manner in which it is directed, (c) the efficiency of production, and (d) the integrity of the producer. A motion picture is not a commodity that can be purchased on a basis of competitive bidding. It is a quality product derived from creative effort, imagination, and experience. In addition to this, many specialized skills enter into the production process. All these things—creative ability, imagination, skill, and experience—cost money. None of them can be left out without the lack showing up in the product. The motion picture producer who can meet the foregoing specifications is in the best position to save the purchaser's money. As H. G. Christensen so aptly remarks in *Television,* May 1946, Vol. III, No. 5:

Have you ever thought of the *high cost of cheap pictures?* There are few places where cheapness shows itself for all its worth as clearly as it does in a motion picture wherein the cutting job was mainly that of cutting corners. . . . No one can deny that motion pictures are created . . . the work of *thought* and *imagination.* . . . This takes creative brains which are not only scarce but expensive. And this is not the place to save money, because right here is where those expensive brains can show you how to cut costs without losing quality . . . There's a whale of a difference between a picture turned out cheaply due to lack of experience . . . and one skillfully written, planned and produced for a limited budget.

Whether the film is made by a commercial producer or by the station personnel, good results cannot be achieved without the requisite creative ability and know-how. The purpose of the film must be clearly set forth; the story it is to tell must be sharply etched; the script must be written by someone who not only knows how to write a good television *movie script* but also knows motion picture production and can write *within the budget*. The director must know his business; he must have at his disposal adequate facilities and production personnel; he must have sufficient time, if he is to do an adequate job. Finally, the whole project must be intelligently planned.

Steps in Sound Film Production

Having established the purpose of the film and the audience it is to reach, a rough treatment is usually prepared in order to indicate the basic theme and how it is to be developed. The shooting script is then written and approved, and the production schedule is set. The scenery is designed and built, properties and costumes are ordered, and locations are selected. Casting is done and music is arranged. Then the shooting begins.

The script is first broken down into a *shooting schedule*. Scenes are not shot in sequence unless they happen to fall into an economical pattern of studio or location set-ups. All the scenes that take place in one set, for instance, are shot while the actors, lights, and all the facilities are right there. If there is lip-sync dialogue the sound is recorded with the picture. But if the dialogue does not have to be accurately synchronized, or if the sound track carries only narration or music, the sound can be recorded separately and "dubbed" in. It is customary to rush through a print of each day's shooting. These "rushes" are viewed by the director, and each scene is approved before the set is "struck."

At this point the picture is on two or more films, one picture film and one or more sound tracks (on some Hollywood productions many tracks may be required). To make this clear, suppose there is to be mood music over dialogue. The dialogue is recorded on one sound track coincident with the shooting of the picture. A print of the picture in its final edited form is made and projected on a screen in the music-recording studio. The orchestra conductor, watching the action on the screen, fits the music to the picture. This is recorded on a separate sound track, a sound track being a run of film on which the sound only is recorded. The cutter synchronizes this music track with the voice track and with the picture, putting leaders on with matching "start" marks, so that when they are run at the same time in separate projectors, with the sound from each controlled by a mixer, the effect of the final combined picture and sound film is produced.

This is called an "interlock" screening and affords the producer and the purchaser an opportunity to pass final judgment on the production.

If the work is approved, the picture and sound tracks are combined in one film, optical effects (fades and dissolves) are inserted, and the release prints are made.

This sketchy outline merely highlights the principal steps; there are many minor details. To the outsider the production of a motion picture, especially on a Hollywood set, seems unnecessarily slow and inefficient. But it must be recognized that when perfection is being striven for in as complex an undertaking as motion-picture production, and where the work of many people must be perfectly co-ordinated, production-line methods cannot be used. The results usually warrant the cost and the effort.

Because of the perfection which can be obtained, motion pictures are the best solution of the spot commercial problem. The sponsor can preview the commercial and there is no danger of a bungled production. Furthermore, a filmed commercial can be given country-wide distribution. Purchased in quantities—enough let us say for a run of twenty-six weeks—a considerable saving in production cost can be effected.

The same reasoning applies to one and two-reel shorts. The "Mr. and Mrs." type of situation comedy or the soap opera (God forbid), if produced in quantity, running through a whole series, and thereby making the most efficient use of talent and production crew, can be produced more economically on film than in live television. In fact, if the script is written and filmed as a *television* production rather than as a motion picture, it is possible to film long runs of sustained continuity and cut down considerably on shooting time. By using two or three cameras a complete motion picture program can be shot in continuous production (except for shifts of equipment from set to set) just as it is in television. If the film is then skillfully edited and optical effects and music are added, the resultant product, though not perhaps up to motion-picture theater standards, will probably be equal in quality to the usual live television production, for the reason that retakes can be made if necessary, editing can be more carefully analyzed, and the sound can be more perfectly balanced.

PRODUCING INTEGRATED SILENT FILM

Continuing our case method of study, we shall take as our problem the film sequence from the play FORGIVENESS outlined in Chapter VI on page 101. It is the sequence at the scene of the accident in which the child was injured by a truck.

1. *Planning the Production*

The producer's first step is to determine the running time of the sequence. He decides, let us say, that it should run 34 seconds and be made up of the following scenes:

Scene 1. Medium shot of front end of truck. The driver has brought it to a stop and is just looking back. He sees Mary lying in the street, gets out, and goes back. Camera pans with him to Mary lying in the street. Passer-by rushes up and they both bend over her. John arrives on the scene as we . . .   Time—20 seconds

CUT to

Scene 2. Closer shot. Luke pushes his way through crowd and examines the child   "   9   "

CUT to

Scene 3. Close-up. Luke picks Mary up and starts toward the house as we . . .   "   5   "

DISSOLVE to studio.

Having analyzed the scenes to be filmed, the producer discusses the action in detail with the cameraman and together they go in search of a suitable location.

2. *Choosing the Location*

The three principal factors in choosing a location are: (1) appropriateness of the setting, (2) lighting conditions, and (3) practicability. For this particular shot it would be better to pick a dead-end street where there is no traffic. Lighting is the important factor. A location should be chosen where the camera can be set up to shoot *across the light or slightly into it.* Shooting with the light gives a flat effect lacking in modeling. Shooting directly into the light is apt to produce shadows that are too dark for television, unless the subject matter is light in value.

In all location work where privately owned property is to be shown, the owner's permission should be obtained. The police department should also be contacted and arrangements made for shooting on streets or public areas.

3. *Location Shooting*

At the time selected for filming, when the light will be right, with the actors and extras present, including properties, the action is roughed in and the equipment set up. The cameraman may find it necessary to use reflectors to throw light into the shadows. These are flat panels covered with aluminum metal leaf and mounted on pedestals. Sunlight reflected from their bright surfaces will lighten up foreground shadows effectively. When shooting more or less into the light, they serve the same purpose as the "front fill" lights used in the studio. They can be constructed in the studio shop.

The producer uses chalk marks or other means to show the actors exactly where they are to stand and the paths of any contemplated movement. The scenes should be rehearsed until they are satisfactory as to camera work and running time. If the cameraman has the slightest doubt about any scene, it should be retaken; a "cover" shot is less expensive than going back on location for a retake.

Before shooting each scene, a "take chart" should be shot in big close-up. This can be either a slate marked with white chalk or a block of paper marked with black crayon. Its purpose is to enable the cutter to identify the scene. It should give the name of the production, the scene number, and the "take." If the cameraman is making an exposure test it is helpful to have this filmed also.

When making a scene where the sound is being recorded at the same time, the practice is to use a "slap-stick." This consists of a hinged upper member of the take chart which makes a slapping noise when brought down sharply. When the scene is to be shot, the order of events is as follows (1) the second cameraman holds the take chart in front of the camera, (2) the director says, "Roll 'em," and when the sound recorder gets up to speed he says, "Camera"; (3) the second cameraman closes the slap-stick, reads what is marked on it, and then walks off the set; (4) the director yells, "Action," and the scene is shot. This makes it possible for the cutter, out of the many pieces of film which literally litter the cutting table, to identify and match up the sound and picture for each scene; he can pick out the picture frame which shows the take chart at the instant it is "slapped" and match it up with this identical point in the sound track.

4. Recording the Sound

If it is desired to record the sound to be used with integrated film, this can be done by the following short-cut method, provided there is no lip-sync dialogue shown in close-up:

In the case at hand the film is put into final form, the action is timed, and the dialogue is written. A sound-effects record of street noises is selected for a background effect. A movie projector is set up in the studio and the film is run for rehearsal of the cast. The sound-effects man is rehearsed in playing the record of street noises until a portion is found that forms a suitable background. With a few rehearsals the cast, watching the action on the screen, can time their dialogue closely enough. The video engineer controls the mixing of the dialogue and the sound effects, and the combined sound is cut on an acetate record. It is then only a matter of cueing in the record at the right instant during the program.

The time and the work involved in recording on film is considerably greater. The negative has to be developed, synchronized, and printed, and for ordinary purposes the cost and effort are hardly justified.

5. Making a Film Loop

Film loops are useful in effecting transitions and as title backgrounds. They can be threaded into a projector and run for as long a time as desired. Only a short length of film is required. In 16mm, a piece about four feet long is sufficient for the ordinary effect.

Suppose a transition is needed for a play in which time is a significant element. The swinging of a clock pendulum is a shopworn device, but it will serve as an example. This is filmed in close-up. The cutter marks a frame in which the pendulum is at its farthest point of travel; he marks another frame about four feet from the first mark showing the pendulum in the same position, and at these points he splices the film together into a continuous loop. When projected, if properly spliced, the pendulum will swing back and forth ad infinitum.

If the sound of the clock's ticking is desired, the sound effects man can provide it. By watching the action on a viewing monitor he can time his strokes. The video engineer can fade the effect in and out. Producers will find many applications for this technique.

PRODUCING THE NEWSREEL AND
SPECIAL EVENTS FILM

The television newsreel constitutes the most extensive application of studio-produced motion pictures. A station producing anything like twenty minutes of newsreel film a day is undertaking a major operation, but at the same time it is probably attracting a sizable viewing audience. People of all ages and classes like pictures—particularly pictures of other people exerting themselves, of people in the limelight, and of people in trouble. The wide circulation of picture tabloids and of "pix mags" (as *Variety* would say) and the attendance at newsreel theaters all testify to the picture-mindedness of the average person.

1. *The Function of the Newsreel*

The function of the newsreel is the *reporting* of events. In its truest form it is not a medium for editorializing. Certainly it should not be used for propaganda, for the motion picture is too powerful a force to be placed indiscriminately in the hands of minority groups.

To present news without some degree of bias is almost an impossibility. Every broadcaster, every newspaper publisher, every news analyst has his own personal beliefs. He will instinctively interpret events and trends in the light of these beliefs. His thinking will be colored, quite unintentionally, by the acts and beliefs of others in the same economic and social strata. Within reasonable limits this spread of thought and action is highly desirable; it often leads to the wise solution of social problems. But when it oversteps the bounds of "the greatest good for the greatest number of people" and becomes an implement of propaganda for the benefit of a few it no longer serves "the best interests of the public."

The radio industry has experienced a considerable amount of rebound of public opinion regarding the presentation of news. Commentators have been accused of bias—of "slanting" the news. The matter has at times been taken before the Federal Communications Commission, and the FCC is much interested in this aspect of radio broadcasting. It therefore behooves the television broadcaster to benefit by this backlog of experience and treat the handling of news with breadth of vision.

The television newsreel, with its dual impact of sight and sound, can be a strong force for good as well as a means of disseminating information. In addition to its more obvious function of reporting sports and local events, it can serve the community by publicizing civic improvements, safety drives, and other worthy causes. In the handling of controversial issues, both sides should be presented. In all news coverage the interests of the public as a whole and the welfare of the local community should be the controlling influences.

2. *The Nature of the Newsreel*

Perhaps the most noticeable characteristic of the newsreel is its vigorous pace. It moves along. Since it is not given to the creation of moods and since there is no plot to be exposed, there is no need for slow pacing.

Then too, the very essence of the newsreel is its visual content, and the eye can take things in quickly—almost at a glance. For this reason the accompanying narrative need not be exhaustive; in fact, it verges on the ridiculous when it overstates what can be clearly seen and completely comprehended.

It is usually the little bits of human interest—the "color" shots—that lift a newsreel above mediocrity. At a fire, for instance, the most moving scenes may be not the shots of belching flames but the look of horror on some bystander's face or a shot of a weeping woman holding some worthless gewgaw she has saved. The cameraman should be on the alert for any bits of human interest that will point up the action.

Since the television newsreel is a potpourri of scattered events, and since the pace should be lively, it is important that the opening shot of each sequence be selected with care. This should clearly establish the "what" and the "where" and should be of sufficient length to allow the audience to become oriented. From then on each sequence should develop rapidly and *build to a climax*. The commentary should be written with these factors in mind. It should bridge the sequences and in the first few words, as each new sequence comes on the screen, should prepare the audience for what is to follow. Subtitles serve as a useful device in effecting transitions between chapters or subdivisions.

3. *Collecting Newsreel Material*

A newsreel crew, if the pick-up is at all complicated, will consist of a producer, a script girl, cameramen, a "grip" or porter, and a spotter or contact man. The producer's job is to run the show and to gather all the information necessary for writing the commentary. He must be able to size up an event and extract its essence with speed and accuracy. He will lay out the pattern of picturization and will disperse the cameramen to their various points of vantage. Through his contact man or scout he will pick up the necessary factual information; in the case of a sporting event this will be the names of players or contestants, who must be identified in the course of the action.

All this information will be taken down by the script girl. The producer at this time may even go so far as to dictate portions of the commentary, since on-the-spot reporting is likely to have more freshness than when written subsequently. All pertinent information should be obtained, because when it comes to writing the commentary there is no telling what will be useful.

The five "W's" of the newspaper business are about the best formula for gathering news: *what* happened; to *whom* it happened; *where, when,* and *why* it happened. If this information is obtained along with an interesting choice of picture material, there is a good chance for the editor to put together a newsreel that will hold the attention of the audience.

In gathering the material on location it should be borne in mind that when the various camera shots are being edited they will be meaningless lengths of film unless they can be identified. For this reason one of the cameras should be used as a *control,* and the script girl should take down all the information pertaining to each scene which is taken by that camera.

The producer and the cameramen should keep in mind that the material they are gathering, perhaps in small bits here and there, must have *continuity* when put together on the cutting table. It should also be remembered that the newsreel calls for action and "color." The picture should carry the story, the narrative adding only those elements which the picture does not make clear or which will create further interest in the picture.

4. *Camerawork*

It is not within the scope of this book to treat the subject of motion-picture photography, but there are a few points which can be touched upon that are of special significance to the television newsreel cameraman.

In order to preserve the essential nature of television, camera work should be intimate. The movie camera, like the television camera, should serve as the eyes of the audience. Most of the shots must of necessity be medium shots or close-ups; otherwise they will not show up well on the screen.

As pointed out in the chapter on Video Techniques, the orientation of the audience should be considered in all camera work. Intercut shots of the same action taken from widely different angles can cause confusion.

Lighting is extremely important. As mentioned on page 188, it is usually best to *shoot across or slightly into the light.* This tends to make objects stand out and separate themselves from what is behind them. It gives modeling and contrast, two qualities essential in a newsreel where clean-cut factual presentation is the vital consideration. The lighting is particularly important where rapid action is involved. Flat lighting is to be avoided in this type of shooting and *the film should be exposed for the half shadows in the important subject matter*. This will give the proper contrast range for television and allow the highlights to burn through while retaining some rich darks.

Newsreel pictures should be composed along *dynamic lines*. This is no place for placid, formal composition. Lineal structures built on strong diagonals and right angles are the best, because these forms have the greatest attraction power. Compositions should be simple and direct. They should be selected with the sole purpose of showing only that which is important to the action or story. They should have vitality and punch. At the same time, the occasional inclusion of a "pretty" shot or an "effect" is desirable, because these are good foils for the action sequences. So too, when appropriately spotted, "crazy angle" shots (made with the camera out of plumb) and "high hat" shots (with the camera close to the ground) are useful for variety.

Needless to say, hand-held-camera shots are to be avoided whenever possible. A heavy tripod is an encumbrance, but it makes steady pictures. In catching human-interest shots, the cameraman is usually more successful if he sets up at some distance from the person being photographed and uses a telephoto lens. This makes it possible to get close-ups without making the subject self-conscious. The equipment, therefore, should include an assortment of lenses, running all the way from the wide-angle type to those of long focal length.

It is probable that some stations will use 16mm film exclusively. If so, the cameras should be provided with motor drives, served by portable 12-volt batteries. A spring-driven camera can be the cause of losing many important bits of action. For the same reason, 200-foot magazines are virtually a necessity.

5. Stills

Although still pictures are static and are not regarded too favorably on television programs, they can be used successfully when skillfully presented. The photographs must have the proper gray scale for television rendition and should not contain much detail. If they are to be used in a sequence it is best to use a dual projection system, in order to get away from the old lantern-slide method of pulling one through after another. With a dual system it is possible to cut, fade, or dissolve from slide to slide.

It is often necessary to include a few stills in a news program to cover items of interest which cannot be presented on motion picture film. If they are to cut into a run of film, the equivalent amount of blank leader can be spliced into the film and the projector will not have to be stopped and started again.

6. *Picture Field Allowance*

In photographing for television there are two factors to be considered in determining the picture field. One is the slight loss in picture size (as seen on the viewfinder) which occurs in the projector gate. The projector manual will give this information. The other is the loss in definition and the distortion around the edge of the picture caused by the curvature of the television tube. The cameraman therefore must make due allowance by taking in a slightly larger field and by not framing too close to any important bit of subject matter.

THE DOCUMENTARY FILM

The documentary film differs from the newsreel in a pronounced way. Whereas the newsreel is purely reportorial in character, the documentary film is *editorial* in the sense that it seeks not only to inform but also to *affect* the audience emotionally and intellectually. The newsreel is content with showing what happened today or yesterday. The documentary is concerned with the social significance of what happened. It is concerned with the *background* of events—what took place in all the yesterdays having a bearing on the subject. It is concerned with the trend of the times and its effect on tomorrow's world.

One of the first truly great documentaries produced in this country, *The River*, written and directed by Pare Lorentz, tells the story of soil erosion with such emphasis and skill that you are moved to feel the social significance of the wasted lands. The story is so gripping that it makes you want to do something personally to prevent a recurrence of such wanton waste of our natural resources. Though made many years ago, before the development of certain modern film techniques, it is worthy of study.

Another distinguished contemporary worker in the documentary medium, who has produced many notable films in all parts of the world, Julien Bryan, president of the International Film Foundation, has this to say:

A document to be genuine, must record indisputable facts. A documentary film, to be true to its name, must present images and sounds which its audience can confidently believe. . . . To give a flow of visual images literal rather than symbolic meaning, we must first decline to use them for advocating anything, and refuse to yield to prejudice or pressure in the selection or omission of certain scenes. . . . Rather, it means filming representative fragments which, taken together, tell the whole story, so far as this is visible. It means photographing those things which all shades of opinion agree are revealing and significant—but for conflicting reasons. . . . Thus the documentary film is the raw stuff of history in the making. Beginning where the news-reel flashes off and the travelogue falters, the documentary film gropes ahead toward recording noteworthy realities on film more expertly and more impartially. It seeks to supplant nothing; yet through its unequalled capacity for bringing facts to life, the documentary film can and does vividly supplement and enrich all other existing media for knowing our troubled and changing world.

Worth-while documentary films are obtainable from many sources and constitute excellent program fare. The medium also falls within the scope of activity available to the television studio having a motion picture unit. Such undertakings must of necessity be kept to simple proportions. However, a clever film producer with a flair for showmanship and a broad knowledge of the business can produce effective documentaries, making use of stock shots, newsreel clips, and material obtainable from film libraries and explorers. As a case in point, a broadcast of "NBC Tele-Scope," in New York, was reported in *Variety* in the following fashion:

NBC television has added another stock feature in its fine news coverage with a new (sic) type of documentary newsreel titled "NBC Tele-Scope." Combined, edited and produced by Edwin S. Mills, the film can be compared favorably with the "March of Time," which it resembles in format . . .

Preem edition, titled "Pall over Palestine," dealt with the question of the Arab-Jewish conflict in that country. . . . Film pointed up in excellent detail the basic reasons for the controversy, quoting the Balfour declaration, alluding to the rich oil deposits . . . and referring to the Arab effendis' reluctance to see the growth of western civilization, as brought in by the Jews, call a halt to their static, feudalistic economy.

By using care in selecting his film shots, Mills was able to maintain some semblance of movement throughout the picture, which is a must for television. Entire production was backed up by a deeply moving score, which included the Jewish national anthem, a cantor reading from the prayer book and a muezzin calling the Mohammedans to pray. Excellent commentary was read in good fashion by Larry Semon.

The technique is subject to considerable variation, including the integration of live talent. It affords an opportunity to add visual and aural interest to a straight discourse by a recognized authority, which, however learned it may be, is apt to be deadly dull if it is ungarnished.

The secret, of course, lies in giving all documentary treatments eye and ear appeal; in bringing movement and flow to the visual continuity; in using music and sound effects for their strong emotional value.

~~~~~~

Chapter X

TELEVISION LIGHTING

TELEVISION originates from and terminates in light. It is light, falling in patterns on the mosaic of the camera tube, that causes the modulated signal. It is light, in recognizable patterns, that forms the picture on the tube of the receiving set. Lighting, in the sense of light control, is one of the major ingredients of television showmanship.

The creation of pictures that will capture and hold the attention of a television audience is a complex problem dealing not only with engineering factors but also with the intangibles of pictorial art and aesthetics. The motion picture industry has conditioned the public to high standards of pictorial excellence. The television audience expects at least an approximation of those standards. Lighting is one of the most important factors in achieving that goal, for the quality of the television picture is largely dependent upon the use and control of light.

Naturally the ordinary program does not call for the full gamut of moods or for the attainment of unusual effects. The simplest television pictures, however, present more complicated problems in lighting than are apparent to the casual observer. They can be solved only with the proper equipment in the hands of someone who understands the principles of lighting and pictorial composition, and in addition has a keen pictorial sense.

THE NATURE OF LIGHT

To understand the principles of lighting it is necessary to understand, at least in an elementary way, the nature of light. One might suppose that any kind of light, provided it is bright enough, would be suitable for television. This is far from the truth, however, for the characteristics of light and the work it will do are subject to wide variation.

When we speak of light we really mean the phenomena which light produces, for even the most advanced physicist cannot tell us what light is, beyond stating that it is a form of energy which at times displays *wave motion* and at other times seems to consist of *tiny particles of energy*. We do know that light travels in straight lines, at the rate of 186,000 miles per second. And we know that light produces color—in fact, that it is made up of color.

1. *Wave Length and Frequency*

The wave theory of light states that the color depends on the *wave length*. In the visible spectrum, red has the longest wave length and violet the shortest. The visible spectrum, however, constitutes only a small segment of the total light band or electromagnetic spectrum. Ultraviolet light, which is invisible, has rays of shorter wave length than has visible violet. At the other end of the visible spectrum, beyond red, we find the infrared (heat) waves, which have longer wave lengths, and beyond these the television and radio waves, which increase in wave length as we move toward the bottom of the spectrum.

The frequency at which light waves vibrate, or, to put it another way, the number of waves which pass a given point in a second, increases as the waves become shorter. The low-frequency television waves currently

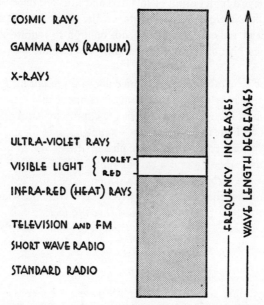

Fig. 28. The Electromagnetic Spectrum. All These Waves Travel at the Same Speed—186,000 Miles per Second.

being used have a higher frequency and shorter wave length than those used in standard radio. Color television waves are still higher in frequency and shorter in wave length. The simplified diagram in Figure 28 shows the approximate relative position of radio, television, and visible light in the spectrum.

Lest it appear that we are exploring territory beyond the boundaries of the subject at hand, we should perhaps state that television lighting is definitely tied in with the characteristics of light energy just referred to as well as with others to be taken up in turn.

2. Color Characteristics

We are concerned with the wave length of light for three main reasons: first, because the wave length determines the color; second, because light sources differ in the amounts of light energy given off in the various color divisions of the spectrum; and, third, because the mosaic of the camera tube is not equally sensitive to all these colors. For example, incandescent lights have a disproportionately high output of red-orange light; hence it is necessary to use strong yellow-red make-up, for otherwise faces have a deathly pallor on the television screen. Incandescent lights also have a high output of infrared and thus are uncomfortably hot to work under. Mercury vapor lights, on the other hand, are lacking in their output of red-orange (though not enough to require much make-up), but they give off little infrared and therefore are pleasant to work under.

It must be remembered that all the colors are present in light. Midday sunlight is nearly white; that is to say, it contains about equal amounts of all the colors. Light from an electric arc approaches sunlight in quality. Late afternoon light is yellow-orange—somewhat like incandescent light. Since the various types of camera pick-up tubes differ in their color sensitivity, and since there is a considerable difference in the light characteristics of the various light sources which can be utilized in television, it is apparent that the tubes must be reconciled with the source of light. In other words, *the gray scale produced on the picture tube depends on the combined characteristics of the camera tube and the type of lights used.*

3. Light Reflection and Absorption

In photographic and television lighting we are concerned principally with *reflected* light. The light emanating from either the sun or an artificial source is reflected from the many surfaces of the subject to the lens of the camera. The amount of light reaching the camera lens depends on two things: (1) the strength of the light source, and (2) the nature or color of the reflecting surface.

Hard surfaces, such as polished metal, absorb little of the light. If the surface is so placed that the *angle of reflection* equals the *angle of incidence,* many of the rays will be reflected directly into the lens, causing glare. Light yellow surfaces reflect more light than dark purple, because less of the light is absorbed. An object appears yellow because all the colors in the light falling on it are absorbed *except yellow.* A dark purple object, therefore, reflects only the dark purple rays, and since these contain less energy than yellow rays the object appears darker.

From this it will be seen that the color and shade of the surfaces being photographed or televised, the strength of the incident light, and the sensitivity of the photographic film or camera tube all have a bearing on lighting. The best results are obtained when a production is planned so as to take all these factors into consideration—when the colors and values used in sets, costumes, and make-up are scaled to fit the lighting and the camera facilities.

LIGHT MEASUREMENT

The familiar photographic exposure meter is the device most commonly used in measuring the strength of light. It contains a photoelectric cell capable of generating a weak electric current which varies in proportion to the strength of the light falling on it. In this sense it resembles one of the minute droplets on the mosaic of the television camera tube.

Most exposure meters are calibrated in foot candles. The *foot candle* unit of measurement is the amount of light "falling on a surface everywhere one foot away from a standardized light source." This source is called the *international candle,* and is the amount of light emitted by five square millimeters of platinum at the point of solidification.

There is barely enough light for reading ordinary print without eyestrain at a level of five foot candles. The image orthicon tube, however, can pick up a good picture at this level, whereas the iconoscope requires a "foundation" light level of 400 to 800 foot candles.

1. How to Use the Exposure Meter

Photoelectric exposure meters differ somewhat in the various makes, but their performance is sufficiently similar for us to speak in inclusive terms. Not all of them, however, cover a sufficient range of foot candles to be useful in television. For outdoor use any of the accepted makes are satisfactory, since they are designed for the range of reflected light encountered in out-of-door photography. But for use in the television studio certain types are not capable of reading the direct or *incident* light from a light source. Even then it may be necessary to obtain a calibrated mask from the manufacturer to cut down on the area of the photosensitive surface, so as to be able to make incident readings at the higher levels normally used in lighting a set.

For studio work, therefore, only those meters which read directly in foot candles should be used, and they should cover a range of 0 to 1500 foot candles. Furthermore, they should be checked periodically for accuracy.

An exposure meter will give misleading measurements if it is used improperly or if its function is not thoroughly understood. It is not a selective device, hence *it must be used selectively.* That is to say, the readings taken must be made in *selected areas* of the subject, rather than used for a general reading of the entire picture field.

An exposure meter has a definite angle of vision, which varies in the different makes. This angle and the distance away from the subject determine the field of coverage. An over-all reading of the entire picture field does not give particularly useful information, for the reason that we are really concerned not with the average light but with the light on the *important parts of the picture.* Individual readings, therefore, should be taken of the important areas, in order that the lighting can be balanced to give good gray-scale rendition to each of those areas.

Taking a simple example, if the shot is a head-and-bust close-up of a person, separate readings should be taken of (1) the highest modeling light on the face, (2) the half light, (3) the shoulders and bust, and (4) the background. With this information, and with allowances for the color and values of the skin, hair, costume, and background, a proper balance of light on each can be achieved. It is not to be inferred that this procedure is necessary in setting each close-up, though it is advisable in the case of announce spots and important speakers. The example is cited to bring out the point that an over-all reading of this subject would not give the needed information, which is *the range of gray-scale values.*

In taking light readings on a full set the problem is much more complex than in the foregoing example. Here the readings must be taken in zones or playing areas. But before discussing this in detail we shall describe the two principal methods of using the exposure meter.

a. Reflected Light Method

The first and most commonly used method is to read *reflected* light. This is done by pointing the meter toward the subject. When used in this way it should be held close to the surface being measured, in order to exclude all other light. A good rule to follow is to hold the meter away from the subject at a distance which is slightly less than the width of the area being measured.

This is the accepted method for out-of-door work. Here the light itself cannot be controlled (except to a minor degree by the use of reflectors and the like). In outdoor work, light control is achieved by adjustment of the camera diaphragm.

Light readings should be taken of the important areas of full light, half light, and shadow. The meter should be held close to those areas. The cameraman should then decide how dark he wishes the principal shadows to be on the screen and set the lens diaphragm accordingly. If the subject is lit by strong sunlight and is light in color, the diaphragm can be "stopped down." If the light is weak and/or if the subject is dark, the lens diaphragm must be opened wider.

The reflected light method can also be used to advantage in the studio for lighting special close-ups where careful control of detail and tonal values is essential.

b. Incident Light Method

The second method is not as generally understood, but it has been adopted by many experts in photographic lighting because of its adaptability to the complex problems of lighting a full set. In this method, readings are taken of the *incident light*. It is done by pointing the meter *directly toward each light source*. The advantage of this method over reading the reflected light from many surfaces is twofold: first, it goes directly to the heart of the problem, the intensity of light falling on the various surfaces; second, the readings are more accurate. A highly experienced person can take fairly consistent reflected light readings, but it is necessary to make allowances for the reflection characteristics of the surface, and the average person will get more consistent results by working from incident light readings.

The incident light method proceeds from two established experience factors: (1) knowing the strength of light which must fall on the subject, and (2) the directions from which the light must come to produce the desired pictorial effect. The lighting director uses the following procedure: He first analyzes the scene and decides on the *scheme* of lighting; he knows from experience the maximum and minimum light levels that are required by the particular camera tube being used and staying within these known limits he measures and adjusts the amount of light coming from the directions specified in the lighting scheme. With this method he is working directly with controllable factors—the relative amount of light supplied by each source and the directional pattern.

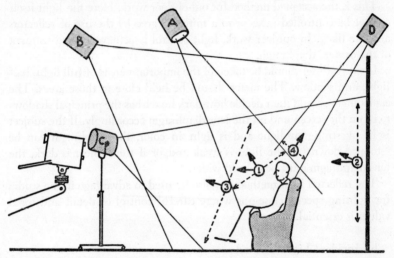

FIG. 29. THE INCIDENT LIGHT METHOD OF MEASUREMENT.

A typical example is shown in Figure 29. The lights indicated should be regarded merely as symbols representing any suitable type of light source. Furthermore, we shall consider at the moment only the *measurement* of light.

Having decided the level of light and the amount of contrast best suited to the action and mood of the scene, and with all lights off, turn on the modeling or *key* light (A). Point the exposure meter directly toward the light at Zone 1, moving it throughout the desired field of coverage. When the light has been brought to the proper intensity, turn it out and follow the same procedure with the *foundation* lights (B), taking meter readings in Zone 2. Now turn on the *front fill* light or lights (C) and measure in Zone 3. Leaving this light on, turn on (A) and (B), and measure the light again at Zone 1 to determine if the combined lighting is satisfactory. By holding the meter just in front of the face of the subject (or where it is to be) and directing the meter first toward the modeling light and then toward the camera, the range or ratio of front fill to key light can be ascertained. Finally, with all these lights on, "hit" the rimming light (D) and measure in Zone 4.

With this system, provided records are kept of satisfactory light patterns for all types of scenes, the lighting director has only to follow the same procedure in lighting the ordinary set. Naturally the exposure meter must be able to read the strongest light beam. In some instances this may go as high as 1500 foot candles if a camera tube of the iconoscope range of sensitivity is used.

LIGHTING TECHNIQUES

Television lighting is limited by a number of conditions inherent in the medium. It is essential that these factors be recognized in order that the lighting techniques used may stay within the limitations yet take full advantage of all the possibilities.

1. Limiting Factors

a) *Continuous production.* Since the production cannot be stopped to make lighting adjustments, it is necessary to accept many improperly lit passages. Although it is possible adequately to light a stationary subject such as an announcer or a harpist, or a sponsor's product, it is often a physical impossibility to maintain good lighting throughout a scene in which players are moving about the set. The correct lighting set-ups for a long shot and for a satisfactory close-up are dissimilar, yet we must cut from one to the other. Players assume all sorts of postures and turn in all directions with respect to the light, and yet we must often catch them in close-up under unfavorable lighting.

b) *Characteristics of the pick-up tube.* The camera tube is capable of only limited gray-scale rendition, and its color response in terms of gray scale values is quite different from that of the human eye. In addition there is a considerable disparity between the color response of the camera tube and the color emission of the artificial light sources available. Consequently the black-and-white television picture reproduces some of the colors in unnatural gray values. Red, for instance, which the human eye normally sees as middle gray, becomes almost white when picked up by the iconoscope under tungsten light. Green becomes dark gray, though the eye normally sees it near the middle of the gray scale.

c) *Costs.* Economic considerations have slowed certain possible solutions of the lighting problem. However, a method of centralized spotlight control is available. This is a method of control over fifty spotlights in a group from a common movable pedestal from which it is possible to select any one of the fifty for control in the following: (1) to switch on and off; (2) to raise and lower; (3) to spot or flood; (4) to pan 360°; (5) to tilt 180°. The development and installation of this equipment was aimed at an important economy in time and money. There is a period when the producer, director and performer-talent meet in the studio with the myriad technicians and their tools—electronic, electrical, and scenic—for the purpose of achieving that blend in finished product which is necessary to high rating, sponsor approval, and viewer acceptance. Costs during this critical period run high. The ability to set, reset, focus, or trim lighting equipment without stopping rehearsals or interfering with any other activity in the studio is a major step in the direction of efficiency and economy. This kind of efficiency results in freeing personnel from preoccupation with equipment, for the more important and satisfying creative efforts of producing quality programs.

d) *Floor space.* Because of the necessity of providing free and unrestricted movement of the cameras, the number of floor lights which can be used is limited and their placement is hampered.

Automation must enter the area of television production. Specifically, the remote control camera and the remotely controlled lighting equipments mentioned can join hands so that when television tape is perfected, the pressure of producing against the little red hand on the clock should be eliminated for all scripted programming. This should result in the ability of the producer and director to set up a shot and light it, position the camera and the lights remotely, and having pleased themselves as well as the designer, audio, and video man, place a card in the machine and punch the master button. From that time, whenever the card is placed into the activating mechanism, the camera and lights will respond to the preset positions, thereby taking the guess work out of fine lighting relating to a specific camera position in a given scene.

2. *Basic Principles.*

Lighting fulfils three main functions: (1) providing adequate illumination so that the subject may be clearly and completely *seen;* (2)

illuminating the subject in such a way that certain attributes of the subject will be *felt;* and (3) localizing the illumination to bring out particular portions of the scene. There are other minor functions, but these are the ones which largely govern television lighting schemes.

Lighting a subject so that it can be clearly seen, either completely or with the light focalized on certain parts, is entirely a matter of applying *engineering* principles. Lighting which causes the viewer to respond emotionally toward the subject involves the application of the principles of *aesthetics.* The lighting director, therefore, must be dually equipped: he must thoroughly understand the physical characteristics of light and the mechanics of handling it, and at the same time he must be emotionally responsive, sensitive to subtle nuances, and endowed with artistic taste.

Even the most factual picture should be interesting, and it can usually be made so with good lighting if it is imaginatively handled. Often a commonplace subject can be made into a charming picture merely through the control and use of light. The elements of control and the aesthetic factors used in achieving effective lighting may be summarized as follows: (a) levels of illumination, (b) zones of illumination, (c) pattern of light and and shadow, (d) range of contrast, (e) lighting of edges, (f) texture, and (g) gradation.

a. Levels of Illumination

The sensitivity of the camera tube determines the levels of light intensity that can be used. The tube most widely used at the present is the image orthicon, and since this is the only one on which sufficient performance records have been accumulated we must restrict our study of lighting technique to its characteristics.

As camera tubes of higher sensitivity are made available the levels of illumination can be lowered, though some of this drop will be absorbed by stopping down the lenses to get increased depth of focus. However, the methods of lighting, the positioning of lights, and the use of light will be altered very little by "faster" tubes.

The image orthicon requires an average basic level of 100 foot candles with the lenses opened up to f 3.5. This is purely an engineering consideration. It is a simple matter to build up this amount of light, but interesting pictorial effects cannot be produced by lighting all portions of a set at the same level. The resultant picture will be flat, the faces of the players will lack modeling, and the visual separation of one object from another will depend entirely on their gray-scale values. If, on the other hand, the light intensities used throughout the set extend over a range, let us say, of from 75-300 foot candles, pictures of pleasing quality can be obtained. If the lights are properly placed, the faces will have modeling and the attention can be focused wherever desired. Furthermore, with this range of light intensity, sufficient scope is provided for the electronic "shading" of the signal, so as to produce pictures which have sparkle and extend over the full range of the gray-scale values obtainable in television.

Since the requirements vary, no fixed rules can be laid down as to the range of intensities, but *a range of one to three may be taken as a satisfactory guide in lighting the average set*. Of course the nature of the program and the gray-scale values used in costumes, properties, and set decorations are the controlling factors here. The lighting equipment should be capable of supplying controlled light (1) from any desired direction, (2) at any desired intensity, and (3) in whatever zones are required.

Taking the example previously used in describing the incident method of light measurement, let us consider how these lights may be balanced to produce an interesting range of gray values and a proper separation of objects. (See Figure 30.)

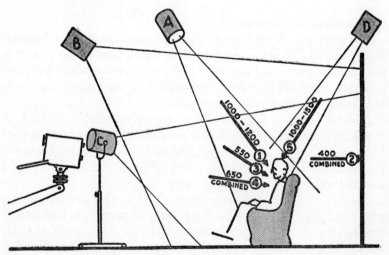

FIG. 30. RANGE OF LIGHT INTENSITIES IN FOOT CANDLES REQUIRED TO PRODUCE MODELING AND SPARKLE IN A TYPICAL SCENE.

The *key* light (A) in this case has been focused so that 1000 to 1200 foot candles (depending on conditions) are falling on the face of the subject, at an angle of approximately forty-five degrees. This light is hung from a point on stage right about forty-five degrees off the line of the camera. In this position the face is given good (standard) modeling. The *foundation* lights (B) are set at 550 foot candles in Zone 3. Two floor lights (C) are used for *front fill*, bringing the front level up to 650. Assuming these to be flood lights (not controlled beam type), the one on stage right is set farther back from the subject, because the key light is on that side of the face. The other floor light on stage left is set somewhat nearer so as to put sufficient half light on that side of the face.

The lights should be moved around and adjusted as to relative intensity until the desired modeling is achieved and a pleasing range of gray values has been produced. With all lights on, the light levels at Zones 2 and 4 will have been raised somewhat above the individual light readings. The combined lighting of 400 foot candles at the rear wall of the set (Zone 2) and of 650 at Zone 4 produces a satisfactory ratio between foreground and background light; it will separate the subject from its background unless it should happen that their relative gray values cause them to merge.

In such an event the *rimming* light (D) may be used to good advantage. If the subject has black or very dark hair and the local color of the background produces a light gray, it is possible that there will be adequate separation. But if the hair is light it may merge into the background to such an extent that the shape of the head will be lost. By *rimming* the head with strong light from behind, the edges of the whole contour—hair, shoulders, and the hands in gesturing—will sparkle with light and stay in the foreground plane. Rimming will also add sparkle to a dark-haired subject.

This is only one of many possible lighting schemes which might conceivably be used for the same subject. The purpose in outlining it has been to show how pictorial interest may be created by the use of varied levels of illumination. To summarize the results: (1) the focus of attention is localized on the principal subject by modeling it with a *key light* whose intensity is at a three-to-one ratio with the background; (2) a two-to-one ratio of key light to *front fill* gives a pleasing balance of contrast between modeling light, the half light on the face, and the shadows in the eye sockets and under the jaw ; (3) a one-and-one-half-to-one ratio of foreground to background lighting gives separation; and

(4) the 1500 foot candle level of the rimming light gives sparkle to the contours. It should be noted that if the ratio of key light to front fill is increased, let us say, to four-to-one, more artistic or dramatic effects can be created.

It is impossible to lay down fixed lighting formulae. Each scene has its own special requirements. However, the above set of ratios with minor variations may be used as a guide in lighting the average television set. The *ratios will remain approximately the same* regardless of the sensitivity of the camera tube.

Due allowance must always be made for the gray-scale value of the background, for this controls its level of illumination. To a large extent it also controls the levels throughout the set. If the background is too light or too dark, or if the reflective characteristics of the surface are not right, good lighting cannot be achieved. Here again no formulae can be laid down, because the type of lighting and the camera equipment used introduce unpredictable variables. It is important that the lighting director and the scenic artist get together and work out background standards, for the purpose of determining the proper colors, values, textures, and reflection characteristics to meet the conditions in their particular studio.

b. Zones of Illumination

In the foregoing example we were dealing with a relatively simple problem—a foreground subject remaining in a fixed position. We shall now consider lighting a set in which there are a number of actors or performers moving about. Here we shall establish *zones* of illumination. In some cases these zones or fields of light will be fixed and the players will be directed to work within them. In others, such as dance programs, the zones of light will *follow* the moving figures.

A simple solution would be to pile enough light onto the set, mostly from the front and top, so that no matter where a performer happened to be there would be enough light for him to be seen. This can be accomplished, with relatively little effort on the part of the production staff, by *floodlighting* the set with a sufficient number of lights hung from the ceiling and on floor pedestals. By careful control of gray-scale values in make-up, costumes, properties, and backgrounds it is possible to achieve passable results with such a system. But this kind of lighting lacks distinction and completely disregards the element of showmanship.

In the previous example the foundation lights (B) and even the front fill lights can be of the floodlight type, but the others must be of the *controlled beam type* to accomplish their purpose, for with lights of this type it is possible to *localize* the light and *control the area* covered. This feature is even more important in the case we shall now consider.

Figure 31 represents the floor plan of a set in which there is a considerable amount of movement. We shall assume that the producer has organized this movement by establishing a number of playing areas where the principal medium shots and close-ups can be picked up to good advantage.

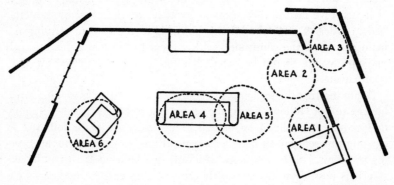

FIG. 31. FLOOR PLAN SHOWING PLAYING AREAS PLANNED TO COINCIDE WITH FIELDS OF KEY LIGHT.

The first scene occurs in Area 1 and involves a character seated at a desk near a window. He rises when a visitor is announced and moves to Area 2. Here he and the visitor play a scene and then move to Area 4, seating themselves on the davenport. A third character enters and dialogue occurs in Area 5; some of the figures are seated and others are standing. One of them crosses and sits in Area 6. From time to time one of the characters moves nervously from place to place, and it is important to show the pieces of business that occur as he moves about. The action takes place in late afternoon, and it is desired to give the illusion of sunlight streaming through the large window on stage right. The nature of the piece is gay and sprightly and calls for high-keyed, edgy lighting.

The first step is to build up the foundation lighting for the entire set. The three walls should be brought up to light levels that will form the proper background for the actors. As shown on page 208, a level of 400 foot candles on the walls and 650 of "front fill" on the faces in the play-ing areas will give good separation. Up to this point the lighting can be satisfactorily built up with floodlight units. But, for the balance of the work, spotlights are required which throw a beam that can be fo-cused, so as to control the intensity and field of light in the several play-ing areas.

In Figure 32, for clarity and simplicity only the modeling, rimming, and accessory lights are shown. The spotlights marked "S" are either hung on battens or, better still, operated from catwalks. The dotted areas represent the aproximate field of coverage of each light or pair of lights. Five medium-shot camera positions are indicated by the letter "C" in order to show the relative positions of the camera carrying the main thread of the continuity, with respect to the key lights for each playing area. It should be noted that the locations indicated are only approximate.

Assuming that the station is not equipped with catwalks making possi-ble the use of "follow" lights, the set-up first to be described will apply to "pre-set" lights hung on battens. The procedure to be followed in lighting this set may be taken as a general guide in practically all light-ing problems. It is best to work with only one light on at a time. In this way it is possible to determine the direction, intensity, and exact field of each light. This is particularly important in the setting of spotlights for modeling and rimming. Ordinarily it is advisable to build up the foundation lighting first; next to set the key or modeling lights one at a time, with the foundation lights off; finally, to do the same thing with the rimming lights. Sometimes, as in the case of a fixed subject, it is best to start with the key light, but the *order* is not so important as the taking of each light *individually*.

Light S-1 is set to cover the figure seated at the desk in Area 1. A num-ber of factors are involved in the positioning and setting of this light: (1) the action takes place in daylight, and the key light coming as it does from the direction indicated will give the illusion of light coming through the window; (2) it must be adjusted so that no light spills on the wall or hits too strongly on the top of the desk (lights of this type are provided with "barn doors" or flaps which can be adjusted to mask off parts of the beam); (3) if S-1 is in this position with respect to S-2, when the actor rises, his head will come into the field of S-2 as he moves upstage to Area 2.

S-2 covers the action in Area 2, where the second player makes his

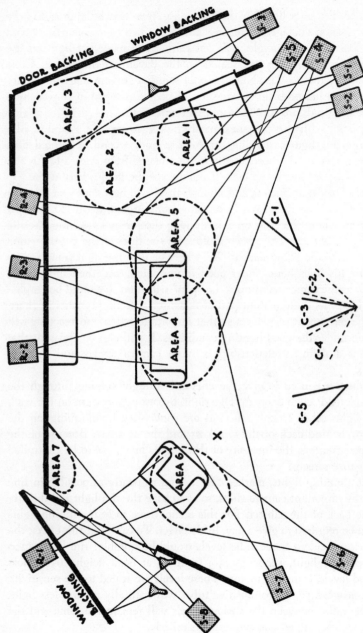

Fig. 32. Key and Rim Lighting of Playing Areas for a Typical Gay Comedy on a Twenty-five Foot Set, Using Pre-set Spotlights.

entrance. S-3 puts light on the player in Area 3 as he approaches the archway from offstage. Lights S-4 and S-7, since they come from both directions at a wide angle, will put fairly good modeling light on the two figures when they are seated on the davenport in Area 4. Cross lighting, by the way, is about the only solution (except flat front light) of the television problem of two-shots of people engaged in conversation where the heads are turned in opposite directions.

S-5 is set with two purposes in mind: first, to provide a field of illumination for figures standing in Area 5; and, second, a lighted area through which the players can move in crossing from Area 2 to Area 4. Two lights will be needed here if the area of the field is very wide.

Light S-6 covers Area 6, and, though there will be a dark spot through which the player must pass in crossing from Area 5, it can be handled either by taking the cross on a fairly long shot or in something like the following manner: The player crosses, on the lines of the person seated in Area 4, to the point marked "X," where he is in the light from S-7; he delivers his lines here, under good illumination, and then moves into Area 6 as the camera continues the "pan" with him. It should be emphasized here that an important part of television directing consists in charting the movement of players so that important action and reaction will be seen under the good lighting conditions. It will also be apparent that there is a definite relationship between camera angles and lighting angles.

Light S-8 is used to give the effect of sunlight coming through the small-paned French doors upstage right, by casting a pattern on the wall. Strip lights set in trough reflectors are convenient for illuminating the backing behind each of the windows and the archway. Because of the cramped quarters, the intensity of these lights may have to be controlled with gauze screens.

The rimming lights, marked "R," are set as nearly as possible in line with the important camera shots, so as to have the rim light fall directly on the back of the subject. For this scene, three to four running lights would be required to give a gay, lively effect. To carry out this effect, the following incident foot-candle levels would be suitable: rim light, 1200 to 1500; key light, 1000 to 1250; front fill at head height, 650; background levels, from 350 to 500. These levels are scaled to the sensitivity of the iconoscope. More sensitive tubes will naturally require less light, but the ratios between the various levels will remain the same and the lights will be angled and positioned similarly.

In dance programs and particularly in audience participation shows, follow spots from overhead or the auditorium are especially advantageous.

With this form of key lighting, care must be exercised not to throw a noticeable spot of light on one of the walls. It is sometimes difficult to angle the light to avoid this, particularly if the action takes place upstage close to the back wall (a condition that should be avoided if possible). There are times, however, when the action cannot be kept away from the set walls, and the best solution is to parallel the wall with the light beam and regulate the barn doors so as to keep the light off the wall. A "gobo" (a piece of cardboard or metal) is occasionally needed to mask part of a beam of light.

It is also necessary with this type of lighting to avoid the use of too high values in properties and costumes. Since the whole purpose of this system is to focus the attention on the faces of the players or on some important object, there should be no disturbing competition. Upholstery should not be too light. Instead of white paper, white tablecloths, or white bedding, *off-white* (ecru, *café au lait*, or light blue) should always be used.

c. Pattern of Light and Shadow

Another factor which has a definite bearing on lighting effects is the *pattern* of light and shadow that is created by the lights. The key lighting just described is only one of a number of schemes which may be used to achieve modeling. This particular method of bringing the key light in at an angle of approximately forty-five degrees with the horizontal plane and at about the same angle with the camera produces a standard form of modeling that happens to fit a large number of situations.

This scheme of lighting presents broad patterns of light to the camera. The opposite and more dramatic effect is produced by moving the key lights upstage and having the modeling light fall on the subject at ninety degrees or more off the line of the camera. If the front fill level is lowered at the same time, a very dramatic effect is created. With this scheme, broader shadow areas face the camera and the pattern of light will flow along the edges. Certain dance routines lend themselves to this treatment; in fact, the dancing figure may be cited as an excellent example of the use of light-and-shade pattern.

Our enjoyment of the dance is derived largely from the pleasure induced by *line* and *lines of movement*. If the lighting develops and accentuates line, therefore, our enjoyment is increased—that is, in certain types of dances. Strong side lighting and back lighting which casts shadows on the floor toward the camera are schemes which produce distinctive effects. Silhouette lighting is useful at times. Interesting effects can be created by the *manipulation* of light during a dance routine—for example, by having strong key light alternate from different directions by turning lights off and on in rhythm with the dance.

In black-and-white television the *patterns of light* produced by the key lights determine, to a large extent, not only the clarity of the important subject matter, but the enjoyment of looking at it.

d. Range of Contrast

The range of contrasts attainable in television is determined by the characteristics of the pick-up tube. White "blooms" and black cause edge flare. Sharply defined, brilliant whites and rich blacks cannot be produced. The lighting director must therefore work within the range of medium high light to medium low dark.

The contrast quality of the picture that is *broadcast* will be the result not only of the lighting effects produced on the set but also of the skill of the engineer in the control room who "shades" the picture; for poor shading can ruin a good effect. Finally, the quality of the picture on the home receiver will depend on the skill of the person who adjusts the set.

The control of contrasts is one of the means to that end. If contrast in pleasing measure is lacking in the lighting, if the lighting is flat, the only contrasts in the picture will be produced by the gray scale of the subject matter and the pictures will resemble newspaper comic strips.

The viewer's emotional response to pictures is affected to a considerable extent by degrees of contrast and contrast range. If the picture is keyed high but also contains a few vigorous darks set against areas of light, the effect will be gay and lively. A low-keyed picture with strong contrasting lights will evoke dramatic suspense. For this reason the contrast range in a given scene should be scaled to the intent or emotional content. *Contrast range can be regulated by the direction and angle of the key lighting and by the levels of light intensity.*

e. The Lighting of Edges

Much of the eyestrain in viewing a television screen results from the effect of separating the important subject matter from its surroundings and its background. The solution of this condition is often a matter of lighting the edges of the subject properly. We have already seen how it is possible to separate a light-haired person from a background that tends to merge by the use of strong back lighting which puts a sparkle of light along the edge. Often this is the only way that separation can be achieved. Hence no lighting system is adequate that does not make it possible to use rimming lights.

Side lighting is also useful in developing edges. Interesting effects are obtained by the use of one strong light from the side and a soft fill light from the opposite side. This develops one light edge (lighter than the background) and a shadow edge that separates from the background because it is darker.

In lighting a set where there is a considerable amount of movement, edge lighting by means of follow lights is usually indicated, not only because it improves separation but also because of the added picture quality. In fact, it may be stated without exaggeration that *back lighting skillfully handled is the final essential ingredient in good television lighting.*

f. Texture

Surface texture is often an object's most important visual feature. In the case of a manufactured product, the sponsor will most certainly be critical of the development of texture—or the lack of it. Because of the limited resolving power of the television tube, it is impossible to bring out anything but fairly coarse texture. But under the proper lighting a certain amount of texture can be developed in a big close-up. If, however, the surface is highly reflective, it will be necessary to "kill" the reflection by spraying the surface with liquid wax or by treating it in some way to give a matte effect.

The angle at which light strikes a surface is the controlling factor in producing texture. Back lighting or cross lighting are needed to produce the shadows which bring out the textural qualities of the surface. The front light ratio must be carefully controlled so as not to cancel out these shadows.

g. Gradation

The gradation of gray-scale values in a picture is analogous to the crescendo and diminuendo in music. A flat tone in pictorial areas is as monotonous as a musical passage which lacks variation.

A plain background can be made interesting by lighting it so that there is gradation in tone. This is a refinement that is often overlooked, but it adds a touch of distinction, and the lighting director who is content with nothing short of perfection will devote as much attention to the rise and fall of tone passages as does the conductor of a symphony.

3. *Lighting Control*

In the foregoing résumé of the basic control elements by which lighting effects are achieved we have touched upon a number of specific lighting schemes and have also outlined the principal aesthetic factors involved in all lighting problems. The application of these basic principles is subject to limitless variation, depending upon the physical and aesthetic requirements of each scene.

The lighting director, in co-operation with the producer, should analyze each problem to determine how their separate functions can be co-ordinated. Neither the lighting scheme nor the direction of the players can be considered without regard for the problems which are involved in each and without adjusting one to the other. The movement and positioning of the players must be adapted to the limitations and potentialities of the lighting system.

This means that *the producer must direct the performers in playing to the lights* as well as to the cameras. The talent should be schooled to avoid casting shadows on each other (a common occurrence) and to assume favorable positions with regard to the key lighting. In many instances this will require a *light rehearsal* as part of the technical rehearsal when the cast is first brought before the cameras. Stand-ins can be used for polishing off the lighting after the action is definitely established.

During the camera rehearsal the lighting director should mark all light cues on his copy of the production script. How he will control the lighting and where he will operate will depend upon the design of the studio. However, he can produce showman-like results only by operating from the control room, where he can see the camera monitors and check the lighting effects as they appear on the picture tubes. He should be provided with talk-back equipment enabling him to direct his light men in the studio through headphones, and he should be stationed at a desk so placed that he has a good view of the monitors and the studio. This desk should house the switches for the lighting circuits, and his cue sheet should indicate when to turn lights on and off. By turning lights off when they are not needed a considerable amount of power can be saved and—of equal importance—the temperature on the sets can be lowered.

LIGHTING SYSTEMS

No one type of light now on the market provides the answer to all television lighting problems. Dollars and energies are being expended on producing the ideal system which would meet the following requirements:

(a) High selectivity and flexibility capable of producing a wide variety of moods and effects.

(b) A sufficient number of lights of the floodlight or combination floodlight and spotlight type, so placed and so accessible that the foundation lighting can be built up under conditions of control—these lights to be hung from overhead battens or catwalks.

(c) A sufficient number of soft-edged spotlights, equipped with barndoors and screen holders, hung from stationary and traveling catwalks or from beams so that they are readily accessible, easily directed at any desired angle, and operated manually as follow lights when desired—these lights to be used for modeling, cross lighting, and back lighting.

(d) Accessory units of various types for lighting cycloramas, backgrounds, merchandise, and title-gadget and visual-effect set-ups.

(e) Remote control from a light director's desk in the control room, equipped with talk back into the studio and switches for all lighting circuits; a multiplicity of circuits so as to provide flexibility of control, with dimming potential in all circuits.

(f) Grid gray-scale rendition of colors to compensate for any inequalities of the pick-up tube.

g) No equipment to be floor borne.

(h) Maximum comfort for talent and staff as regards heat and glare.

(i) High operating efficiency and reasonable operating costs, with a minimum of interruption to production from servicing the lights.

A basic system including complete remote control is obtainable today through the Century Lighting Company, New York City. This particular system is so designed as to accept seventeen messages from the control panel to the specific lighting units, is over-designed to be able to include up to fifty-two messages, later functions being possible of addition. The determining factor in the widespread use of this kind of equipment will be the standard of showmanship which the broadcaster wishes to achieve. If he is content with mediocre results, it is only necessary to flood the set with "plenty" of light, and a system can be installed quite inexpensively. But if normal standards of excellence, characteristic of the field broadly referred to as "show business" are to be achieved, the lighting system will be expensive to install and will require an operating budget commensurate with the results; economy of studio operation and excellence of lighting values.

Lighting sources suitable for use in television fall into three general categories: (1) incandescent, (2) fluorescent, and (3) carbon arc.

1. *Incandescent Light*

The light energy from incandescent lamps is disproportionately high in the red-yellow end of the spectrum. With incandescent light, the red and orange in properties and costumes is translated into unnaturally light grays. Photographic filters will correct the balance somewhat, but the "factor" is so high for these filters that the light intensity must be raised to an excessive degree.

The efficiency of incandescents is low, because most of the energy goes into heat. Lamps in the higher wattages have a short life and must be replaced frequently, especially when used in enclosed mountings such as spotlights. This is often due to softening and distortion of the glass brought about by uneven heat when the light is tilted down at a sharp angle. To avoid having lamps go out during a performance they should be inspected daily, and any lamp showing bad bulges or one over its rated hours of life should be replaced.

In spite of the many objectionable features of incandescents, they are extensively used in television lighting. The following types may be used to fulfill specific requirements:

a. Birdseyes

This type of lighting unit possesses the unique feature of having a self-contained reflector which throws a floodlight. They are obtainable in wattages of 150, 300, 500, and 1000. The efficiency is low and an excessive amount of heat is given off. Yet, because they are light and easy to use, some television stations have used them exclusively. The Birdseyes are arranged in banks hung from the ceiling (remotely controlled for rotation and tilt) and mounted on floor pedestals. They are capable of supplying sufficient over-all light, but they are totally inadequate in modeling and selective lighting since there is no means of controlling the beam.

As accessory units, however, Birdseyes are useful, particularly in the middle or lower wattages. Arranged in banks of four or six or in strips, they are adptable for lighting small cycloramas, backdrops, and areas where space is restricted and a lightweight fixture is needed. They can also be used for footlights in banks and strips. When not housed in metal the birdseye lamp is an extremely dangerous piece of equipment since any contact with wood or metal brings down a shower of glass upon the performer.

b. Floodlights

Incandescent floodlights utilizing 750-, 1000-, 1500-, or 2000-watt Mazda lamps deliver a fairly satisfactory foundation light. Their efficiency is higher than Birdseyes and their color response is better (bulbs may be purchased having various Kelvin ratings). They are mounted in reflector housings which can be hung from overhead battens or catwalks, or they may be set in floor pedestals. The spread of the beam and the intensities at useful distances vary somewhat with the different makes; it is advisable, therefore, to investigate the market and select the product which meets the requirements of the particular application. Special hanging structures can be devised for rotating and tilting groups of these lights by remote control.

Since floodlights cannot be focused, they are incapable of providing selective modeling or localized zones of key light in large playing areas. Even in a small set, such as a single figure or the display of a product, the usefulness of this type of light does not extend beyond supplying foundation light, on account of the excessive amount of "spill" caused by the wide angle of divergence, usually in the vicinity of 120 degrees.

c. Spotlights

Incandescent spots, obtainable in wattages from 500 to 5000, use Mazda globes. These units are fully enclosed and are equipped with a lens and a focusing mechanism. The lens most commonly used is of the Fresnel type and, if properly designed, will throw a beam of light which is uniformly intense in the center of the field over a useful area, vignetting to a soft edge. This last characteristic is important, and since some makes produce hard-edged, uneven beams it is advisable to investigate thoroughly before purchasing.

The spotlight beam can be regulated over a considerable range of divergence—from something like 20 to 80 degrees. Here again there is a wide difference in the performance of the various makes, some of them giving uneven distribution as the angle of the beam is increased. Certain makes are improperly ventilated, and this results in short lamp life. Hence spotlights should be purchased on the basis of performance rather than of first cost.

Spotlights should be provided with lugs for mounting the shutters (commonly called barn doors) which are used to mask and regulate the field of light, and also for mounting diffusers for softening the beam and cutting down on glare. The spotlights may be hung from battens, mounted on catwalk brackets or supported by floor pedestals. Their weight (5 k.w. spots will run to about 100 pounds including the pedestal) makes them unsuitable for floor use, except in special applications. Furthermore, the glare of spots is objectionable, though it can be reduced with a diffuser.

The virtue of the spotlight for overhead use is the controllability of the beam, both in area of field and in intensity. Hence it is a useful tool in creating controlled key lighting and in modeling, cross lighting, back lighting, and rimming.

d. Incandescent Color Temperatures

Reference has already been made to the fact that light sources vary as to color characteristics. Lord Kelvin discovered that the color emission from a heated light source varies with the temperature. From this a standardized color temperature scale has been established which makes it possible to rate lighting units according to their color output. Mazda lamps manufactured for the motion picture studios, for black-and-white-photography, have a color temperature of 3250° Kelvin; they are listed under the trade symbol "MP." For color work, lamps of 3380° Kelvin are used because they have a better color response; these are listed under the symbol "CP" and are better for television use because of the improved color rendition, though they are more expensive.

As a matter of comparison, the high-intensity arcs used in technicolor photography have a color temperature of 6400° Kelvin and produce a light that closely resembles sunlight at sea level. This kind of light is ideal for television, and the carbon arc would be the answer were it not for other considerations which will be discussed later.

2. *Fluorescent Light*

The fluorescent light is used extensively, especially by stations with small studios. The color temperature is at 6400° Kelvin. However, the energy output of fluorescence is so low per unit that a large number of units have to be used to build up the required level. Where the fluorescent is interspersed with incandescents in small areas an extremely high intensity fill is accomplished.

The fluorescent is a long-lived lamp and recent developments have placed a dimming device for these lamps on the market.

The fluorescent is comparatively free of glare, has a low heat output, approximates daylight (6400° Kelvin), has a lightweight housing, has extreme brilliance, long lamp life, easy maintenance, and high light output verses current input. The bulk of the fixtures and the inability to focus make them a not highly desirable television lighting source.

3. *High-Intensity Carbon Arc Light*

The high-intensity carbon arc comes the nearest to providing the perfect light for television because it so nearly duplicates sunlight. Its 6400° Kelvin means that all the colors in the spectrum are present in approximately normal amounts. Although a considerable amount of ultra-violet light is radiated from the arc itself, most of this is filtered out by the glass lens or diffuser. In the improved makes there is practically no noise that can be picked up by the microphone unless they are brought into much closer proximity than is ordinarily necessary. The new types, furthermore, can be "struck" remotely by merely turning on the switch. The replacement cost of carbons is low.

The objectionable features of the carbon arc are three: (1) the short burning time of the carbons (in the vicinity of one and three-quarter hours in present equipment) interferes with rehearsal and production; (2) a certain amount of noise is unavoidable in recarboning; (3) the units are heavy. Carbon arc lamps are more expensive watt for watt than incandescents, and since they require direct current the cost of converters must be added if the studio is supplied with alternating current. The higher efficiency and lower maintenance cost, however, make them a better investment over a period of time.

Carbon arcs may be used for floodlighting as well as spotlighting. A type of lamp known as the "Duarc," developed by Mole-Richardson for technicolor filming, produces an excellent foundation light. This lamp contains two arcs, each controlled by a separate motor and fed in such a manner that the operation is steady and flickerless. The lamp is equipped with a glass diffuser which delivers a soft, even light free of glare. They are most adaptable to overhead use, and, though the light is ideal for front fill, the total weight of 150 pounds for lamp and pedestal makes them cumbersome for floor use.

The Duarc is capable of delivering 135 foot candles at a distance of 15 feet, within an angle of 40°, spread quite uniformly over an eleven-foot field. Its total effective divergence is an angle of about 150°, which means that the light falls off sharply on either side of the 40° zone in the middle of the beam. These characteristics make it possible to overlap and overlay the beams from a number of Duarcs and build up the desired level. The manufacturers advise that they intend to increase the burning time to three hours and to make other adaptations to television requirements.

The carbon arc may be used as a spotlight, but the types now manufactured are for the most part too highly powered and unwieldy for television use. The light, however, is ideal for key lighting, and as time goes on the manufacturers will doubtless find it profitable to develop equipment which meets television's requirements, including longer carbon burning time.

From the foregoing brief outline of the various types of lights it is evident that incandescents are the cleanest, most efficient, least costly to operate lighting source available today. Some of the possible combinations of the lighting sources available are incandescent spots for key lighting and rimming with either incandescent or fluorescent foundation or fill light; incandescents and arcs used in the same manner; arcs for foundation lighting, incandescent spots combined with fluorescents for key lighting and rimming. Incandescents used alone produce an extraordinary amount of heat but they are most efficient from a point of view of space consumed.

4. Control Equipment

Control of intensity and field is ordinarily accomplished either by moving the light nearer to or farther away from the subject, or by "pinning" or spreading the beam. There are conditions, however, where neither of these methods can be employed in sustained production. In such cases the intensity can be controlled in the manner widely used in motion picture and theater production—by the use of dimmers.

a. Dimmers

The function of the dimmer is to regulate the current supplied to the lamp in varying degrees by changing the amount of resistance in the circuit. Dimmers are made to serve a multiplicity of circuits, with an indexed control lever for each circuit and provisions for interlocking any number of them.

These circuits should be numbered so that the lighting director can call for changes in light level by circuit number, as indicated on his light-cue production script. In this way, if for instance it is necessary to reduce the intensity of a spotlight or a group of lights during a scene, he has only to speak into his microphone to the man on the dimmer, who can effect an instant change noiselessly and in timing with the action.

The ultimate in cross-connecting, presetting, and dimming control is available in the C-I Board. Here is a highly sensitive and well designed piece of equipment which gives the operator one control per inch so that the lights may be played with the fingers implying the sensitivity of a musician at the piano or organ.

b. Light Control Circuits

The lighting system should provide enough circuits to facilitate all conceivable combinations of interlocking for dimmer control and switching. The system should be flexible and mobile, so that lights can be used wherever desired. Each outlet should terminate in an interconnect plug at the switchboard position and on a lighting batten or outlet in the side walls and back walls of the studio. There can never be too many outlets in a studio and only the dollars available should dictate the number that will be installed. Plugging boxes and jumpers should be discouraged as they take floor space and are dangerous, lending themselves to disconnects at the least propitious moment and to accidents of personnel tripping and falling.

c. The Light Control Desk

As noted before, the light-control desk should be located in the control room, where the lighting director can see the camera monitors and the action in the studio. Through the talk-back equipment he can direct his lighting crew and handle the switching. Thus he has the situation under control and can achieve distinctive results, provided he has the full co-operation of the producer, a good lighting crew, and a flexible system.

The lighting equipment is to the producer and the lighting director what the palette is to the painter—a means of painting with light. Good lighting is a creative activity and, like good painting, requires not only skill but aptitude. Television demands good lighting.

COLOR DEMANDS ATTENTION

Another dimension has recently been added to the picture—*color*. It has given rise to some anxious questions in television studios.

Is more skill required of personnel? Functions performed by operating personnel familiar with black and white can be performed in color tele-vision by people of the same occupational skill.

How does color television differ from black and white? Fundamentally it does not differ at all.

Are different operating techniques required? Basically, no.

Can the television worker in black and white function in color? Yes, we all function in color every day, and color is the normal condition no matter what our job or environment.

The compatible color system as developed by The Radio Corporation of America and approved by the Federal Communications Commission is the most sensitive color palette yet developed. A twist of the dial and a picture rich with color is tinted blue, another twist and a roseate hue accents the image. Such sensitivity and immediate response carries with it the potential for imposing upon the picture and therefore the viewer the color sense of the man with the knob in his hand.

The electronic color system has limitations, which the future must overcome through constant refinement of techniques. Today's limitation is replaced by another tomorrow, and this must continue until the knob-less system will convey faithfully the yellow-green grass of Arizona, the blue-green grass of Kentucky, and the green-green grass of New Eng-land.

The design of setting, lighting, or costumes for color television in-volves the same principles of good design basic to black and white tele-vision or motion pictures. Color will not substitute for size, shape, or scope. High reflective surfaces in black and white or color are an obvious danger. Full skirts make short women look shorter, horizontal lines make stocky people look stockier, perpendicular lines accent height—whether they are reproduced in color or black and white.

No special equipments are required for lighting in color television. The instruments and lamps are the same as those used for monochrome production. Color in lighting is achieved by the use of gelatine, silks, or glass filters as used in theater or color motion pictures.

At a lens opening of f 5.6 the image orthicon requires lighting levels ranging between 250 and 400 foot candles, depending on the reflective qualities and color of the subject being televised. Standard incandescent lamps of 2900° Kelvin are used and color temperature changes of approximately 300°, up or down, are tolerable before blue light deviation is noticeable on skin tones.

Atmosphere and mood may be established, maintained and resolved by changes in color. Settings may be so painted as to reflect the varying shades or hues of colored light washed over them.

Time may be established by the judicious use of color—the low cool light of dawn, the high hot light of noon, the warmth and glow of the setting sun, and the blue-black of night (with or without the steel blue moon cutting through).

Place or environment may be implied by the off-camera reflections of fire, water, desert, or snow.

Skin color is a standard of reference. No matter how insensitive we may be to color in our surroundings, skin color is an index with which we are all familiar, the baby-pink, the lily-white, the ruddy, the tan. Accepting a color combination on the control room monitor stemming from the blond, brunette, or red-headed central figure is as good a yardstick as can be used.

However, a word of consideration, rather than caution. A color standard may be established in the studio, and with slight degradation it leaves the transmitter and is faithfully reproduced by the home receiver. What of the surroundings in which it is being viewed? Are there yellow lamp shades and green walls? Highly reflective painted surfaces or absorbent wall hangings? Will not the reflections and refractions, in color, react upon the standard? Doctor Matthew Luckiesch compounds our dilemma when he states, "Color-blindness in its common meaning, a deficiency in the visual sense, is a rare condition, generally existing from birth. It descends in complete form upon only a few in each million persons. It is not a disease, but a congenital misfortune. However, mental color-blindness is in many respects a disease. Not only endemic —but at times epidemic. Mental color-blindness is a very general affliction of civilized adults."

Color will not replace nor substitute for program content. The use of color in television is guided by the same factor that dictates the use of color in any other facet of our culture—taste. The use of color is not a science. It is an art. Television is an art. Television demands attention.

Index